Establishing Self-Access
From Theory to Practice

CAMBRIDGE LANGUAGE TEACHING LIBRARY

A series covering central issues in language teaching and learning, by authors who have expert knowledge in the field

In this series:

Affect in Language Learning *edited by Jane Arnold*

Approaches in Methods in Language Teaching *by Jack C. Richards and Theodore S. Rodgers*

Appropriate Methodology and Social Context *by Adrian Holliday*

Beyond Training *by Jack C. Richards*

Collaborative Action Research For English Language Teachers *by Anne Burns*

Collaborative Language Learning and Teaching *edited by David Nunan*

Communicative Language Teaching *by William Littlewood*

Communicative Methodology in Language Teaching *by Christopher Brumfit*

Course Design *by Fraida Dubin and Elite Olshtain*

Culture Bound *edited by Joyce Merrill Valdes*

Designing Tasks for the Communicative Classroom *by David Nunan*

Developing Reading Skills *by Françoise Grellet*

Developments in ESP *by Tony Dudley-Evans and Maggie Jo St John*

Discourse Analysis for Language Teachers *by Michael McCarthy*

Discourse and Language Education *by Evelyn Hatch*

English for Academic Purposes *by R. R. Jordan*

English for Specific Purposes *by Tom Hutchinson and Alan Waters*

Focus on the Language Classroom *by Dick Allwright and Kathleen M. Bailey*

Foreign and Second Language Learning *by William Littlewood*

Language Learning in Intercultural Perspective *edited by Michael Byram and Michael Fleming*

The Language Teaching Matrix *by Jack C. Richards*

Language Test Construction and Evaluation *by J. Charles Alderson, Caroline Clapham and Dianne Wall*

Learner-centredness as Language Education *by Ian Tudor*

Managing Curricular Innovation *by Numa Markee*

Materials Development in Language Teaching *edited by Brian Tomlinson*

Psychology for Language Teachers *by Marion Williams and Robert L. Burden*

Research Methods in Language Learning *by David Nunan*

Second Language Teacher Education *edited by Jack C. Richards and David Nunan*

Society and the Language Classroom *edited by Hywell Coleman*

Teacher Learning in Language Teaching *edited by Donald Freeman and Jack C. Richards*

Teaching the Spoken Language *by Gillian Brown and George Yule*

Understanding Research in Second Language Learning *by James Dean Brown*

Vocabulary: Description, Acquisition, Pedagogy *edited by Norbert Schmitt and Michael McCarthy*

Vocabulary, Semantics and Language Education *by Evelyn Hatch and Cheryl Brown*

Voices From the Language Classroom *edited by Kathleen M. Bailey and David Nunan*

Establishing Self-Access
From Theory to Practice

David Gardner and
Lindsay Miller

CAMBRIDGE
UNIVERSITY PRESS

PUBLISHED BY THE PRESS SYNDICATE OF THE UNIVERSITY OF CAMBRIDGE
The Pitt Building, Trumpington Street, Cambridge, United Kingdom

CAMBRIDGE UNIVERSITY PRESS
The Edinburgh Building, Cambridge CB2 2RU, UK
40 West 20th Street, New York, NY 10011–4211, USA
477 Williamstown Road, Port Melbourne, VIC 3207, Australia
Ruiz de Alarcón 13, 28014 Madrid, Spain
Dock House, The Waterfront, Cape Town 8001, South Africa

http://www.cambridge.org

© Cambridge University Press 1999

First published 1999
Second printing 2003

Printed in the United Kingdom at the University Press, Cambridge

Typeset in Sabon 10.5/12pt   [CE]

A catalogue record for this book is available from the British Library

Library of Congress Cataloguing in Publication data applied for

ISBN 0 521 58482 5 hardback
ISBN 0 521 58556 2 paperback

Contents

Contents

List of figures

List of tables

Thanks

We are particularly grateful to the following colleagues who took the time to show us around their self-access centres and explain what goes on there: Ahmed B. Buyong and Jesintha Jeamalar (Sekolah Rendah Kebangsaan (L), Kuala Lumpur, Malaysia), Poon Noor Rezan and Mazwin Tajuddin (Sekolah Menengah Wangsa Maju 2, Kuala Lumpur, Malaysia), Richard Pemberton (The University of Science and Technology, Hong Kong), and Felicity O'Dell (Eurocentres, Cambridge, UK).

We are also grateful to Christine Heuring for discussions about counselling in SALL, Paul Raj for co-ordinating the Malaysian school visits and Chan Chap Choi, Jasper for art work.

We are grateful to the numerous colleagues who have discussed our ideas with us over the years, especially the members of the Hong Kong Association for Self-Access Learning and Development. Members of the Association have provided a stimulating environment by talking about self-access and listening to us talking about it.

Felicity O'Dell is already mentioned above for her kindness in showing us around the Eurocentres SAC but she has done much more. We are grateful to her for reading the manuscript and making many invaluable comments and suggestions for improving it.

We would also like to thank Alison Sharpe and Mickey Bonin, our editors at Cambridge University Press. The former for initiating the project and the latter for bringing it to fruition.

Finally, we would like to thank Rocío Blasco García whose amazing eye for detail while proof-reading our manuscript has improved it considerably.

If we have inadvertently forgotten to acknowledge anyone else who has helped us please excuse us and put it down to failing memories caused by spending too long in front of the word processor.

David Gardner and Lindsay Miller
Hong Kong, June 1998

xiv

Acknowledgements

The editors, authors and publishers are grateful to the authors, publishers and others who have given permission for the use of copyright material identified in the text. It has not been possible to identify, or trace, sources of all the materials used and in such cases the publishers would welcome information from copyright owners.

Richards, J. C. and C. Lockhart. 1994. *Reflective Teaching in Second Language Classrooms*. Cambridge University Press on pp.38, 39 and 40; Nunan, D. 1988a. *The Learner-Centred Curriculum*. Cambridge University Press on p.41; Littlewood, W. 1996. *Autonomy in Communication and Learning in the Asian Context*. In Proceedings of *Autonomy 2000: The Development of Learner Independence in Language Learning*. Bangkok: King Mongkut's Institute of Technology on p.42; Dickinson, L. and D. Carver. 1980. *Learning How to Learn: Steps Towards Self-Direction in Foreign Language Learning*. In *ELT Journal 35*. Oxford University Press on p.44; Horwitz, E. K. 1985. *Using Student Beliefs about Language Learning and Teaching in the Foreign Language Methods Course*. In *Foreign Language Annals 18 (4)*. ACTFL on pp.45 and 46; Adult Migration Education Program (AMEP). 1989. *Review of Individual Learning Centres*. National Centre for English Language Teaching and Research (NCELTR): Macquarie University, with permission of the Department of Immigration and Multicultural Affairs (DIMA): Australia on pp.52, 53 and 54; Dwyer, R. 1996. *Building Thoughts*. In D. Gardner and L. Miller (Eds.). *Tasks for Independent Language Learning* (adapted with permission). Alexandria, VA: TESOL on p.132; Nunan, D. 1996. *What's My Style?* In *Tasks for Independent Language Learning*. Alexandria, VA: TESOL on pp.159 and 160; Thomson, C. K. 1992. *Learner-Centred Tasks in the Foreign Language Classroom*. In *Foreign Language Annals 25 (6)*. ACTFL on pp.166 and 167; Self-Access Centre *Test Your Knowledge* Worksheet. Hong Kong University of Science and Technology: Language Centre on p.176; Kelly, R. 1996. *Language Counselling for Learner Autonomy. The Skilled Helper in Self-Access Language Learning*. In R. Pemberton et al. (Eds.). *Taking Control: Autonomy in Language Learning*. Hong Kong University Press on pp.183 and 184; Rogerson-Revell, P. and L. Miller. 1994. *Developing Pronunciation*

Skills Through Self-Access Learning. In D. Gardner and L. Miller (Eds.). *Directions in Self-Access Learning.* Hong Kong University Press on p.187; Heuring, C. *What Makes a Good Counsellor?* Worksheet (adapted with permission). Hong Kong Polytechnic University on p.191.

Introduction

This book aims to bridge the gap between theory and practice in self-access language learning (SALL). While much of this book presents practical ideas dealing with issues related to SALL, they are supported by references to relevant literature and research. This link between theory and practice makes the debate about SALL accessible and makes this book a useful resource for establishing and running self-access learning facilities. SALL is an approach to language learning not an approach to language teaching. It is applicable in all educational contexts and with all kinds of learners. The many and varied examples in this book are taken from as wide a range of situations as possible.

Self-access has been applied in many different ways and forms all over the world. Our approach in writing this book has been to show how SALL encompasses all this variation; it has not been to constrain self-access within a narrow definition. In order to describe SALL in all its variations we have developed new terminology and new concepts. These are particularly evident in the typology of self-access systems we have developed, the models of self-access management we have proposed and in the suggestions for creating and exploiting learner profiles. By developing these we are better able to describe self-access in an international context.

The international interest in SALL and autonomous learning in recent years has manifested itself in a proliferation of papers, books and conference presentations. There has also been an increase in the incorporation of self-access as a component in teacher education. There have been a number of key papers in leading language and linguistics journals dealing with self-access and autonomy (Sheerin 1991; Miller and Rogerson-Revell 1993; O'Dell 1992; Kenny 1993; Crabbe 1993; Dam 1994; Dickinson and Wenden 1995; Gardner 1996). Several books have been written in the area (Dickinson 1987, 1992; Brookes and Grundy 1988; Little 1989, 1991; Sheerin 1989; a series of booklets published by the British Council [McCall 1992; Moore 1992; Sturtridge 1992; Carvalho 1993; Booton and Benson 1996]; Gardner and Miller 1994, 1996; Esch 1994; Dam 1995; Broady and Kenning 1996; Pemberton et al. 1996; Benson and Voller 1997; Karlsson et al. 1997). There have been international conferences organised round the same themes (University of Cambridge, UK, 1993; University of Hong Kong,

Hong Kong, 1993; Hong Kong University of Science and Technology, Hong Kong, 1994; King Mongkut's Institute of Technology Thonburi (KMITT), Thailand, 1996; AILA, Finland, 1996; University of Nottingham, UK, 1998). Some examples of SALL as a component of teacher education are as follows: the Institute of Education (Hong Kong) incorporates SALL into their refresher courses for school teachers, KMITT (Thailand) runs a post-graduate diploma and a masters programme in resource-based language learning, and the Bell School at Saffron Walden (UK) runs a teacher training course in SALL.

In different parts of the world there have been different focuses in the way these concepts have been implemented. In Western Europe the development of self-access centres (SACs) has resulted from an ongoing debate about autonomous learning. Well known examples of implementing self-access learning in Europe come from the Centre de Researches et d'Applications Pédagogiques en Langues (CRAPEL) at the University of Nancy in France; from the Language Centre at the University of Cambridge, UK; and from the Bell School in Saffron Walden, UK. In addition to these individual sites the British Council, through its Direct Teaching Operations, has established a number of showcase SACs throughout Europe.

Southeast Asia has seen a recent surge in the development of self-access centres. A major influence in this development has been links with European proponents of self-access through consultants from European universities and through sponsorship and advisory services provided by the British Council. Among the countries in this region with a large commitment to self-access learning the focus of development has varied. In Hong Kong there has been a focus on developing SACs at tertiary level and this focus is now broadening to encompass secondary schools. The situation in Singapore is somewhat similar to that of Hong Kong with well developed tertiary level SACs. In Malaysia, the initial impetus came from teacher-training colleges and has since spread rapidly to primary and secondary schools. In Thailand, the focus has been on the training of school teachers at diploma and degree level.

Australia became committed to self-access learning through its development of the Australian Migrant Education Program (AMEP) which caters to the needs of new immigrants to the country. This has resulted in the establishment of many self-access centres. These centres are known by a variety of names and function in different ways. The centres are used by adult learners from a variety of ethnic, social and cultural backgrounds. The focus of the centres is on work-related language needs.

The North American influences related to self-access language learning have been mainly through intensive work into learners' styles and strategies. This is where the concept of the 'good language learner' was first developed. This stimulated teachers to consider how they might encourage their learners to develop effective learning techniques based on the experiences of successful learners. This concept was later developed to include all the individual approaches learners may have when learning a language. With insights into learners' styles and strategies, teachers have become more aware of the roles they need to adopt. The work into learners' styles and strategies has taken place in classroom-based learning in North America and this adds another dimension to the concept of self-access.

The layout of this book is in three parts. The four chapters in Part 1 are important for discussion before establishing self-access. In Chapter 1 we give the background to self-access language learning. Here we discuss issues central to understanding what 'self-access' means. We place the learner at the centre of focus and show how all issues related to establishing self-access revolve around the learner. The elements of self-access are described, and we raise issues related to resistance to implementing self-access. In Chapter 2 we show how, before self-access can be established, discussion and fact-finding about learners' beliefs and attitudes about language learning in general, and self-access in particular, has to be undertaken by teachers. Teachers also have to be able to express their own beliefs and attitudes and compare and contrast these with their learners' views. The understanding that teachers gain by doing this will help them prepare for introducing self-access, and help them prepare their learners for self-access. Chapter 3 introduces a typology of self-access. We have developed this typology in order to categorise the many and varied types of self-access systems. This framework is referred to in Part 2 of the book when we discuss practical issues about self-access. The typology also shows the flexibility of self-access which enables it to be implemented in many different situations. The last chapter in Part 1 is about managing self-access. Issues related to how to manage self-access are important to consider before setting up a system. This ensures that an appropriate management model is developed before a self-access system is implemented.

Part 2 of this book contains eight chapters. Each chapter focuses on particular practical issues related to establishing self-access. Chapter 5 is about learner profiles. We show how these are important in helping both learners and teachers plan and keep track of work done in self-access. The information from developing and monitoring learner profiles ensures that the most appropriate self-access opportunities and facilities can be provided for learners. Chapter 6 deals with self-access materials. We describe the many and varied ways in which self-access materials can be developed and we suggest a framework for the development of specially written materials for self-access. In Chapter 7 we look at self-access activities. We give examples of the types of activities which can be developed for different levels of language learners, and we discuss some general uses which can be made of self-access facilities. In this chapter we argue for teachers to be innovative in the implementation of self-access activities. Chapter 8 deals with physical settings and resources. We discuss classroom, library and self-access-centre environments. We illustrate how the establishment of self-access in each of these settings is different. We also comment on the types of resources needed in each of these environments. In Chapter 9 we review a number of ways in which the classroom can be used as a starting point for SALL. We look at ways of designing and implementing classroom-based SALL, and also the importance of learner reflection. Chapter 10 deals with counselling. Counselling in self-access requires teachers to take on many different roles and their relationship with their learners has to change. In order to achieve this shift in teachers' roles we suggest teacher-training workshops and give examples of how these may be organised. Chapter 11 focuses on assessment in self-access. We show the relevance of conducting 'small' and 'large' assessments and how these can form part of learners' profiles. We also discuss ethical issues in monitoring learners' assessment in self-access. In the last chapter of Part 2 (Chapter 12) we look at evaluation of self-access. Here we discuss issues related to the effectiveness and efficiency of conducting self-access evaluations. We also provide a six-step guide to conducting an evaluation.

Part 3 of this book consists of four case studies of self-access centres. The case studies are of self-access centres in a primary school, a secondary school, a university, and a private language school. We provide these case studies to illustrate the theoretical and practical issues raised in Part 1 and Part 2 of the book.

Part 1   Theoretical perspectives

1   Background to self-access language learning

1.1 Introduction

Our intention in this chapter is to provide an overview of issues concerning learner autonomy and other related areas which have an influence on self-access language learning (SALL). We begin by examining the debate surrounding autonomy and identifying the major influences which have contributed to this debate. This debate will not be discussed after this chapter because it is not central to the purpose of the book. It is, however, an important starting point for talking about SALL. The remainder of the chapter focuses specifically on SALL by identifying:

- its characteristics
- the beliefs and attitudes which affect the acceptance of SALL
- the change in roles which is required of both learners and teachers
- the challenges of promoting speaking in SALL
- the differences between self-access centres (SACs) in native and non-native speaking environments
- the kinds of learning environments in which SALL can take place
- possible areas of resistance to SALL.

Finally, we discuss issues related to the costs of establishing and maintaining SALL. Many of the points related to SALL which we touch on in this chapter are developed more fully in the rest of the book.

1.2 Definitions

It is difficult to define concepts like 'autonomy' and 'independent learning' for three reasons. First, different writers have defined the concepts in different ways. Second, they are areas of ongoing debate and therefore definitions are continuing to mature as more discussion takes place. Third, these concepts have developed independently in different geographical areas and therefore they have been defined using different (but often similar) terminology.

1.2.1 Autonomy

The concept of 'autonomous learning' stemmed from debates about the development of life-long learning skills and the development of independent thinkers both of which originated in the 1960s. By 1981 Holec (1981: 3) had defined autonomy as 'the ability to take charge of one's own learning'. He developed this definition further in 1985 by talking about autonomy as a conceptual tool. Holec has been a major influence in the debate about autonomy in language learning and his initial definition has been taken as a starting point in much subsequent work in the area. Dickinson (1987: 11), for example, accepts the definition of autonomy as a 'situation in which the learner is totally responsible for all of the decisions concerned with his [or her] learning and the implementation of those decisions'.

Other definitions of autonomy have situated it within three major schools of thought. Some see it is a personal characteristic, some see it as a political concept and others see it as a definition of educational practices. Two writers who see autonomy as a personal characteristic are Little (1990) and Kenny (1993). Little (1990: 7) sees learner autonomy as 'essentially a matter of the learner's psychological relation to the process and content of learning'. Kenny (1993: 436) states that autonomy is not only the freedom to learn but also 'the opportunity to become a person'. An example of viewing autonomy within a political framework is found in the work of Benson (1997: 29) who defines learner autonomy as representing 'a recognition of the rights of learners within educational systems' and, within the context of teaching English as a Foreign Language, as 'a recognition of the rights of the "non-native speaker" in relation to the "native-speaker" within the global order of English' (Benson 1997: 29). An example of viewing autonomy as an educational practice comes from Boud (1988: 17) who suggests that, as well as being an educational goal autonomy is 'an approach to educational practice'.

The above definitions deal with the concept of learner autonomy. In this book, which places the learner at the centre of focus, it is important to identify the characteristics of an autonomous learner. In a colloquium in which an attempt was made to define the characteristics of an autonomous learner, Dam et al. (1990: 102) defined one as 'an active participant in the social processes of classroom learning ... an active interpreter of new information in terms of what she/he already and uniquely knows ... [someone who] knows how to learn and can use this knowledge in any learning situation she/he may encounter at any stage in her/his life'. In addition, Dam et al. (1990: 102) characterise learner autonomy as 'a readiness to take charge of one's own learning'. Gardner and Miller (1996: vii) define autonomous language learners as those who 'initiate the planning and implementation of their own learning

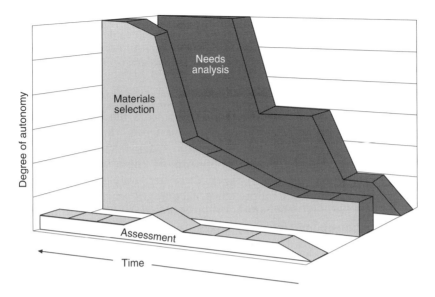

Figure 1.1.   Example of changes in autonomy in learner decision-making regarding reading

program'. These definitions go some way towards clarifying the characteristics of autonomous language learners. However, as Nunan (1997: 193) points out 'it may well be that the fully autonomous learner is an ideal, rather than a reality'. He argues for degrees of autonomy and that learners' potential for achieving different degrees depends on factors like their personality, their goals, institutional philosophy and cultural context (Nunan 1997).

In addition to the differences in degrees of autonomy suggested by Nunan, there may also be fluctuations in the degree of learners' autonomy over time and from one skill area to another. For example, a learner may attain a high degree of autonomy in listening but could remain teacher dependent in learning about writing. Levels of autonomy may vary even within single language skills, for example in reading. Figure 1.1 shows an example of the development of a learner's levels of autonomy in three aspects of reading. First, the learner's autonomy in analysing needs has developed rapidly. It should also be noticed that this development went through two stages where each time a plateau was reached and then passed. Second, the learner's willingness to select materials has developed more slowly. However, there is a sudden rise in autonomy in materials' selection which occurs shortly after passing the second plateau of autonomy in needs analysis. Third, the learner's willingness to accept responsibility for assessment of reading has hardly changed. There was a small increase in autonomy at one point but this was not sustained. This may be due to the learner's lack of confidence in the reliability of self-assessment.

1.2.2   Approaches to encouraging autonomy

Approaches which assist learners to move from teacher dependence towards autonomy are described in various terms, the most common are: self-directed learning, self-instruction, independent learning, and self-access learning. Although proponents of these approaches may argue for differences between them, there are more similarities than differences. Each of the approaches encourages learners to set and pursue their personal language learning goals. Holec (1988) states that learner responsibility is a necessary requirement for self-directed learning. He identifies two kinds of learner responsibility. In what he describes as *static*, learners, either by themselves or with the help of others, set a programme of language learning and follow it through. He describes this responsibility as a 'finished product' (Holec 1988: 174). The kind of responsibility he describes as *dynamic* is more flexible because learners take on responsibility for their learning as the learning programme develops. Dickinson (1987: 11) sees self-direction as an 'attitude to the learning task' within which learners accept responsibility for decision-making but do not necessarily implement the decisions. He also makes a distinction between self-direction and self-instruction, the latter being a neutral term describing a context where learners are not under the direct control of their teachers (Dickinson 1987).

Independent learning is seen by Sheerin (1997) as an educational philosophy and process, whereas Gardner and Miller (1996) see it as one stage in a process in which learners are moving towards autonomy in their learning. Self-access is probably the most widely used and recognised term for an approach to encouraging autonomy. Sheerin (1991: 144) refers to self-access as 'a means of promoting learner autonomy'. We certainly see self-access as a way of encouraging learners to move from teacher dependence towards autonomy and it is for this reason that we use the term 'self-access' throughout this book.

1.3   Elements of self-access

Self-access language learning is an approach to learning language, not an approach to teaching language. There are misconceptions in the literature about self-access. It is sometimes seen as a collection of materials and sometimes as a system for organising resources. We see it as an integration of a number of elements (Table 1.1) which combine to

Table 1.1.   *Elements of self-access*

Element	Function
Resources	To provide:
	• learning materials • authentic materials • activities • technology • access to authentic language users • access to other language learners.
People	Teachers to perform the roles of:
	• information provider • counsellor • authentic language user • manager • materials writer • assessor • evaluator • administrator • organiser.
	Learners to perform the roles of:
	• planner • organiser • administrator (record keeping) • thinker (about learning) • evaluator of SALL • self-assessor • self-motivator.
	Other learners to perform the roles of:
	• partners • peer-assessors.
Management	To provide:
	• organisation • overseeing of the system • coordination • decision-making • interfacing with the institution.
System	To organise SALL facilities in a way or ways that best support the needs of the learners.

Table 1.1. (*contd*)

Element	Function
Individualisation	To acknowledge individual differences in: • learning styles • learning strategies • time and place of learning • quantity of time spent learning • learning level • content of learning • commitment to learning.
Needs/wants analysis	• To identify learning goals. • To facilitate the creation of study plans.
Learner reflection	To consider: • language ability • progress in language learning • suitability of SALL for self • goal setting.
Counselling	To provide: • advice on language ability • advice on learning methods • negotiation of study plans.
Learner training	• To enhance understanding of SALL. • To experience a variety of methods. • To increase effectiveness in learning.
Staff training	• To enhance understanding of SALL. • To increase effectiveness of services.
Assessment	Kinds of assessments: • self-assessment • peer-assessment • external-assessment. Purposes of assessment: • self-monitoring • certification • evaluation of SALL.
Evaluation	• To decide suitability of SALL for self. • To provide feedback about SALL to teachers/manager.
Materials development	• To support individualisation. • To improve learning opportunities.

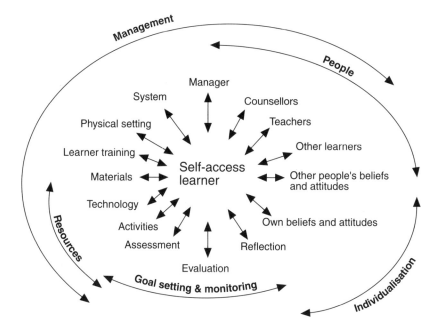

Figure 1.2.   Interaction between the learner and the self-access environment

provide a learning environment. Each learner interacts with the environment in a unique way (Figure 1.2). The elements of self-access and the ways in which learners interact with them are dealt with in greater detail in Part 2 of this book.

1.4 Issues in establishing self-access

Self-access is very flexible. It can be used on a large scale or a small scale. It can be conducted in a classroom, in a dedicated self-access centre or elsewhere. It can be incorporated into a language course or it can be used by learners who are not taking courses. It can function at all learning levels. It allows for different levels of independence among learners encompassing both teacher-directed groups of learners and virtually autonomous learners. It allows individualisation but also supports groups. It is not culture specific. It is not age specific. In effect, self-access learning can benefit all language learners. However, for many learners it is a new concept with which they are unfamiliar. Learners' attitudes to SALL are based on their own incomplete knowledge of self-access and may be conditioned by outside influences.

1.4.1 Influences on self-access learners

Some learners may be predisposed to self-access learning while others may not. Riley (1988) suggests that this applies not only to individuals but also to identifiable groups of learners. He found, for example, that as groups of learners Danes, Americans, Moroccans and Vietnamese each reacted differently from the other with respect to a self-access project. The Danes completed the project satisfactorily and had no problems in accepting their 'new' roles. The Americans, although stating that they were in favour of the project, had difficulty in organising themselves and comprehending the purpose of the task. The Moroccans accepted the theory behind completing a project but were unable to complete the task in practice. The Vietnamese 'said nothing and did nothing' (Riley 1988: 14).

Learners' attitudes towards self-access may be affected by four main influences. These are: their teachers, their educational institution, their peers, and society. Teachers are an important influence because it is they who are most likely to first introduce learners to self-access. Teachers who do this because of their own commitment to self-access learning are likely to have an enthusiastic attitude and are likely to communicate that enthusiasm to the learners. The attitudes of teachers who introduce self-access to learners simply because of institutional policy are likely to be more variable. In a study of learners' and teachers' attitudes to self-access language learning Gardner and Miller (1997) found that learners were, in general, more positive about the benefits of self-access than their teachers.

Institutional attitudes to self-access can be an important influence in the way self-access is introduced, or whether it is introduced at all. In highly structured institutions, the introduction of self-access needs to become a policy issue. In cases where funding is required for self-access resources, the institutional influence becomes even more important.

Peer pressure is recognised widely as an important influence on learners. Where groups of learners have successfully used self-access learning other learners are likely to want to try it. In situations where self-access is a totally new concept it may be difficult to encourage learners to move away from the traditional approaches with which they are familiar. Learners need to be exposed not only to self-access learning but also to information about how it is different and why.

Society can also be an important influence on the up-take of self-access learning. Parental pressure, culture and power hierarchies can all potentially influence the introduction or inhibition of new approaches to learning. Kennedy (1988) suggests that there are multiple levels of influence in bringing about change. He suggests a knock-on effect where wider ranging systems influence those below them, which in turn influence the next level and so on down from the cultural system at the highest level through political, administrative, educational and institutional levels to the classroom. The introduction of self-access learning may occur at one or more levels of this hierarchy. Gremmo and Riley (1995) have also identified socio-cultural factors as well as institutional, learner and staff characteristics as important influences on the establishment of self-access. They suggest that these influences are so powerful that self-access can only be planned locally and that 'there is no universal model' (Gremmo and Riley: 156) for setting it up.

1.4.2 Changing roles

The introduction of self-access language learning requires changes in the roles of learners, teachers and the institution. Learners need to become more aware of their central role in the decision-making process (see Figure 1.2). They have to learn to take an increasing amount of responsibility for their learning. They have to learn about the importance of reflection on their learning and how it can help them to redefine their goals to make them constantly relevant to their needs and wants. The changing role of learners requires an increase in learner training which should be incorporated into self-access materials, activities, counselling and classroom work rather than becoming a stand alone set of instructional activities.

The roles of teachers change dramatically as their learners engage in self-access learning. Teachers need to relinquish some of their control over learners, even allowing them to make mistakes. Teachers need to learn new skills to take on their new roles (Figure 1.3). Some of the 'new' roles for teachers in SALL may look familiar. Teachers may already be administrators and organisers of learning. However, these roles have to be redefined when the new roles of learners (Figure 1.4) are also taken into account. In order to adapt to their new roles successfully teachers need training.

As learners and teachers change their roles so too must the institution. It needs to move from a directive stance to one of being a provider of learning opportunities. These opportunities may be used by different learners in different ways and the choices about how to use them must lie with the learners and not with the institution.

1.4.3 Speaking as part of SALL

We have singled out speaking as a special issue in the establishment of SALL because it can create special difficulties and because it is the cause of some misconceptions among staff and students. Many teachers, students and administrators have a view of self-access which likens it to

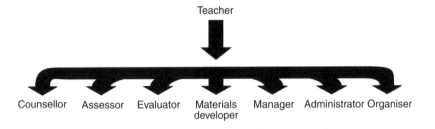

Figure 1.3. Changing roles of staff in SALL

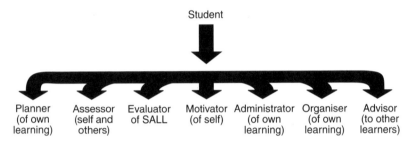

Figure 1.4. Changing roles of learners in SALL

quiet study or library work with learners studying individually and (most importantly) quietly. However, self-access is an opportunity for learners to learn and practise the kind of language they need and want. In many cases this involves speaking and this should be encouraged not stifled. There are, however, two major problems related to self-access speaking. First, it is noisy and, second, it can be difficult to provide opportunities for speaking as part of self-access.

The issue of noise is one which needs to be addressed when planning SALL because of its implications for the rest of the institution. Speaking makes noise and when lots of learners speak a lot of noise is made. If SALL is being implemented in a classroom, the noise may disrupt students and teachers in nearby classrooms. If SALL materials are stored in a library, the noise level created may be inappropriate for a library atmosphere. Even where a dedicated SAC is available, noise may interfere with other users of the SAC and the SAC itself may be too closely situated to other quiet areas of the institution.

Thus, creating noise is a problem; however, not allowing noise is a bigger problem. Self-access learners who are prevented from working on oral skills may lose interest in self-access learning. In addition, maintaining a quiet atmosphere throughout a SAC excludes many opportunities for pair and group work that focus on other language skills. Imposing a rule of silence is not the solution to the noise problem. The solution is to implement SALL in a way which takes account of the noise. Table 1.2 suggests some practical steps.

The second problem to be faced is that of providing speaking opportunities in SALL. Such opportunities can vary from practice at the segmental level (e.g. vowel and consonant practice) to authentic oral communication (see suggestions in Table 1.3). In Chapter 7 we discuss a variety of activities which can be used to encourage learners to work on their speaking skills. We begin, in Chapter 7, by including speaking as an important part of learners' analyses of their language strengths and weaknesses (Activity 1) and as an element in the process of becoming familiar with SALL (Activity 7). When we suggest learner participation in the administration of self-access facilities (Activity 5) and in the preparation of self-access materials (Activity 12) we envisage this involving communication in the target language. We also suggest a number of activities which will involve learners in oral use of the target language such as: developing descriptive skills (Activity 8), participating in a conversational exchange (Activity 9), using a puppet theatre (Activity 10) and developing oral presentations (Activity 11). These are just examples of the activities that can encourage use of the target language. Wherever possible, learners should be provided with authentic needs for speaking the target language. This may involve inviting native speakers or other authentic users of the target language into the institution to interact with learners; conducting language counselling sessions in the target language where possible; or making a teacher or counsellor available for casual interaction with learners.

Some students feel awkward about using a foreign language, especially with their classmates and friends. Some institutions try to overcome this by establishing rules to encourage a target-language environment in their SACs or classes. However, students need to know what the rules are and understand the reasons for them. They also need to be reminded of them from time to time. Establishing and explaining the rules can be done in a number of ways: through learner training programmes where students can discuss how best to increase use of the target language; by the teachers/counsellors always using the target language, or at least using it as much as possible; and by requiring student helpers in a SAC to use the target language with each other, thus providing a good example to other learners of the rules in action. Flexibility is required in establishing such rules. If students feel uncomfortable they may begin to hate self-access learning or at least stop participating orally. The level to which the rules are strictly maintained could be varied according to the language level of the learners and other

Table 1.2.   *Planning for noise in SALL*

Action	Explanation
Accept	Teachers implementing SALL should accept for themselves that noise is important for language learning. Not all teaching/learning is quiet: e.g. sports, woodwork, cooking.
Refuse to accept	Teachers should never accept that SALL is complete without speaking opportunities.
Explain	Colleagues, especially those with no knowledge of language teaching, are probably unaware of the need for noise. They need to understand that noise indicates learning not anarchy. They could be invited to observe a SALL session or they could be shown a video of speaking activities.
Separate	Quiet areas and speaking areas can be designated. In a classroom they may be different corners of the room, in a SAC they could be different rooms or separated physically by bookcases. McCall (1992) suggests for SACs that noisy areas should be near the entrance with quieter areas further in.
Raise awareness	Learners should be made aware of the noise levels they create, why noise is important and also why it needs to be controlled.
Direct	Learners should be provided with speaking activities which direct them towards controlled speaking (e.g. 'take it in turns to comment on . . .', 'First write notes then discuss'). These activities will reduce the overall amount of speaking (and noise) and will encourage learners to think about what they are going to say.
Discourage	Learners should be discouraged from seeing self-access as a time for chatting to friends in their native language. Such chats often lead to an escalation in noise levels.
Encourage	Learners could be encouraged to chat to friends but only in the target language. This will slow down the pace of communication and usually prevents escalation of noise levels.
Allow	Learners should be allowed to use their native language if they need to but only for certain activities, e.g. reflecting on their learning. This 'serious' use of language will probably keep noise levels relatively low.

Table 1.3. *Some suggestions for speaking activities in SALL*

Activity	Methods
Sounds: e.g.: • single vowel/consonant sounds • minimal pairs • sentences containing difficult sounds.	• Provide published materials like 'Ship or Sheep' (Baker 1981). • Create a list of problem sounds specific to the learners (with tape recording). • Assess as individual or peer assessment.
Vocabulary	• Provide a list and tape for vocabulary groups (e.g. shopping terminology, medical terminology). • Provide a multimedia talking dictionary with record option. • Provide printed dictionaries with pronunciation symbols (e.g. International Phonetic Alphabet). • Select words from a movie in pairs and peer-assess each other. • Use workshops dealing with specific vocabulary (video tape these for use later by other students).
Phrases	• Provide tapes with tapescripts and self record options. • Provide multimedia materials with record options. • Use workshops dealing with specific kinds of language (e.g. useful phrases for everyday conversations).
Teaching	• Ask more advanced students to teach some vocabulary to less advanced ones; preparing to teach something is a great way of learning about it. • Ask students to prepare self-access speaking materials for other students (for a fuller discussion see Chapter 6).
Discussion groups	• Run regular discussion groups. Make the topics serious but within reach of the learners' language skills. A facilitator should be present at least for the first few meetings otherwise learners find it too daunting to get started. • As discussion groups mature teachers/counsellors should withdraw.

Table 1.3. (*contd*)

Activity	Methods
Conversation	• Set up conversation exchanges (discussed in Chapter 7) between learners of different languages. • Set up pair/group discussions (provide starting materials). • Invite native or near-native speakers to join SALL sessions. • Provide people for a casual conversation in a SAC (e.g. teachers or student helpers).
Interviewing	• Invite outsiders in to be interviewed. • Send learners out looking for people to interview. • Learners can interview each other. • Learners can interview counsellors (videotape these for students to use when preparing for interviewing).
Presenting	• Learners can make presentations to each other. • When learners are ready they can present to an invited audience (videotape for other learners to watch).
Debating	• Set up a debating competition (provide practice materials for use beforehand). • Encourage competition between different groups of learners (e.g. different classes). • Invite learners from other institutions to compete. • Invite outsiders to attend the finals of a debate to add authenticity. • Ask a native speaker to be the judge.
Poetry readings	• Invite learners to prepare to read poems to an audience. • In preparation, ask learners to discuss the content of the poems.
Plays	• Involve learners in performing a play. • Provide preparatory materials to help learners understand the play and the language in it. • Invite an audience to the play. • Stage an 'academy awards' session after the play (of course, the session will be in the target language, and everyone should get a prize).

factors which teachers/counsellors deem important, like, for example, self-consciousness of students or their level of motivation.

Speaking has a special status in SALL because it is a problem and it creates a problem. The former because it is sometimes difficult to find activities which promote speaking, and sometimes even more difficult to persuade learners to try them; the latter because speaking creates noise which can disrupt the work of other learners and colleagues. The easy solution is to prohibit speaking but this is not a good solution since it leads to very dull SALL and may demotivate the learners. The best solution is to plan for speaking from the start by making sure it is optimally located and encouraged through well-constructed materials and activities.

1.4.4 SACs in native-speaking and non-native-speaking environments

Some of the functions of self-access centres vary according to whether the commonly used language of the world surrounding the learning environment is the target language or not. In other words, a SAC supporting a foreign language may be different to a SAC supporting the language of the host country. Before discussing differences we should clarify two of a SAC's major functions which remain the same in each case. First, the provision of self-study language-learning materials (grammar, listening, etc.) which independent learners can use to satisfy their own needs and wants. Second, the preparation of learners for greater independence in their learning by encouraging the development of individualised strategies, reflection on learning and taking responsibility. Where a SAC's functions will differ most, depending on whether it is located in a native or non-native speaker context, is in relation to authentic uses of the target language.

Where learning is taking place in a non-native-speaking environment, SACs offer language-learning opportunities that would not be possible in formal lessons. In particular, SACs can offer some kind of simulation of a native-speaker environment where learners can choose to immerse themselves in their target language, interact with authentic materials and perhaps also talk to native, or near-native, speakers. We discuss more fully the issue of using authentic materials in Chapter 6 and give an example of a conversational exchange in Chapter 7.

In native-speaking environments in which learners are surrounded daily by authentic language opportunities and native speakers, these attributes of a SAC become less important. This does not mean a SAC loses its function but simply that the function changes. In a native-speaker context a SAC takes on a bridging role. Its job is to help learners gain the confidence to move out from the classroom into the native-speaker environment. This is important at all language levels but is particularly crucial for lower-level learners. The learners can use their SAC to prepare themselves for authentic interaction. They can also return to the SAC later to understand more about what happened in their interactions. Once they have had an authentic language experience, the support materials of the SAC are invaluable in helping them to gain from the experience and prepare for the next.

Because some of the purposes of SACs differ according to the learning environment it is not surprising to find that a comparison of SACs in native-speaking and non-native-speaking environments shows variance in the advantages and disadvantages of SACs. These differences are listed in Table 1.4.

1.5 SALL environments

The environments in which self-access learning can take place fall into two categories, these are *controlled* and *uncontrolled* environments. The former includes classrooms, libraries and self-access centres. These are places in which self-access materials and activities can be made available in an organised way. These environments may also provide counselling services and may encourage (or sometimes compel) self-access learners to keep records, submit to assessments and participate in evaluations.

The other category of environments is labelled uncontrolled because the environments are beyond the control of teachers/counsellors. These are environments in which self-access learners see potential for language learning and take advantage of it. Such environments include public environments, like airports and the World Wide Web, semi-private environments, like student clubs and student residences, and private environments, like a learner's own home. The best use of uncontrolled environments may be when learners make use of them in conjunction with controlled environments, thus maintaining the integration mentioned in Section 1.3 which we see as an essential feature of self-access.

1.6 Justifying SALL

There are some major differences between the characteristics of classroom teaching/learning and those of self-access learning (Table 1.5). The appropriateness of classroom teaching is rarely questioned. It is a time-honoured approach which is generally accepted because it is traditional. Self-access learning does not have the same seal of approval and may be questioned by those who are unknowledgeable about it or hostile to it. There are a number of grounds on which educators,

Table 1.4. *A comparison of SACs in native speaker and non-native speaker environments*

	Native speaker environments		Non-native speaker environments	
	Advantages	Disadvantages	Advantages	Disadvantages
Authentic target language	• students will have greater access to native speakers of the language • authentic target language materials will be readily available	• dealing with native speakers may be frightening especially for lower level learners • authentic materials are unlikely to have bilingual support	where native speakers and authentic materials are scarce they will probably be supported to ensure maximum benefit	students may not have much access to native speakers or authentic materials
Counsellors	students may have more confidence (rightly or wrongly) in taking advice from a native speaker of their target language	counsellors probably will not be able to speak students' native languages. This is a particular problem for beginner students	counsellors who work in the SAC may be able to speak the mother tongue and so appear more approachable to weak students	counsellors may not be native speakers of the target language. This may reduce students' motivation to use them
Language of communication	the SAC environment is usually multi-lingual, therefore, students have to use the target language with other students	students may have difficulties and feel frustration when working with other learners who have different pronunciation/accents	lower level students could choose to communicate with their peers in their own language to solve learning problems	students may not use the target language much as they will feel more comfortable speaking with the counsellor and classmates in their mother tongue

Table 1.4. (contd)

	Native speaker environments		Non-native speaker environments	
	Advantages	Disadvantages	Advantages	Disadvantages
The real world	• the SAC may act as a bridge to the outside, unstructured environment • learners can build up their confidence in the SAC before trying the real world • it is possible to blur the lines between a SAC and the real world by inviting the real world in and sending the learners out • the SAC can protect lower level students from the real world until they are ready for it	students may continue to use the SAC instead of the real world, i.e. they may spend all their time in a SAC practising the language and rarely take advantage of the English-speaking environment around them	where access to a target language real world is impossible a SAC can provide a simulation	a simulation is never as good as the real thing
Learner involvement	a SAC provides support while learners are adjusting to the environment	students may never become fully involved because they tend to be on short courses and because there are other attractions outside the SAC	if the SAC is in a school where the student spends several years, students may become involved in developing materials and/or decorating the SAC and have a greater sense of ownership	if learners do not see the benefits of SALL they may not become involved in the SAC

Table 1.4. (*contd*)

	Native speaker environments		Non-native speaker environments	
	Advantages	Disadvantages	Advantages	Disadvantages
Materials	there may be greater access to up-to-date material obtained from the native speaking environment	usually the materials in the SAC cater to mixed nationalities and cultures and therefore cannot cater fully to the specific needs of particular groups of learners	• the SAC can cater to the specific language learning needs of the students • materials can be developed with a focus on the local environment which the students are familiar with	it may not always be possible to obtain authentic materials
Culture	the culture of the host country can be expressed in the SAC	learners' cultures may be ignored in the quest to cater for a large number of different learners. Therefore the style of self-access may not be what the student is used to	the SAC can be oriented to the cultural values of the local society	if the local culture does not value autonomy in learning, a SAC may be considered of no value
Motivation	learners have an immediate need for the target language	the 'protected' world of the SAC may seem less attractive than the real world	opportunities to interact with the target language and culture demonstrate the utility of language learning	if it is difficult to obtain authentic materials, or if the range of materials is restricted, the SAC may appear boring and students may prefer not to go there

Table 1.5.   *Characteristics of taught courses and self-access learning*

	Taught courses	Self-access learning
Goals	• very specific • restricted in range • established and controlled by educators.	• specific or vague • single goals or extremely wide ranging • established by educators; students; both; or non-existent.
Level of learner autonomy	Ranges from none (i.e. complete teacher-direction) to partial group autonomy (e.g. a learner-centred or a negotiated syllabus).	Ranges from none (i.e. students required to do self-access) to absolute autonomy (e.g. students who elect to use self-access).
Learning gain	Relatively easy to measure with pre- and post-course tests.	Difficult to measure because: • learners work independently, thus, standardised tests are impossible • duration and intensity are flexible so tests are difficult to position • effects may be extremely long term so true gain may only appear years later.
Duration of study	Limited by length of the course.	From one off use to life long learning.
Intensity of study	A feature of the course and therefore controlled by the teacher.	May be controlled by the teacher or the individual depending on the degree of learner autonomy.
Learner motivation	• Sometimes evaluated through pre-course and/or end-of-course questionnaires. • Observations of in-class participation.	Important for establishing level of learner support.
Cost effectiveness	Can calculate the cost per student for: • a specific quantity of teacher input • the degree of learning gain (in gross terms).	Currently neither input nor learning gain are calculated. Individualisation in self-access makes this challenging.

Table 1.5 (*contd*)

	Taught courses	Self-access learning
Teacher attitudes	• Teachers' attitudes often stem from the way they learned and from training courses. • Taught courses are accepted as the 'normal' way of teaching. No justification is expected.	Teachers' attitudes to self-access can be affected by the following: • they have traditional views of how knowledge should be imparted • they fear being usurped by SALL • they think students will not be motivated to study independently.
Attribution	Taught courses are often the only input students are receiving. Learning gain can be attributed to those courses.	Self-access is rarely the only input received. It usually combines with other forms of input making it difficult (or impossible) to isolate attributable learning gain.

students or administrators (the stakeholders) may question the introduction or continuation of self-access learning (Table 1.6). In Table 1.6 we have also suggested ways in which these questions can be answered. These are general answers on which more detailed answers relevant to individual contexts can be built.

To summarise our justification of SALL we would say, although it is difficult or impossible to show that SALL alone is directly responsible for learning gain, this is also true of most other language-learning activities. There is, nevertheless, some evidence that learners find SALL useful (and sometimes enjoyable), and our informed common sense as teachers leads us to believe that extra exposure to language is beneficial. If SALL is organised and systematic it allows maximum exposure to a wide variety of language-learning opportunities for a large number of learners in the least time-consuming and least costly way. Quality control can be undertaken through an active counselling service and through the monitoring of learner behaviour and feedback, for example through the use of learner profiles (see Chapter 5).

In addition to supporting language learning, SALL can result in increased learner autonomy; however, this depends to an extent on the way in which it is organised. SALL may favour certain skills over others but this can also be true of classroom teaching. In the case of SALL an imbalance in the focus on skills is largely a result of individualised learners responding to their own needs and wants. SALL is appropriate

Table 1.6. *Grounds on which the use of self-access language learning (SALL) might be questioned*

Grounds	Questions	Some Answers
Efficiency	Time available for learning/teaching is limited. Is SALL the best way to spend this time? Is it faster or slower than classroom learning?	SALL exposes learners to a wide variety of language learning opportunities which stimulate them, meet their individual needs, suit their individual learning styles and promote autonomy. If it does these things in an organised and systematic way which complements classroom teaching then it is probably an efficient use of an institution's resources and of learners' time. Evaluation of the efficiency of learning in SALL is, however, an area where more research is needed (see Chapter 12).
Cost	SALL will incur additional costs. Is self-access learning the best use of the institution's finances?	Some implementations of SALL are high cost especially some dedicated self-access facilities. However, there are also many examples of low cost SALL in operation (see Chapter 9) including some dedicated facilities (see Case Study 1). Nevertheless, institutions should not see SALL as a cheap alternative to teaching.
Effectiveness	The goal of SALL is to encourage learner autonomy while learning a language. Does SALL actually result in increased autonomy? Does SALL result in learning?	There are different stages of autonomy in learning (see Section 1.2.1). Students and teachers need to be realistic about what can be achieved by learning in SALL environments especially as the benefits may not be immediately apparent. Sensitisation needs to be built into learner training. It is usually impossible to evaluate exactly how much SALL has contributed directly to learning gain; however, this can also be said of other parts of the learning environment, e.g. group work, projects or homework. All of these, including SALL, are part of the teaching/learning toolkit.

Table 1.6. (*contd*)

Grounds	Questions	Some Answers
		We rely on a number of sources to evaluate effectiveness including teacher and learner perceptions, observations of behaviour and general evidence of learning gain (see Chapter 12).
Quantity of learning	Self-access learners may make their own decisions about how much to learn. How can an institution determine whether students have learned enough? How do institutions usually define 'enough' learning?	• Teachers who work in SALL need to be prepared to justify what their students are learning via SALL. They can do this by encouraging their students to prepare Learning Portfolios (see Chapter 11). • It may be appropriate to define 'enough learning' in relation to individual needs and wants.
Quality of learning	Some self-access learners may make decisions which result in them not fully mastering their chosen topics. How can quality controls be implemented to ensure the quality of learning is consistently high? How do institutions usually ensure the quality of learning is high?	As with all language learning, students need to be allowed to make mistakes and to learn from them. The key to quality control in self-access learning is counselling (see Chapter 10). Accountability (or self-accountability) can be introduced through the use of learner profiles (see Chapter 5).
Coverage of skills	SALL may be perceived as favouring some language skills over others. Are some skills easier to deal with in self-access than others? Do self-access learners favour working on certain skills and, if so, why? Does classroom teaching give all skills equal treatment? How much practice with particular skills do individual students get in classroom teaching and in SALL?	• Many self-access centres begin by offering materials for the receptive skills: listening and reading. These skills are easier for individual students to deal with, in terms of not having to find others to work with, and they can often check their work easily with answer cards. As self-access matures in institutions, productive skills are often added. This is often at the request of students who want to develop their oral or writing skills. It also develops from teachers' desires to produce a wide range of activities which cater to their students' needs (see Chapter 7).

Table 1.6. (contd)

Grounds	Questions	Some Answers
		• The skills self-access learners favour will vary according to institutional requirements (e.g. examinations) and availability of appropriate materials but also largely because of individual needs and wants. The same influences may apply in the classroom but without learner individualisation. SALL allows learners to decide for themselves how much practice they need.
Language level	SALL may be perceived as too difficult or unnecessary for certain levels of language learners. Is SALL suitable for learners at all levels?	SALL is beneficial for all kinds of learners although, as with other kinds of learning, it needs to be adapted to its users. There are successful implementations of SALL at all levels of learning and in all age ranges. Throughout this book we discuss SALL for a variety of learners. We describe self-access facilities for all age groups from young learners to adults (see Chapter 3 and the case studies in Part 3), we give examples of self-access activities which span the range from beginners to advanced learners (see Chapter 7) and we discuss issues related to learner levels of self-access materials (see Chapter 6).
Culture	SALL is sometimes considered to originate from western culture (although there are also counter-claims). Is it appropriate for learners who traditionally learn by rote? Is it appropriate for learners whose culture does not emphasise individualism?	Each implementation of SALL is unique and should be tailored to the cultural context (see Section 2.5). There are many successful implementations of SALL in non-western cultures, some of them are described in this book.

Table 1.6. (contd)

Grounds	Questions	Some Answers
Autonomy	SALL encourages learners to make decisions. Is the encouragement of autonomy consistent with the goals of a particular institution?	• To answer this question for a specific context it would be necessary to look at the goals of the institution. However, in most cases one goal of education is to create independent thinkers which is consistent with autonomous learning. • Where the concept of 'autonomy' is difficult to accept a rewording of the term may go some way to solving the problem. 'Self-direction' or 'self-study', for example, may not sound so worrying as 'independence' or 'autonomy'. Perhaps even the introduction of 'good' or 'modern' language teaching practice would ensure some degree of autonomy in all language classes (see Chapter 9 for ways of doing this).
Organisation versus anarchy	Self-access learners are encouraged to customise their plans of study so that each learner may have completely different objectives and methods to all other learners. Can such diversity be organised to prevent anarchy? Does orderliness enhance learning? Does anarchy prevent learning?	There is no evidence that being organised enhances learning. However, it is reasonable to assume that a total lack of organisation might decrease efficiency and possibly effectiveness. Thus, self-access systems need to encourage an organised approach without stifling diversity. This can be achieved through learner profiles (discussed in Chapter 5).
Maturity level	SALL encourages learners to take responsibility for their own learning. They make lots of decisions about what, when, where and how to learn. Does this increased level of responsibility require a level of maturity that only exists in adult learners?	A number of studies we refer to in this book and in particular Case Studies 1 and 2 in the final part of the book demonstrate that SALL can be implemented successfully with pre-adult learners.

Table 1.6. (*contd*)

Grounds	Questions	Some Answers
Devaluation of teachers	SALL encourages learners to be less teacher-dependent. Does this undermine the status of teachers? Does this mean SALL will eventually make teachers redundant?	It is true that SALL tends to diminish the traditional teacher role but this is replaced by a range of new roles (see Chapter 1, especially Section 1.4.2) which require a new range of skills (see Section 2.7, Section 4.5, Chapter 9, Chapter 10). Teachers are as integral to SALL as they are to classroom teaching; however, their presence is less immediately obvious. It would, therefore, be wise to make sure administrators and managers know about the new roles undertaken by teachers and their unique qualifications for undertaking these roles (e.g. knowledge of language learning, student behaviour, learning styles and strategies). In addition, SALL should not be viewed as a replacement for teaching but as a complement to it which allows greater individualisation and a wider range of learning opportunities.

to all levels of learners and to all ages of learners. This is supported in the literature by examples of successful SALL implementation in all categories. SALL is not suitable only for students from western cultural settings and this is demonstrated, for example, by the many successful implementations in Asia. SALL does not threaten teachers' jobs: it creates new and important roles for teachers to which they have to adapt. Teachers remain an integral part of the learning process.

In cases where justifications for existing SALL implementations must be made it is wise to find ways to record: what activities, materials and resources learners have used; learning gain (even if it cannot be directly attributed to SALL some responsibility can be claimed); and perceptions of learners and teachers of the usefulness and enjoyability of SALL activities and materials. This data will provide some evaluative evidence to justify SALL; for a more detailed discussion on evaluating SALL, see Chapter 12.

1.7 The costs of SALL

It may be tempting to present SALL as a cheap alternative to teaching, especially when looking for arguments to justify funding. However, this would be erroneous, partly because SALL does not replace teaching but complements it and partly because SALL is not cheap (although it may be an efficient use of resources). The cost of SALL varies considerably according to the system implemented and the extent to which it is implemented. In Chapter 3 we suggest a typology of self-access systems some of which clearly cost less than others (see Table 3.1). Institutions get what they pay for and in some cases a low-cost system is suitable for the context.

There are two kinds of costs involved in SALL; the start-up costs and the recurrent costs (see Section 8.4 for more details). The former are easy to calculate and often become the focus of attention in making decisions about SALL. Recurrent costs are less obvious but if funding is not forthcoming they can lead to the failure of SALL. A key element in successful SALL is pedagogical input and this is relatively expensive. Only teachers can adequately perform many of the roles created by SALL, like, for example: selecting materials (Chapter 6), writing materials (Chapter 6), creating learning activities (Chapter 7), running workshops (Chapter 7), language counselling (Chapter 10), creating links with the curriculum (Chapters 7 and 9), designing and implementing assessment (Chapter 11), and evaluating (Chapter 12). (These roles are further discussed elsewhere in this book; the respective chapter numbers are given above.) SALL involves teacher time on an ongoing basis and that costs money. The costs may be hidden (e.g. where SALL happens in the classroom) or they may be obvious (e.g. in a SAC which provides a counselling service). Pedagogical support is what makes SALL different from what could be provided in a library.

Institutions may be able to benefit from economies of scale when introducing SALL. Thus, although low-cost classroom-based SALL appears to be cheap it may be more cost efficient (and perhaps also more pedagogically effective) to provide a SAC as a central facility which would reduce the quantity of materials required, to centralise the use of teacher time and to enhance the opportunities for interactions between learners. When an institution commits itself to providing a SAC it may still opt for a relatively low-cost implementation. Pedagogical staff would still be required for counselling and some decision-making but much of the administrative work could be undertaken by student helpers. In addition, teachers could be asked to volunteer their time or they could be asked to accompany their classes to the SAC and help out with counselling or other duties. The cost of updating and improving materials would still occur but this could be reduced to a minimum in a number of imaginative ways (e.g. by providing laminated worksheets instead of take-away copies, by asking teachers and publishers for donations of materials, by asking learners for a subscription). One large area of expenditure is technology. A low-cost solution is to do without technology. There is a tendency in some parts of the world to think of SACs as high-tech environments; however, this is not the only option as is demonstrated by some of the examples of successful low-tech SACs in this book. In deciding about technology it is important to consider the expectations of teachers and students.

It is not easy to secure funding for SALL, especially adequate funding which covers the costs of pedagogical support. Ways of securing funding will vary in different contexts; however, in all contexts a well-grounded proposal which draws on all available evidence is essential. In Table 1.7 we suggest the kind of documentation that could be used to support a proposal. In addition, it is useful before making a proposal to find ways to enhance awareness about SALL. Awareness-raising should aim at staff as well as students of an institution but can also be conducted on a more public level where this will bring benefits. Table 1.8 suggests some ways in which awareness-raising exercises can be conducted. Teachers proposing SALL should also be aware that there are often alternative sources of funding or alternative ways of looking at the funding issue. Table 1.9 suggests some techniques for actively seeking funding.

Implementing SALL should not be seen as a cheap alternative to teaching. It should be seen as a useful complement to teaching which enhances language-learning opportunities and provides learners with

Table 1.7. *Documents to provide in support of a proposal for SALL*

Provide	This Demonstrates
• a rationale for the introduction of SALL	• benefits to learners which cannot be gained any other way
• a literature review showing the arguments for SALL	• academic support for SALL
• a list of countries and kinds of institutions where SALL has successfully been implemented	• that SALL is in widespread use and at a variety of levels and with a variety of age groups
• a report on local implementations of SALL	• that SALL is applicable within the cultural setting and within local funding possibilities
• a review of new skills required of teachers (see Chapter 10)	• the professionalism required of teachers in SALL
• an explanation of language counselling	• how the funding needed for pedagogical support will be spent
	• the benefits to students
• results of a staff survey	• level of support from colleagues
• results of a student survey	• level of interest among students
• a management plan	• understanding of management issues (see Chapter 4)
• the results of a pilot study (e.g. an implementation of SALL with one class)	• the practicality and validity of SALL
	• the hidden costs (like teacher time)
• a projection of numbers of SALL users	• cost efficiency

the independent learning skills to continue learning language after they have finished formal studies. In this light it may be judged to be relatively cost efficient. SALL can be implemented at different cost levels and institutions need to decide what is appropriate for them. Where implementation is to be widespread it may prove to be more efficient to provide a SAC than to implement small-scale SALL in each classroom. There are a number of ways in which the success rate of funding applications can be improved. Many of these are context specific; however, in general, applications have a greater chance if they are well supported by documentary evidence and if the proposers take the trouble to learn about specific funding systems and their alternatives.

Table 1.8. *Ways of raising awareness about SALL*

Way	Effect
• Produce some simple but effective self-access materials which meet widespread learning needs in the institution. Make them widely available to students and also to colleagues.	• Practical demonstrations of SALL will help learners and colleagues to see its value. They will also provide feedback which can be summarised in a document to the funding body.
• Offer workshops which introduce students to some easily applicable self-access ideas.	• ditto
• Reproduce testimonials from satisfied SALL users.	• Students are more likely to pay attention to accreditation of SALL which comes from their peers. Teachers and administrators might also be influenced by it.
• Produce a focused article for an institutional publication (e.g. staff magazine, student magazine, parent–teacher newsletter).	• Raise awareness among relevant people about the potential of SALL in the institution.
• Produce a general newspaper article about SALL.	• Raise public awareness (institutional administrators also read newspapers and are often sensitive to public opinion).

1.8 Summary

In this chapter we have laid out the background to self-access language learning. We have shown how it is an approach to language learning which has as its ultimate goal the moving of learners from teacher dependence towards autonomy. We have given a brief review of the debate about autonomous learning and how it is defined. We have also mentioned other labels for approaches similar to, but not synonymous with, self-access language learning. We have also provided an overview of self-access language learning, discussing: its characteristics, the issues related to establishing it, sources of influences on learners, the changing roles of those involved, the kinds of environments in which it takes place and, finally, its validity.

Table 1.9. *Techniques for actively seeking funding*

Technique	Explanation
• Find out how to acquire the right information.	• Library staff are often good at knowing where to look.
• Find out about existing funding.	• Knowing how current funding is calculated and distributed can help in discussions with administrators.
• Reorganisation.	• Look at current funding for ways of reorganising distribution of funding to allow some SALL.
• Find out about special funding.	• Ask in your own institution (head and financial administrators), public authorities (local and central government officials), foreign government sources (e.g. embassies, educational missions), private educational funding bodies (e.g. charities, educational trusts), other private sources (e.g. company sponsorship).
• Be creative.	• Find alternative ways of wording funding requests to suit the occasion, e.g. 'self-access learning' for educational funding, 'evaluating self-access learning' for research funding or 'raising linguistic and cultural awareness through self-access learning' for cultural funding.
• Talk to other proponents of SALL.	• If SALL is already working in a similar institution ask how they got their funding.
• Talk to local SALL researchers.	• They often know a lot about what other institutions are doing and how they do it. They sometimes also know about funding opportunities. Occasionally they have some funding which they might share in exchange for research collaboration.

1.9 Tasks

1. Define in your own words one of the following terms and give an example:
   • Self-access language learning
   • Autonomous learning
2. Identify the influences on learners (and perhaps also teachers) within your own context which would most likely inhibit the establishing of self-access learning.

3. Select the new role your learners would have most difficulty accepting (see Figure 1.4). Then list the ways in which you would help them adapt to that role.

1.10 For discussion

1. Discuss why the terminology in the area of autonomous learning is so confusing.
2. If you were establishing self-access language learning which of the elements from Table 1.1 would you prioritise and why?
3. Which of the arguments in Table 1.6 is most likely to be raised in your institution? How would you respond to this argument?

2 Learners' and teachers' beliefs and attitudes about language learning

2.1 Introduction

Accepting 'new' ways of language learning requires a fundamental, and sometimes drastic, change in perceptions from both learners and teachers about how languages are learned. Learners who have undergone a systematic education process develop certain beliefs about how learning should take place. Everyone is, to some extent, conditioned by the educational environment they experience. In language learning, beliefs and attitudes are shaped not only by the educational environment but also by family and societal values. These influences on approaches to learning a language may encourage learners to experience new methods of learning, or conversely constrain and restrict their desire for a new learning experience. In this chapter we explore the complex issues of learners' and teachers' beliefs and attitudes towards learning and teaching a foreign/second language.

We begin this chapter by looking at some of the influences on how learners and teachers form their beliefs about language learning. We then discuss some studies which highlight the differences that may be found between learners' and teachers' beliefs. It is important for teachers to recognise these differences by finding out about their learners. We demonstrate one way to achieve this by investigating cultural perceptions of learners and their learning styles. Next, we discuss how communication between learners and teachers about their beliefs and attitudes is important in preparing for self-access language learning. We then present studies which show a reluctance on the part of learners to change their beliefs about language learning. We argue, however, that with preparation and training, beliefs about self-access language learning can become more positive and learners can see the potential of this approach for their language learning.

2.2 Learners' beliefs about language learning

Learners bring their own beliefs, goals, attitudes and decisions to learning and these influence how they approach their learning. Their learning experiences, in turn, either reinforce or alter these beliefs, goals, attitudes and decisions. Richards and Lockhart (1994) classify learners' beliefs into eight categories. We summarise their categories in Table 2.1. These categories are relevant to self-access language learning because learners' beliefs may inhibit attempts to introduce them to flexibility in their learning and to greater learner responsibility.

Richards and Lockhart (1994) suggest that some teachers discourage learners from using learning strategies of their choice. The individualisation offered by self-access learning encourages learners to develop strategies they find useful. As Oxford (1992: 20) points out, 'when allowed to learn in their favourite way, unpressured by learning environment or other factors, students often use strategies that directly reflect their preferred learning'. Learners' beliefs about appropriate classroom behaviour have an impact on the use of self-access within the classroom environment. Within a traditional educational context learners' expectations may not include learning activities which are not teacher-centred. This will make it difficult for them to adopt new roles in the classroom.

Learners' beliefs about themselves often include perceptions of their ability as language learners. Victori and Lockhart (1995) conclude that learners' beliefs (which they refer to as metacognition) interact with autonomy and language learning. Learners' beliefs, whether true or not, can be simplistic. One study showed that learners believed that to be successful language learners they had to be extrovert, intelligent and have started learning the language as a child (Victori 1992, cited in Victori and Lockhart 1995). Learners' views may affect how they respond to self-access learning opportunities.

2.3 Teachers' beliefs about language learning

While learners' beliefs influence the way they learn, teachers' beliefs are also important as they have a strong influence on the learning environment. Richards and Lockhart (1994) suggest five categories of teachers' beliefs which are summarised in Table 2.2. They also suggest that the beliefs are constructed in the following ways:

- their own experience as language learners
- experience of what works best
- established practice
- personality factors
- educationally-based or research-based principles
- principles derived from an approach or method.

Table 2.1. *Learners' beliefs about language learning*

Beliefs about …	Description
the nature of English.	Learners often see learning a language in different ways. Some perceive grammar as being difficult to master, others find a problem with pronunciation. Some may have a very positive attitude towards a language like English, whereas others may see it more negatively as something they have to learn rather than something they want to learn.
the speakers of English.	Learners may have stereotypical perceptions about speakers of their target language which influence how they themselves use the language. For example, some learners may perceive Australian people as very friendly but British people as more reserved. These beliefs may affect individual learner's own use of English, especially when interacting with native speakers and/or their teachers.
the four language skills.	Learners may be instrumentally motivated to learning the language, e.g. they want to pass the end of term test. If the learners believe that concentrating on one of the language skills will help them achieve their goals then they may ignore other learning opportunities.
teaching.	Learners have very definite perceptions of what teachers should do in class, e.g. provide information, follow the book, give examples.
language learning.	Learners have definite learning strategies which they bring with them to their learning. However, in a classroom situation they are often forced into adopting learning strategies imposed on them by the teacher and/or the materials.
appropriate classroom behaviour.	Learners from different cultures often have different perceptions about what is or is not appropriate classroom behaviour.
self.	Learners may view themselves as good or poor language learners, or may know that their strengths as a language learner lie in one area but not in others.
goals.	Different learners may have different personal goals in learning the language. For some, being able to pass a test or have minimum competence might be the goal, for others they want native-like pronunciation and full command of the language.

Adapted from: Richards and Lockhart 1994

Table 2.2.   *Teachers' beliefs*

Beliefs about ...	Description
English.	Teachers have different beliefs about why their learners should learn English (or any other language). This may be because it is an international language, because it will help the learners get better jobs, or because of the perceived beauty of the literature associated with the language.
learning.	Teachers' beliefs about *how* languages are learned affect their approach to the language. These beliefs come from how they were taught, their training and their experiences as teachers.
teaching.	Teachers' beliefs about how they should teach are based not only on their training but also their personalities. Different teachers approach the same teaching situation in different ways because of this.
the program and the curriculum.	Some teachers have distinct personal philosophies about the program and curriculum they are using, others may follow the institutional or government dictates.
language teaching as a profession.	Some teachers have a distinct view of their profession as a career with goals and career opportunities. Others may not have such clearly established perceptions of their roles in teaching.

Adapted from: Richards and Lockhart 1994

2.4 Differences between learners' and teachers' beliefs about language learning

In a large-scale study of 517 learners of English in Australia, Willing (1988) found that certain classroom activities were rated very highly by the learners, while other activities received a low or very low rating. Learners responded favourably to statements in Willing's questionnaire such as:

I like to practise the sounds and pronunciation.	62%
I like the teacher to tell me all my mistakes.	61%
In class, I like to learn by conversations.	55%
I like the teacher to explain *everything* to us.	54%

(Willing 1988: 116)

Statements which elicited a low or very low response included:

I like the teacher to let me find my mistakes.	27%
In class, I like to learn by pictures, films, videos.	19%
I like to learn English by talking in pairs.	15%
In class, I like to learn by games.	10%
I like to study English by myself (alone).	3%

(Willing 1988: 117)

Nunan (1988a) replicated part of Willing's study but this time with 60 teachers. He asked them to rate the following on a four-point scale according to their degree of importance in classroom teaching: pronunciation practice; explanations to class; conversation practice; error correction; vocabulary development; listening to/using cassettes; student self-discovery of errors; using pictures, film and video; pair work; and language games. Nunan states that 'items were rated and scored in an identical fashion to the Willing study' (Nunan 1988a: 92). The results, however, were not identical. Table 2.3 shows a comparison of the results between learners and teachers in the areas identified above.

The results of the studies of Willing (1988) and Nunan (1988a) show that in the ten areas compared there is complete agreement on only one activity (conversational practice). In all other areas there is some disagreement, and in several the perceptions are almost opposite. As Nunan (1998a: 93) states, the data presented 'reveal clear mismatches between learners' and teachers' views of language learning'. These mismatches of beliefs and attitudes between learners and teachers may prove to be serious obstacles when introducing self-access.

Table 2.3. *A comparison of student and teacher ratings of selected learning activities*

Activity	Student	Teacher
pronunciation practice	very high	medium
explanations to class	very high	high
conversation practice	very high	very high
error correction	very high	low
vocabulary development	very high	high
listening to / using cassettes	low	medium high
student self-discovery of errors	low	very high
using pictures, film and video	low	low medium
pair work	low	very high
language games	very low	low

After: Nunan 1988a: 92

2.5 Cultural influences

Much of the work into learning strategies seeks to find out not only how individuals approach their learning, but whether or not there are any cultural traits or approaches by which certain groups of learners can be categorised. If culture does influence learners' beliefs and attitudes the provision of self-access learning opportunities should cater to these beliefs and attitudes. Littlewood (1996) compiled a list of predictions about Asian language learners. These predictions are based on a review of the literature into Asian students' beliefs and attitudes towards language learning. The predictions are that Asian learners are likely to:

1. have a strong inclination to form groups which work towards common goals.
2. be eager to engage in activities which involve discussion within groups.
3. be concerned to maintain harmony within their groups.
4. be reluctant to 'stand out' by expressing their views or raising questions.
5. perceive the teacher as an authoritarian figure.
6. see knowledge as something to be transmitted by the teacher rather than discovered by the learners.
7. expect the teacher to be responsible for the assessment of learning.
8. show strong motivation to follow through learning tasks of which they perceive the practical value.
9. be more motivated when success contributes to the goals or prestige of significant in-groups.
10. be very concerned to perform well and correctly in what they do in class.

Similar lists of predictions about other homogeneous groups of learners would be useful. These predictions can either be based (as Littlewood's are) on the relevant literature, or on the personal experiences of teachers. They could then be used as a framework within which to develop a view of 'typical' learners. However, caution should be exercised in utilising this framework for two reasons. First, a fundamental precept of self-access is that it encourages learners to develop as individuals, therefore frameworks should not be used to constrain learners. Second, frameworks are based on predictions which should inform but not constrain teachers' attempts to introduce self-access. By reading Littlewood's (1996) predictions, for example, it would appear that Asian learners (and this is a very large group of learners all lumped together) would not take any interest in developing their independent language learning (predictions 4, 5, 6, 7, in particular, indicate this).

However, a study conducted by Gardner and Miller (1997) demonstrates that at least some Asian learners (i.e. Hong Kong Chinese) do accept and work well within self-access environments.

2.6 Preparing learners for self-access language learning

In order for SALL to be successful, teachers must prepare their students to accept more responsibility for their learning than they may be accustomed to. In order to do this, teachers must initiate discussions and activities in the class which challenge students' traditional beliefs about learning a language and their expectations of their abilities as language learners. This preparation must begin in the classroom and can become part of the teaching strategies adopted by teachers.

Dickinson and Carver (1980: 1) maintain that 'there would need to be a shift of emphasis and a gradual change of attitude on the part of both the teacher and the pupils' when preparing learners for independence. They list ten techniques (summarised in Table 2.4) which could be used to promote learner independence in the class. Many of these will already be familiar to teachers who use a communicative approach to their teaching and emphasise the close links which already exist between some classroom practice and SALL.

When preparing learners in the classroom for the shift to independent learning individual differences of the learners have to be taken into account and some of the techniques suggested in Table 2.4 may not work well with all learners. Wenden (1986) shows how a variety of learners have different beliefs about what is important in language learning. If, for example, learners believe that language is systematic and should be learned in a systematic way it may be difficult to get them to engage in activities which require them to guess and take risks. Johnson (1995) cites several studies in which cultural upbringing has a competing effect on language education in schools. She cites examples from Japanese students learning English, Australian aboriginals in Western-style classes, and Mexican students who attend an Anglo-American school. In each of the examples, the students' pre-school culturally-learned styles are at odds with those of the classroom. Teachers, therefore, have to become aware of their learners' beliefs and attitudes to learning and try to accommodate them in their choice of classroom activities.

2.7 Preparing teachers for self-access language learning

An essential part of the success of self-access is in having teachers well prepared to introduce it to their learners. Therefore, teachers need to be

Table 2.4.   *Techniques for promoting independence in the classroom*

Technique	Description
Self-monitoring	Learners keep a record of their language learning and perhaps rate themselves.
Self-correction	Correcting or checking one's work: this may most easily be done in writing, but can also be applied to the other skills also.
Variable pacing	Learners work at their own pace during a lesson.
Group work	Learners work in groups of 3 or 4 to complete a task.
Project-work	An extended piece of work where learners co-operate to gather and organise information; this may then be presented orally or as a written report.
Trouble-shooting sessions	Learners are encouraged to talk about their language learning problems.
Extensive reading and listening	Learners are encouraged to read novels or extended texts for pleasure, they may also be exposed to TV or radio programmes.
Choice of activities	Learners have the freedom to choose which activities to do. Can be related to homework tasks or voluntary attendance at an English club, for example.
Use of pupil teachers	Learners may be encouraged to teach each other.
Sharing objectives	Teachers involve the learners in helping to plan or order the teaching objectives for a period of study.

Adapted from: Dickinson and Carver 1980

sensitised to their own beliefs and attitudes as a first step in becoming aware of any changes in their roles when working with their learners in self-access mode (see Chapter 1 for further discussion on teachers' changing roles). Several instruments are available which help teachers think about their attitudes and beliefs towards language learning. Two of these are notable. The first is the Foreign Language Attitude Survey (FLAS). The FLAS was developed by de Garcia et al. (1976) to enable teachers to think about and discuss their attitudes towards language teaching. The original survey contains 53 statements which range from

Below are beliefs that some people have about learning foreign languages. Read each statement and then decide if you: (1) strongly agree, (2) agree, (3) neither agree nor disagree, (4) disagree, (5) strongly disagree. Questions 4 and 11 are slightly different and you should mark them as indicated. There are no right or wrong answers. We are simply interested in your opinion.

1.	It is easier for children than adults to learn a foreign language.	5	4	3	2	1
2.	Some people are born with a special ability which helps them learn a foreign language.	5	4	3	2	1
3.	Some languages are easier to learn than others.	5	4	3	2	1
4.	The language I am planning to teach is: a) a very difficult language b) a difficult language c) a language of medium difficulty d) an easy language e) a very easy language	a	b	c	d	e
5.	It's important to speak a foreign language with an excellent accent.	5	4	3	2	1
6.	It is necessary to know the foreign culture in order to speak a foreign language.	5	4	3	2	1
7.	You shouldn't say anything in the language until you can say it correctly.	5	4	3	2	1
8.	It is easier for someone who already speaks a foreign language to learn another one.	5	4	3	2	1
9.	It is better to learn a foreign language in the foreign country.	5	4	3	2	1
10.	It's OK to guess if you don't know a word in the foreign language.	5	4	3	2	1
11.	If someone spent one hour a day learning, how long would it take him to become fluent? (1) Less than a year, (2) 1–2 years, (3) 3–5 years, (4) 5–10 years, (5) You can't learn a language in 1 hour a day.	5	4	3	2	1

Figure 2.1.   The Beliefs About Language Learning Inventory (BALLI)
Source: Horwitz 1985

		5	4	3	2	1
12.	Learning a foreign language is mostly a matter of learning a lot of new vocabulary words.	5	4	3	2	1
13.	It's important to repeat and practice a lot.	5	4	3	2	1
14.	If you are allowed to make mistakes in the beginning it will be hard to get rid of them later on.	5	4	3	2	1
15.	Learning a foreign language is mostly a matter of learning a lot of grammar rules.	5	4	3	2	1
16.	It's important to practice in the language laboratory.	5	4	3	2	1
17.	Women are better than men at learning foreign languages.	5	4	3	2	1
18.	It is easier to speak than understand a foreign language.	5	4	3	2	1
19.	Learning a foreign language is different from learning other school subjects.	5	4	3	2	1
20.	Learning another language is a matter of translating from English	5	4	3	2	1
21.	If students learn to speak this language very well, it will help them get a good job.	5	4	3	2	1
22.	It is easier to read and write a language than to speak and understand it.	5	4	3	2	1
23.	People who are good at math and science are not good at learning foreign languages.	5	4	3	2	1
24.	Americans think that it is important to speak a foreign language.	5	4	3	2	1
25.	People who speak more than one language well are very intelligent.	5	4	3	2	1
26.	Americans are good at learning foreign languages.	5	4	3	2	1
27.	Everyone can learn to speak a foreign language.	5	4	3	2	1

Figure 2.1 (contd)

considering the importance of teaching grammar to cultural aspects in teaching a language. Although the survey can be used in its original form to gain a perspective on teachers' attitudes, it should be noted that some of the statements might now appear a little dated, or may have to be changed to suit the context in which the survey is administered. The second is the Beliefs About Language Learning Inventory (BALLI) developed in the USA by Horwitz (1985) (Figure 2.1). Horwitz (1985: 334) developed the BALLI 'to assess teacher opinions on a variety of issues and controversies related to language learning'. She claims that the instrument may be used to: (1) better understand why teachers choose particular teaching practices and (2) determine where the beliefs of language teachers and their students might be in conflict.

The FLAS and BALLI are useful tools in helping teachers express and discuss their attitudes and beliefs about language learning and teaching. By using them, teachers become more receptive to making assessments about attitudes and beliefs they hold, many of which may have been acquired from their own experiences as language learners. They may then be more receptive to making shifts in their attitudes and beliefs about their learners and about innovations in language teaching.

2.8 Learners' and teachers' beliefs about self-access language learning

2.8.1 Resistance to autonomy

There are various reports in the literature about learner resistance towards autonomy. Sinclair and Ellis (1984), reporting on language enhancement programmes for overseas students in England, make the point that many of the students considered that it was the responsibility of the teacher to ensure that learning took place and 'encouragement to work independently of the teacher was rejected and dissatisfaction with the course and loss of motivation the result' (Sinclair and Ellis 1984: 46). Farmer (1994) reported that many of the students participating in a self-access programme at tertiary level expected 100% teacher contact. In Willing's (1988: 117) study of migrant adults' learning styles, only 3% of those surveyed responded positively to the statement 'I like to study English by myself (alone)'. In his discussion of these results Willing states that the majority of learners in his survey had negative associations with the proposal of 'self-teaching'.

2.8.2 A positive example of learner autonomy

What is not clear from the studies cited in Section 2.8.1 is whether the learners had been trained for self-access learning. Gardner and Miller

Table 2.5.   *Students' responses to selected questionnaire statements*

	Yes (%)	No (%)
I like to use a self-access centre for learning a language.	86.14	13.68
I think self-access is a good way to learn.	88.91	9.24
The SAC is **as** effective **as** classroom lessons in improving my English.	58.78	38.63
The SAC has clear objectives.	80.78	16.27
I benefit by using the SAC.	84.10	14.60
Self-access work helps me develop good study habits.	63.59	34.38

Note: Some respondents chose not to respond to some statements.
After: Gardner and Miller 1997

(1997) sampled 541 learners and 58 teachers in self-access centres using both quantitative instruments (questionnaires) and qualitative instruments (interviews) to investigate learners' and teachers' perceptions about self-access learning. Some of the results of this study are presented in Tables 2.5 and 2.6.

Gardner and Miller's study was conducted in five SACs each in a different institution. All of these institutions conducted learner training as part of their induction programmes to their self-access centres. The questionnaire results show a high degree of satisfaction with the self-access facilities, and most of the learners considered it worthwhile to use the SAC to improve their English. A large number of these learners even considered self-access learning to be as effective as classroom-based learning.

In-depth interviews with 50 learners reflected the results of the questionnaire survey. The overriding belief among the learners interviewed was that English was a 'need'. Learners needed to learn the language whether they liked to or not and the self-access facilities helped them in achieving their language learning goals. One user was particularly perceptive in putting into words the position of English with regard to Hong Kong students:

> Basically, learning English has been just as an arranged marriage to me since I was young. It was compulsory to learn English. After more than ten years of learning English, I now have an interest in it and understand how important it is.

In order to compare responses of learners and teachers, the latter

Table 2.6. *Teachers' responses to selected questionnaire statements*

	Yes (%)	No (%)	Don't know (%)
Chinese students like self-access learning.	43.10	15.51	39.66
The students think self-access is a good way to learn.	56.90	8.62	32.76
The SAC is **as** effective **as** classroom lessons in improving students' English.	41.38	39.66	17.24
Our SAC is successful in achieving its objectives.	55.17	13.79	29.31
Students benefit by using the SAC.	86.21	3.45	10.34
Self-access work helps students develop good study habits.	63.80	6.89	29.31

Note: Some respondents chose not to respond to some statements.
After: Gardner and Miller 1997

were given a 'mirror' questionnaire, that is, one which contained similar statements to the learners' questionnaire. The teachers' responses to a selected group of statements are summarised in Table 2.6.

When the responses of the learners and teachers from Tables 2.5 and 2.6 are compared it can be seen that there is a high degree of agreement in two of the statements: learners benefit by using the SAC and self-access work helps students develop good study habits. However, the learners were much more positive than the teachers about the perceived benefits of using a SAC and considered it an effective way to improve their English. Teachers, on the other hand, were unsure about their learners' attitudes and beliefs towards self-access learning. Simply because teachers work in a self-access centre does not mean that they have in-depth knowledge about their learners' beliefs and attitudes. The results of studies like that of Gardner and Miller (1997), when made available, help inform teachers of their learners' beliefs and attitudes and may play an important part in helping teachers re-focus their own beliefs and attitudes.

2.9 Summary

In this chapter we have shown how current research has demonstrated that both learners and teachers hold specific views on language learning and teaching. It is therefore important for teachers to become aware of their own and their learners' beliefs and attitudes when working in self-access learning. Teachers can become better informed about their learners by gathering information about their beliefs and attitudes and then developing a framework within which to introduce self-access.

Any innovation in teaching and learning requires a shift in beliefs and attitudes for both teachers and learners. We have shown that without sensitising teachers to their own beliefs and attitudes and some form of learner training for students, negative attitudes towards self-access learning may develop.

2.10 Tasks

1. Look at Section 2.2. Consider a group of learners you are familiar with. Make a list of what you think their beliefs about language learning are.
2. Look again at the predictions made by Littlewood (Section 2.5). Now make your own predictions about a group of homogenous learners' beliefs and attitudes. You could use the same list of beliefs as Littlewood or you could make your own list.
3. Complete the BALLI in Section 2.7. What does this tell you about your own beliefs towards language learning and teaching?

2.11 For discussion

1. Look at Table 2.2 (teachers' beliefs about language learning). Under each section, discuss what your beliefs are.
2. Look at Table 2.4 in Section 2.6. How many of the techniques in the table do you regularly use in your teaching? Do you think that these techniques lead learners towards independence?
3. Discuss different ways by which you can collect information about your learners' beliefs and attitudes. Consider how easy or difficult it may be to collect such information.

3 A typology of self-access

3.1 Introduction

In this chapter we propose a typology of self-access systems. Our reasons for doing this are:

- to sensitise the reader to the variety of systems which exist
- to illustrate the different ways of structuring self-access support
- to demonstrate that self-access can be applied in many different physical settings (e.g. classrooms, self-access centres, the home environment)
- to demonstrate that self-access works with any group of learners
- to encourage readers to consider self-access systems as flexible.

We first review two important attempts at categorising self-access systems and how they operate. Then we suggest ways in which learner support within self-access systems can be structured. We then construct a typology of self-access systems by describing a series of scenarios. This typology is useful when considering the practical applications of self-access language learning which is the focus of Part 2 of this book. This chapter ends with a short discussion of how the typology can be used as a way of conceptualising self-access systems within different learning contexts.

In attempting to develop a typology for self-access it is important to keep in mind the enormous variety that exists in self-access systems. This variety of systems along with the varied contexts in which they are applied make each self-access facility unique. It is not our intention, therefore, to say that what we describe in the following pages are the only types of self-access systems in existence. There is a wide spectrum of possible self-access systems. Those we describe in this chapter should be seen as points on this spectrum which we have isolated in order to describe them but which, in reality, overlap with each other. Our purpose in developing the typology is to provide a framework for future discussions of self-access systems.

3.2 Types of self-access facilities

3.2.1 Adult learners

In this section we review two typologies that are already used to describe self-access systems. This first is taken from the Australian context and the second comes from self-access centres in France and South-East Asia.

In the Adult Migrant Education Program (AMEP 1990), six models of Individual Learning Centres (ILCs) are described. These six models differ in the degree to which they offer learner autonomy, Model 1 being the least autonomous, and Model 6 being the most. To determine where a centre lies along the continuum of lesser or greater autonomy, a series of questions was devised. These questions are as follows:

1. Is the classroom teacher available to help clients?
2. Are the students enrolled in the class?
3. Are the classroom students required to attend during class time?
4. Is the ILC teacher expected to provide intensive one-to-one tuition in language learning?
5. Is the range of learning opportunities/materials narrowly focused?
6. Are induction sessions for new clients considered essential?
7. Is there provision for small group activities?
8. Is it essential for the ILC teacher to be available to help students select materials?
9. Is an ILC teacher expected to monitor the progress of clients?
10. Is an ILC teacher available to help students manage their own learning?
11. Is it essential that the materials are designed for self-instruction?
12. Can the student attend the ILC at any time during opening hours?
13. Does the student require access to a catalogue or a guide to using the ILC?
14. Is the student expected to select/choose the materials from the collection?
15. Does an ESL teacher provide intensive one-to-one tuition in learning strategies?
16. Is the client expected to make a regular appointment with a self-directed learning counsellor?
17. Are clients able to borrow materials?

(AMEP 1990: 20)

In each of the six models described in the report, the ILCs are dedicated facilities for self-access language learning. They are separate rooms with their own furniture, equipment and specially prepared materials. The following brief descriptions are of ILCs found in Australia.

Model 1: Study centre
Example: Macquarie University, NSW. NCELTR – Individual Learning Centre.

In this type of ILC the main purpose is to complement classroom teaching. The materials are narrowly focused and if learners have any problems in their classroom-based work they can go and work independently in the ILC on that aspect which is causing them difficulty. A teacher is always on hand to help individual learners choose the most appropriate materials. The time learners spend in the ILC is timetabled for a certain number of hours each week.

Model 2: Withdrawal centre
Example: Freemantle, WA – Self-Access Centre.

This type of ILC is described as a 'withdrawal centre', that is, learners can be withdrawn from their regular language classes to attend the centre and study there under the direction of an ILC teacher. Its main function is for remedial teaching. Here again the material is narrowly focused and is aimed at the most common problems learners at particular levels face when learning a language. This type of centre provides intensive one-to-one tuition which is deemed essential for learners to progress any further with their language learning.

Model 3: Programmed learning centre
Example: Belmore, NSW – Individual Study Centre.

A programmed learning centre is basically a 'writing centre'. It does not complement any specific classroom-based language course but is established to provide a means for learners to improve their writing skills in their own time. The centre offers a series of pathways from which learners can choose how to develop their writing skills. The materials have been pre-selected and designed in such a way that only a certain number of options are available. The learners work mostly on their own but may consult a teacher if necessary.

Model 4: Drop-in centre
Example: Adelaide. Renaissance House – The Link.

This type of ILC offers a wide range of materials for learners to choose from. After the initial induction into the centre and the organisation of the materials, the learners choose which areas of language development they wish to work on. The learners may attend the ILC at times convenient to themselves. An ILC teacher is available to help learners develop and understand their own learning styles.

Model 5: Self-directed learning centre
Example: RMIT Melbourne. Centre for English Language Learning
– Self-Access Centre.

The focus of this type of ILC is on helping learners develop skills in becoming more independent in their language learning. The learners may attend the centre at times convenient to themselves. Following an induction session about the centre, the learners meet with an ILC counsellor to work out appropriate strategies that will enable them to further their language learning on their own while working with the materials in the centre.

Model 6: Learning resource centre
Example: Hobart. Adult Migrant Education Centre – Library.

The primary role of the learning resource centre is to provide learners with as wide a range of materials as possible to assist them develop their language ability within or outside the ILC. The learners are fully autonomous in that they know their preferred learning strategies and how to get resources to aid in their language learning. The centre is staffed by a librarian whose job it is to help learners locate resources, and when necessary to lend them out.

The second typology we report on is taken from Miller and Rogerson-Revell (1993). They describe self-access systems according to the following four categories:

Menu-driven
Example: Nancy, France. University of Nancy – CRAPEL (Centre de Recherches et d'Application Pedagogiques en Langues).

In this situation the learners need to be sophisticated language learners who can plan and implement their own language learning. In such a system the learner accesses materials by way of a catalogue which they have to be trained to use. They must know their preferred learning strategies and the most appropriate materials which will help them develop their language skills further.

Supermarket
Example: Malaysia, Kuala Lumpur. The Specialist Teacher's Training Institute – Self-Access Centre.

Here the self-access system offers a wide range of materials clearly labelled and accessible to the users. The emphasis is on allowing learners to browse through the materials to see what they want to do. It is similar to AMEP's Model 4 above.

Controlled-access

Example: Thailand, Bangkok. Chulalongkorn University Language Institute – Self-Access Centre.

A controlled access system lies closer to the AMEP's Model 1 than any of the others. However, the focus here is very much on homework-based activities. The materials are all carefully selected by the teacher to complement the learners classroom-based work and it is mandatory for learners to attend sessions in a controlled-access centre.

Open-access

Example: Hong Kong. The British Council – Library.

An open-access system has features in common with the AMEP's Model 6 above. The learners must be sophisticated in their language learning in order to determine what they want to do and then locate the most appropriate materials. This type of system is usually part of a main library with no specialist teacher on duty to help the learners with their language learning decision-making, but a librarian is available to assist in locating materials.

3.2.2 Adolescent learners

Tibbetts (1994) implemented a self-access reading programme for her sixth-form students in a secondary school in Hong Kong (King's College). Her reasons for doing this were to give a specific group of students extra practice in preparing for the Advanced Supplementary Examination. Her materials were therefore tailor-made. Because of the lack of space in the school the materials were incorporated into the existing library and students were time-tabled to spend some of their English lessons there. Tibbetts' self-access facility resembles a Study-Centre or a Controlled-Access Centre.

Forrester (1994) describes the self-access component of an intensive language-bridging program offered by the British Council to ESL secondary school students preparing for entrance to an English-medium university. Self-access was allocated one sixth of course time. The aim was not to replicate the learning that had already taken place in secondary school classrooms (e.g. grammar and vocabulary development) but instead to focus on the macro skills required for tertiary level study (e.g. extensive listening and reading authentic texts). The self-access system was designed to be temporary so that it could be set-up quickly each summer to meet the specific needs of this group of adolescent learners. This self-access facility is similar to a Study Centre or a Controlled-Access Centre.

3.2.3 Young learners

We will now look at some examples in which young learners develop their language skills by using self-access facilities. Veado et al. (1993) describe a self-access centre for 8-to-11 year olds in Brazil (Cultura Inglesa, Higienopolis – Self-Access Centre). The centre started as part of library facilities where the pupils often waited after school to be collected. The opportunity was taken to develop language learning activities and incorporate them into the library. The scheme was so successful that a self-access centre was established in what can best be described as a 'fun' drop-in centre for young learners. The emphasis here is on the young learners playing language games in English.

Dam (1995) illustrates a complete programme at a secondary school in Denmark during which 11 year olds are encouraged to become more aware of their language learning. Dam encourages her pupils to bring their outside experiences of English into the classroom. Her pupils make their own decisions about what they want to learn and share their experiences with their classmates. The self-access facility in this case is the classroom.

Ruechakul (1996) illustrates a self-access listening programme for secondary school students in her own school in Thailand. She and her colleagues decided to establish a listening corner in a self-access centre first, and to focus on preparing listening materials for M1 students (11 year olds). The rationale for this was that the students' listening skills were weak because in the small town setting where the school is situated there are few opportunities to practise listening to native speakers of English. After setting up the listening corner with suitable equipment and materials teachers took students to the self-access centre for two periods per week. Students then worked on listening tasks 'independently under teacher supervision' (Ruechakul 1996: 198). Interviews with pupils showed that young learners 'enjoyed learning with self-access listening material' (p. 197). For Ruechakul 'the most significant quantifiable success factor' (p. 201) is the substantial improvement in grades on listening tests.

From this brief review of some of the types of self-access facilities in operation around the world it is apparent that there is a great amount of diversity. The one thing that all the examples above have in common is the establishment of some form of learning environment in which self-access can take place. The structuring of learner support within such environments can vary considerably. We categorise learner support structures in the following section.

3.3 Learner support structures

By 'structure' we mean the level of guidance which is provided to learners in order for them to learn through self-access. In Chapter 1 we discussed the importance of learner responsibility for decisions about their language learning and the implications this has for the structuring of support available to the learners in a self-access system. There are three main types of support structures: structured, semi-structured and unstructured.

In a *structured* system of self-access complete guidance is given to the learner on how to enter the system and how to move through it. This starts with a needs analysis for individual learners or whole groups of learners by a tutor who then recommends a course of study (see Chapter 5). The learners report to the tutor at certain stages about their progress either face to face or by handing in a written account in the form of a journal. There is little flexibility for the learner to experiment with the system and/or the materials. Models 1, 2 and 3 (AMEP 1990), and the controlled-access system (Miller and Rogerson-Revell 1993) operate on a structured system of self-access.

A *semi-structured* approach to self-access relies on the learner taking, at some stage, responsibility for choosing the materials and skills they want to work on. Learners have access to tutors and can obtain guidance if they require it, but are encouraged to explore the system and see how they can best make it work for themselves. This system is seen in the following types of self-access centres: Models 4 and 5 (AMEP 1990), and the supermarket system (Miller and Rogerson-Revell 1993).

In an *unstructured* self-access system the learner works with little or no guidance. The resources are made available, in one form or another, and the learners have to put together their own learning agenda and monitor their own progress. Typical environments for unstructured self-access learning are Model 6 (AMEP 1990) and the open-access system and the menu-driven system (Miller and Rogerson-Revell 1993).

3.4 A self-access typology

It is sometimes difficult to assign a self-access system to one particular category within a typology. In any discussion about self-access systems it should be kept in mind that very often a single system may simultaneously be used in different ways by different people. An example of this might be an open-access centre which is also used for directed work when teachers take their classes there during English lessons to complete specific tasks. A second example is when a supermarket-type centre becomes a self-directed learning centre because a learner decides to use the resources along with a tutor's guidance. This multi-system dimension of self-access systems is to be welcomed and encouraged, and it should be kept in mind when we begin to describe systems within our typology.

The terminology used in the AMEP report (1990) and by Miller and Rogerson-Revell (1993) serves well to illustrate the centres they are describing. However, on the generic level it is important to have terminology which could be applied to any self-access system. Our own typology is presented in Table 3.1 where types of self-access systems are arranged in order of possible size: smallest to largest. We have opted to use a shopping metaphor here for two reasons: the names are easy to remember and the self-access systems are well represented by the names of the shop types.

3.5 Self-access system flexibility

While our typology documents points on a spectrum of self-access systems it must be applied flexibly. Each implementation of a self-access system is unique because it is *adapted* to suit the context in which it occurs. The adaptation is influenced by the needs of the learners, the availability of resources and the philosophical stance of the teachers and the institution in general. A benefit of a flexible approach is the ability to change the system if and when required.

One example of adapting a self-access system is given by Farmer (1994) who describes the establishment of a SAC which catered to learners who made choices from menus and pathways (catalogue shop). However, in response to learner demands the system was radically changed to one in which teacher-directed group tasks were the main focus (cash and carry). Changeability is an essential feature of self-access systems. As a system matures the wants and needs of the learners become clearer. Also, as teachers gain more experience in working in self-access, their confidence encourages them to find ways to make the system more effective. The system must adapt to the new requirements of both learners and teachers.

A self-access system may conform to a single type in our typology; however, it may also be a combination of several types. This is particularly true where different groups of learners use it for different purposes. No self-access system should be considered 'better' than any other. What works well for one group of learners in one situation may not be appropriate for another group of learners in a different context. It is important, however, for those working in self-access to be aware of the many possibilities of the self-access systems which are available

Table 3.1. *A self-access typology*

Type of self-access system	Description	Type of learner for which system is most useful	Advantages and disadvantages of the system
Telephone sales	This is a system with no specific location. It relies on technology, specifically the use of computers. Learners interact with their teachers by telephone or electronic mail (e-mail). Teachers act as resources from their offices answering learners' questions and queries which are usually focused on writing, grammar and vocabulary.	University students	• Apart from computers, few additional facilities are required. • The contact with a teacher is initiated by the learner on a need-to-know basis.
Mobile shop	This type of self-access system is based on providing a limited amount of material on a trolley so that it can be moved from class to class and be made available to a large number of learners. The material is aimed at a very specific group of learners and the skills developed are dictated by the teachers responsible for stocking the trolley. Typically, the material on offer develops reading and listening skills.	School students	• Can be easily moved around. • If there is only one trolley then only one class can use the materials at any given time.
Market stall	This type of self-access system only operates on certain days and/or certain times. Typically, the materials are kept in a cupboard in a classroom and at the allotted time the teacher opens the cupboard and displays the materials for the learners to select from.	School students	• Can be timetabled into the learning situation. • The choice of materials is limited because of space limitation.

Table 3.1. (contd)

Type of self-access system	Description	Type of learner for which system is most useful	Advantages and disadvantages of the system
Bring-and-buy sale	Learners bring to class something about the language – some new words, a poster, a magazine, something they have collected on holiday in the target language country, and share this with the other learners. It is a very unstructured system and relies on the impetus from the learners' experiences and what they bring to class. Its main value is in motivating the learners to take part in their language learning and in creating a fun environment in which to explore the language.	School students	• High face validity as learners bring to class things which interest them most. • This system works only when the learners are actively involved and bring things to class.
Postal sales	This type of self-access system is similar to a correspondence course or a distance-learning programme. The material is centrally co-ordinated and sent out to learners as they request it. Learners complete tasks and exercises, which are often based on listening and reading skills, and plot their own progress rate with the aid of answer keys.	Adult learners	• Learners can study anywhere and do not need to be near an educational institution. • There is very little, if any, face-to-face contact between learners and self-access counsellors.
Boutique	This is a specialist system which operates within self-access centres designed for specific groups of learners, e.g. engineers. The materials in this type of facility often complement the course of study which	University students	• Material development can focus on one specific group of learners. • Only useful to specialist groups

Table 3.1.   (contd)

Type of self-access system	Description	Type of learner for which system is most useful	Advantages and disadvantages of the system
	the learners are involved with. There are other materials of interest to the target group of users to browse through.		of learners. It is not useful to general learners of English.
Video-rental shop	In this self-access system the emphasis is on entertainment by way of movies. Learners watch a film. There are no worksheets and no obvious language work expected of the learners. The pedagogical purpose behind this type of system is language immersion.	Adult learners	• Highly motivating, learners generally enjoy this type of learning. • Language learning objectives may not be clear to learners. It is expensive to operate and videos need to be updated regularly.
Technology shop	This system relies on technology. There is a large amount of audio, video and computer technology often with less attention paid to pedagogical input. The emphasis is on motivating learners into using the target language with the aid of technology. It is commonly found in well-funded university self-access centres and in some private language schools.	All learners	• Certain learners are highly attracted to language learning via technology. • It is a very expensive system to install, run and keep up-to-date. It needs technical assistance to maintain.
Catalogue shop	This runs on a menu-driven system. The learners need to know what they want before they enter the system and need to be able to use the catalogue (computer or manual) to search for and locate the	University students; adult learners	• Staff control the materials so the security is high. • Requires some learner-training in order to use the system.

Table 3.1. (contd)

Type of self-access system	Description	Type of learner for which system is most useful	Advantages and disadvantages of the system
	material. Materials are checked out from a counter and browsing may not be allowed.		
Fast-food restaurant	The needs of the learners are immediate. Most of the learners need survival language quickly, in order to listen to a conference presentation, read an academic paper, survive for a short period in a foreign country, pass an exam and so on. The system relies on materials that can be used over a short period of time and focus on specific skills.	University students/staff	• Provides a 'quick fix' for language learning. • The system may not meet the needs of every learner who wants to use it.
Games arcade	This type of system focuses on allowing learners to learn via games or fun activities. The emphasis here is on creating a friendly, unthreatening environment for learners to enjoy 'playing' in the target language. Materials in such a system include board games, drawing boards and puppet theatres.	Young learners	• Promotes motivation for learners to want to learn. • Some teachers (and learners) need convincing that this system has pedagogical value.
Discount store	The emphasis of this system is on producing a lot of materials cheaply in a semi-structured environment. Most of the materials are donated, and the system's main value is to motivate the learners to explore the language and offer language opportunities which they may have difficulty finding outside of the classroom. Typically, material is arranged under general	All learners	• Cheap. • The pedagogical value of some of the donated materials may be questionable.

Table 3.1. *(contd)*

Type of self-access system	Description	Type of learner for which system is most useful	Advantages and disadvantages of the system
	categories, e.g. all the reading material is in one section but not necessarily catalogued according to level or anything else.		
Supermarket	This system offers learners the opportunity to look around and choose what to study. The system displays materials under clearly marked categories: listening, reading, phonology, games, etc., which in turn are usually colour-coded according to level. In this way, learners can independently gain access to the system and easily find the area they wish to study.	All learners	• A user-friendly system. It can vary from cheap to expensive to establish and run. • This system needs a lot of materials to work well.
Cash and carry	This kind of system caters to the masses. There is a limited range of materials but lots of copies. The material is mostly teacher-directed and the focus is on the pedagogical value of the material as perceived by the teacher.	School students	• Cheap. For learners who are unsure about self-access this system offers a lot of support. • There are fewer opportunities for learners to explore the materials by themselves.
Department store	The focus for this type of self-access system is on offering a large number of boutique-like centres within one large self-access centre. This centre caters for a large number of learners with differing specific needs, e.g. engineers, medical students, social workers.	University students	• Many different types of learner can use the system. • This system is expensive to develop and run.

3.6 Summary

Our purpose in setting out the typology in this chapter has been to make the reader aware of the diversity of self-access systems. These systems can incorporate learner support at a variety of levels from complete guidance (*structured*) to little or no guidance (*unstructured*). The systems can be implemented in a variety of physical settings as is clear from the typology. All learners can benefit from some kind of self-access system. A key concept of self-access systems is that they must be flexible thus allowing systems to change as the requirements of their users change.

3.7 Tasks

1. Look at the typology (Table 3.1) and decide on the most appropriate *learner support structure* (see Section 3.3) for each system. Then choose one system and decide on the kinds of support the learners would need to use it effectively.
2. Consider a group of learners you are familiar with. Decide which type of self-access system would be most suitable for them. Make a list of reasons.
3. Choose the self-access system from the typology (Table 3.1) which best suits a context you are familiar with. List the advantages and disadvantages, and explain how you would overcome the disadvantages.

3.8 For discussion

1. Using the questions from the AMEP report (see Section 3.2.1) and applying them to a SAC you know, decide what degree of autonomy the centre allows its users.
2. The typology of self-access systems describes them as individual entities. Think of ways in which different types of systems can be, or are, combined. What is the pedagogical rationale for having more than one system within an independent learning facility?
3. Think of other types of self-access centres you are familiar with. Where do they fit into the typology (see Table 3.1)? If they do not fit exactly, give them a suitable shop name which reflects how they are organised and work.

4 Management of self-access facilities

4.1 Introduction

This chapter looks at management issues. It first considers management in a general context and then focuses on managing self-access facilities. Good management is relevant whether the facilities are large scale like the supermarket type in our typology (Chapter 3), small scale like the mobile shop type or somewhere between these extremes. Not all of the issues discussed in this chapter will be relevant to all kinds of facility; however, some of the issues, for example managing learners, are relevant in every context.

Very little has been written specifically about the management of self-access but there is a large body of literature from two other fields of study which can be drawn on for guidance in establishing good management practice. First, 'management' is a field of study in its own right which is actively studied and researched. It covers both commercial management and public administration. The field of management is wide and provides a rich source of informed discussion on different approaches to management. It also provides us with philosophical debate about management issues and case studies based on practical experiences.

The second field of relevance is that of educational management. This is a field in which commercial management techniques are adapted and applied to meet the specific and unique requirements of educational institutions. Indeed, it is also a field in which there is still debate on whether commercial management techniques are appropriate for education. The study of educational management tends to concern itself with management at an institutional level. Little has emerged which is subject specific, with the exception of work on the management of English Language Teaching (ELT). Professionals and academics in this area have been engaged for some years in discussing ELT management and in particular the management of change (for example: White 1988; White et al. 1991; Kennedy 1987, 1988). Perhaps there has been more interest in management in ELT than other subject areas because it has been a forerunner in commercialising its educational services.

In addition to looking at the practices of business management and educational management, managers of self-access facilities can also learn a lot about practical management issues by examining the methods employed by librarians. They have for many years managed large collections of materials as well as managing facilities, staff and users. Of particular interest are the school library media centres documented in United States publications (Anderson 1990; Prostano and Prostano 1987; Woolls 1994; Stein and Brown 1992) and learning resources centres in the UK (Raddon and Dix 1989). These centres specialise in providing focused learning opportunities.

4.2 Defining management

The task of management is about operating an organisational unit in a way which makes the best use of its resources in the pursuance of its goals and the goals of any governing bodies. This is a very broad definition which encompasses managerial roles in all kinds of organisations from commercial to state-run, from profit-making to charitable. One issue which is interesting to consider and is widely debated is whether educational institutions can or should be managed in the way that commercial institutions are. Even if the above definition of management is accepted, further definition is needed:

- How is the organisational unit defined? Is it a group of people or is it a set of facilities? Does the size of the unit vary or is it fixed?
- What are the resources? Where do they come from? On what criteria is the further provision of resources dependent? What are the special features of the human and material resources?
- Where does the unit fit in an organisational hierarchy? Does it have responsibility for other units? Who is it responsible to?
- What are the goals of the unit and of its governing bodies? Are the goals clearly defined? Are they rigid or are they flexible?
- How are goals pursued? Are there defined procedures? Are procedures open to interpretation, adaptation or disregard?
- How is 'best use of resources' defined? Does this mean 'efficient use', 'effective use' or a combination of the two? If a combination, how is the ratio decided and who decides it?

4.2.1 The role of management

The process of defining what management means in a self-access context is an important first step in deciding how the management of self-access should function and what its purpose is. Defining management function should not be seen as a one-off process. It is useful to review definitions periodically as this encourages management structure and procedures to be dynamic.

A number of authors in the field of educational management agree with White et al. (1991: 192) when they state that 'management is not simply concerned with maintaining the status quo'. It is generally recognised that failure to adapt and to move forwards will be detrimental to the management of organisations (Middlehurst 1995; West-Burnham 1992; White 1988) and this is also true of managing self-access facilities. However, it is not always easy to effect change. Burton (1989: 76), for example, has noted that organisations can 'take on a life of their own and become resistant to change'. When this happens operational methods take precedence over effective goal achievement.

Despite the importance of a dynamic management structure White et al. (1991) also suggest that an institution should not be in a permanent state of change, some stability is required. Wynn and Guditus (1984) suggest that the reality of life in organisations is that there is never complete stability. It seems clear that self-access management needs to provide a stable environment while at the same time leading a process of gradual innovation.

4.2.2 Management and managers

So far we have been defining management as a concept. Later we will also discuss a variety of approaches to implementing a management system. The interface between the concept of management and the methods of implementing it define the managerial role. Once this role is clear a list of duties and responsibilities attached to the role can be produced. This list will define the attributes of a person or people who are to undertake the management role. The attributes will consist of a combination of skills, past experience and qualifications. The specific attributes will vary according to the way in which the management role is defined. In the case of new posts this list of attributes will become a job definition which will aid in recruitment. In the case of existing posts such a list can help define training needs. The process of defining and fulfilling the management role is summarised in Figure 4.1.

4.2.3 Managers versus leaders

Some authors discuss the difference between managers and leaders (e.g. Scott 1989; West-Burnham 1992; Wynn and Guditus 1984). The crux of the distinction being made seems to be a perception of differences in responsibilities. Managers are seen as administrators who are essentially concerned with implementing defined procedures and who are consequently mostly involved with maintaining the status quo. Wynn and Guditus (1984: 28), for example, feel that managers are 'typically involved with maintaining existing structures and procedures'. Leaders, on the other hand, appear to be defined as more dynamic people who

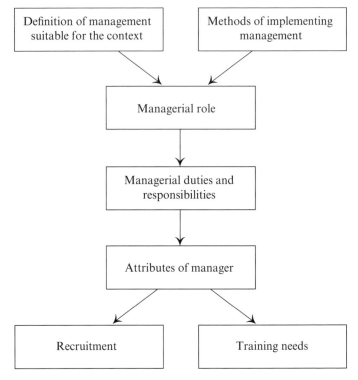

Figure 4.1   Defining and fulfilling the management role

are constantly looking for ways of moving forward. Wynn and Guditus (1984: 28) define leaders as people who 'must respond effectively to the real and perceived needs of the individual, as well as the goals of the organization'. West-Burnham (1992: 117) claims that 'no leader has ever been regarded as great because of her or his ability to maintain the status quo'. He sees leaders as managers of change who welcome the challenge and facilitate the change of others (learners and staff). It is important for self-access managers to understand both these roles.

Some authors make no distinction between managers and leaders, selecting either term for their purpose. For example, Woolls (1994: 89) delivers a series of platitudes like 'a good leader manages time wisely' which are equally applicable to managers. For some, however, the distinction is clearly real. The conclusion of Wynn and Guditus (1984) is that while management and leadership are different, management skills will be part of the portfolio of an effective leader. Thom (1993) argues that managers' leadership abilities will be affected by their attitudes to power.

The differences between managers and leaders, whether perceived or real, may be seen as paralleling the distinction made by Scott (1989) between accountability and responsiveness. Perhaps the managers who follow standard procedures and maintain the status quo do so because they are required to be highly accountable. The leaders, on the other hand, who avidly pursue change may be less accountable but feel a greater pressure to respond to the demands of teachers and students.

The job title assigned to people undertaking a management/leadership role has some significance. It is important for the role holders to feel that the importance of this role is recognised. It is also important that other people interacting professionally with the manager/leader have an understanding of the role. It may be tempting for higher management not to define middle management roles clearly as this allows for flexibility in assigning future workloads. Pugsley (1991: 315) argues forcefully against the 'short-term gains ... in maintaining a certain ambiguity as to who does what and why'. Defining a self-access manager's role in as unambiguous a way as possible is important. There is a great deal of overlap between the roles of managers and leaders and it is probably more fruitful to see them as two aspects of a single role.

4.3 Approaches to management

There are many different models of management proposed in the literature. Some of the more common ones to be seen in educational contexts are described by White et al. (1991). These are briefly summarised in Table 4.1. A problem which has been identified with all models of management has been that of assessing effectiveness. Variation in context may influence the form of management used and may also determine the criteria used for judging effectiveness. Commercial organisations have long scrutinised their managerial effectiveness; on the other hand, educational organisations have been slow to follow. Holmes and Neilson (1989: 70), for example, note that 'the acceptance of a patchy record of managerial effectiveness in education is almost universal'. Some argue that this is because in the commercial world effectiveness can be measured in money whereas in the educational world it must be measured by quality which is more difficult to achieve.

One attempt to measure managerial effectiveness has been to develop the notion of competence and the meeting of standards. Definitions of competence and standards have been adapted from those used in commercial management. Standards can be expressed as expected outcomes. Competence can be measured by comparing these standards with actual outcome.

Participants in this system collect evidence of their performance (usually a portfolio). This evidence is then assessed to see if it meets the

Table 4.1.   *Some common models of management*

Model	Emphasis	Process
Formal	The power of the manager (authority of position)	Hierarchical structure characterised by a top-down approach
Democratic	The importance of people's skills (authority of expertise)	Consensus rather than conflict. This is achieved through collegiality and committees
Political	Interest groups rather than the larger organisation	Acknowledges conflict and expects some ambiguity of goals. Decisions emerge from bargaining and negotiations
Subjective	Individual goals (not organisational goals)	Allows personal interpretation by individuals of how the organisation functions
Ambiguity	Uncertainty and unpredictability. Organisational goals are unclear and ambiguous	Decision-making is unplanned. There is fragmentation of the organisation

Adapted from: White et al. 1991

standards. One of the potential problems with this approach lies with the setting of the standards. It is relatively easy to define competence in dealing with paperwork; it is much less easy to define competence in providing quality independent language-learning opportunities. While the former may be an important part of the job of a manager of self-access facilities the latter has a much greater impact on learners.

The use of a 'standards' approach to help provide an organisational framework can be criticised for a number of reasons. First, the standards tend to ignore the personal attributes of a manager. For example, an ability to manage crises is not covered by the standards but for many educational managers it is a highly desirable attribute. Second, comparing managers' performance with specified standards gives weight to past events thus discouraging prediction of and planning for the future. These are both important events in education. Third, judging whether performance has met standards is, in at least some cases, subjective. Earley (1993: 13) suggests that a standards-based approach can be helpful but should not be used to the exclusion of other approaches to management. The view of Esp (1993) is that this approach is only worth pursuing if it helps to 'improve the effectiveness of teaching and . . . learning'.

Also borrowed from the world of commercial management is Total Quality (TQ), also known as Total Quality Management (TQM). Sallis (1993: 34) describes TQM as 'a philosophy of continuous improvement, which can provide any educational institution with a set of practical tools for meeting and exceeding present and future customers needs, wants, and expectations'. Parker et al. (1995: 208) support this by stating that in using a TQ system 'improved quality will satisfy customers and make organizations more successful'. Other authors also support this approach in education (e.g. Bateman and Roberts 1995; West-Burnham 1992; Wolverton 1995; Woolls 1994).

Applied to a self-access centre (SAC) TQM would require the manager and the self-access team to work together to find ways in which they could improve the service for their 'clients' or 'customers' (i.e. learners). Unlike some of the management models described above TQM can only be achieved when all staff are committed to it and when it is applied to all aspects of the SAC's operations, in other words, the management must be 'total'. Commitment is important because TQM 'cannot be done to you or for you' (Sallis 1993: 34): it must be done *by* you.

Perhaps the most serious management problem a SAC can suffer from is a lack of management. It might be tempting to philosophise that a centre in which learners are encouraged to be autonomous should also allow staff to be autonomous. While it would be wrong to stifle staff initiatives it would also be counter-productive if individual members of staff, through lack of coordination, were undermining each other's work, as reflected in the 'ambiguity' model in Table 4.1. Different institutions will want to manage their self-access resources in different ways but they *must* be managed in some way. This is only common sense in a world where educational resources are finite and learners' needs are almost infinite.

4.4 Managing a self-access centre

4.4.1 The manager's position within the institutional management structure

Whichever model of management is used the self-access manager is a middle manager accountable for a set of resources and the activities of a group of people. The self-access manager reports upwards to a more senior level (this could be the head of department, the head of the institution or a committee). It is the manager's responsibility to make sure that information flows in both directions. Information is power, but only when it is shared. Easy access to information results in a more productive working environment. Figure 4.2 illustrates how the self-access manager is a focal point in the management structure of the SAC.

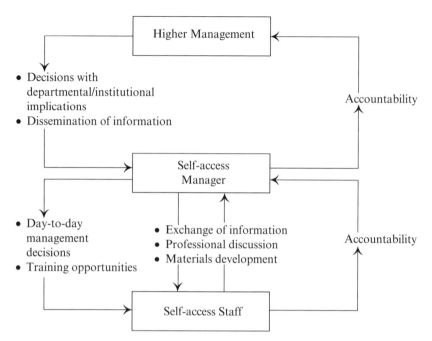

Figure 4.2.   The location of the self-access manager within the management structure

Dennison and Kelly (1989) found that even when a breakdown in communication is beyond the control of managers, it is they who are associated with inefficiency and ineptitude.

In some institutions SACs may not have a full-time manager. This may be because self-access is not organised on an institutional level. Alternatively, commitment to self-access may be small and is coordinated by a member of the teaching staff as an extra duty. In some cases institutions may not have recognised the amount of work and level of expertise required to manage self-access effectively. Institutions which provide insufficient management for SACs are wasting their resources because this results in under-use by learners.

In a study of five tertiary level institutions Gardner and Miller (1997) found all had made similar investments of large sums of money in their self-access centres. Only one of them, however, had appointed a full-time manager who calculated that the job required about 60 working hours per week. This involved running a centre which operated a cash-and-carry-type self-access system (see Chapter 3) which catered to the diverse language needs of several hundred university students each week. The manager was responsible for pedagogical development, financial planning and personnel management (about 20 staff). The other centres in the study, with similar management requirements, were being managed by teachers who were given some hours per week of release from other duties.

4.4.2 Managing staff

Ambiguity about the roles of self-access centre staff can cause problems. Pugsley (1991), in discussing ELT management, argues that there are long-term gains in having established procedures. In terms of SAC management the following points need to be clarified:

- methods by which staff have input to the decision-making process
- procedures for defining standards of work (e.g. materials, workshops)
- requirements of posts (job description, working hours, responsibilities)
- rewards of posts (pay, bonuses, benefits)
- appraisal (ways in which staff and the manager are assessed, how feedback is given, the purpose of appraisal)
- procedures for staff to make complaints

Appraisal should be part of a staff development scheme aimed at 'developing skilled, well motivated and effective staff who understand what they are attempting to achieve' (Hitt 1990: 27). It is the manager's responsibility to see that staff reach their optimum performance. If an appraisal scheme is also linked to benefits such as promotions the criteria should be made public so that all staff understand why some are rewarded and others not.

Managers should not concentrate their efforts exclusively on the work of educational staff in the self-access centre. The important contribution of technical and clerical staff should also be recognised. On a practical level it is worth noting that discontented or misguided clerical and technical staff can place numerous obstacles in the way of educators. It is the manager's responsibility to make sure that support staff feel included in the aims of the centre and that their work contributes to, rather than hinders, the achievement of pedagogical goals.

4.4.3 Managing learners

The management of learners in a self-access centre is much less clear cut than in a classroom. The potential range of attributes of learners (ability, level, motivation, time available) is much wider in a self-access centre. In addition, it is more difficult to collect this information because there may be little direct contact between learners and staff. Monitoring of learning can also be a problem. Learners in a classroom may benefit from negotiated syllabuses but the teacher still retains control. In a self-access centre there is likely to be little control over many of the learners. A risk is that learners might only select easy options, thus not benefiting fully.

The challenge for the self-access manager is to help self-access learners define their goals and, where necessary, find ways to persuade them to experiment more widely. Some of the ways managers may do this are as follows:

- needs analyses (could be self-administered by learners)
- assessments (could be self-assessments)
- providing orientation sessions
- providing pathways through materials
- providing workshops (for skills or particular materials)
- providing counselling services (for individual learners)
- assigning learners to a mentor
- forming learners into study groups
- requiring/encouraging learners to report on what they have done/ learned
- requiring/encouraging learners to make study plans
- focusing materials acquisition in certain areas
- restricting access to certain kinds of materials for certain kinds of learners
- recording attendance
- accrediting self-access work

Deciding whether to make elements from the above list part of an obligatory system or make them voluntary would depend on the under-lying philosophy of the self-access centre. If the intention is to provide an environment in which learners act completely autonomously then compulsory activities would be out of place. In such a case the manager would need to be sure the learners could cope with such a high level of autonomy. In a SAC with more tightly focused objectives the manager might want to impose a certain level of compulsory guidance on the learners (Figure 4.3). It is also possible that some centres will have different categories of learners, some of which are expected to be less autonomous than others. So, for example, new users of a SAC might be required to undertake certain activities whereas more experienced users would not. A distinction might also be drawn between more mature and less mature users of SACs. Immature users might need more direction whereas more mature users might only need clarification on the benefits of trying a range of activities.

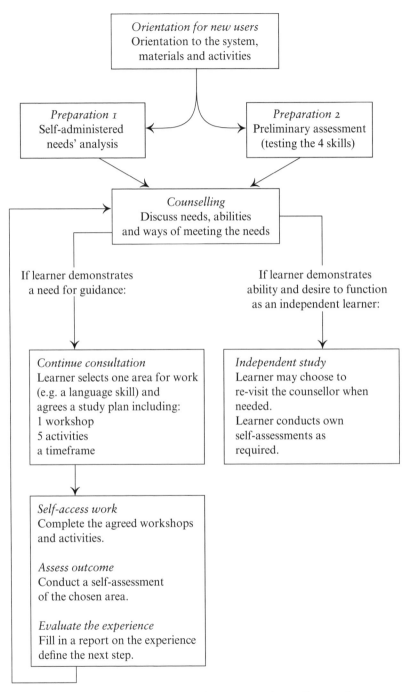

Figure 4.3. Example of a compulsory guidance imposed on self-access learners

4.4.4 Managing resources

Optimum management of resources requires a knowledge of the following:

- the needs of the learners
- the wants of the learners
- learners' goals
- learners' achievement of their goals
- learners' perceptions of current resources
- the amount of time learners spend using the resources
- the uses to which current resources are put
- the effectiveness of current resources
- capability of production of in-house materials
- sources of published materials
- the self-access requirements of taught courses.

Measuring the effectiveness of resources is not easy in self-access contexts. It may be tempting to count usage as a measure of usefulness. Raddon and Dix (1989: 84) claim that 'to a certain extent the use made of resources is also an indication (although not the only one) of the relevance of those resources'. While this may be true in some contexts in others it is less likely. Gardner and Miller (1997) found self-access language learners reported a heavy use of videotapes for entertainment purposes; however, entertainment was rarely given by learners as a goal in using their centres.

It is easy to measure how many learners come into a SAC each day or how many times a particular piece of material or equipment is used. These statistics are useful but they do not measure effectiveness. This can only be measured by assessing the extent to which set goals have been achieved. In a classroom setting the goals are generally set by the teacher or an educational board. Whether they have been achieved can be measured through assessment. In self-access learning the goals are often individualised and thus not always evident to the manager. It is important to gather information about the goals learners are setting in order to see whether current resources can help with those goals or need supplementing.

On a practical level there are things managers can do to make sure that resources are used to the optimum advantage. First, they must make sure that there are no mismatches between resources. For example, if learners are recommended to videotape themselves doing group role plays there must be video equipment located in an area sufficiently large for the activities and blank videotapes must be available (perhaps for purchase if the learners want to keep them). Second, managers can establish routine procedures in a way that makes them efficient and easy to follow. For example, if learners need to use a videotape with a book, they should not need to go to two different locations to find them even though it is administratively easier to store books and tapes on different shelves.

4.5 Managing classroom self-access

Much of what has been said in the previous section about the management of learners and resources is also relevant to managing classroom self-access although it will probably be on a smaller scale. The management of learners should be easier than in a SAC. Teachers are familiar with their own learners in a way that SAC managers and staff cannot be. Self-access in the classroom is a good opportunity to individualise both the learning programme and the attention learners receive. However, teachers need to guard against the complacency that may arise from feeling they know everything about their students. The relationship between teacher and students is a different one to that of counsellor and self-access learner. To maximise the benefits to learners, teachers need to be aware of this and explore the role of learning counsellor (for a fuller discussion of this role see Chapter 10).

Resource management of classroom self-access may, by comparison with a SAC, be easy and difficult at the same time. It may be easy because classroom self-access is unlikely to have huge resources and thus little time needs to be spent on managing them; difficult because, when resources are limited, teachers need to be creative in ways of using them if all learners are to benefit. For example, in a SAC there may be 20 audio tape recorders making it possible for learners to engage in individual listening practices. In a classroom there may be only one tape recorder. Teachers need to decide in these circumstances whether to group self-access listening activities or work out a schedule for individual listening activities.

However large or small the scale on which self-access is offered, the same basic principles underlie its management. The needs, wants and abilities of the learners must drive its development. Even when teachers are offering self-access to learners they know well they should still take them through a process of needs analysis. The outcome may offer some insights to the teacher but, most important, will be an awareness-raising exercise for the learners.

4.6 Involving learners

Self-access learners can contribute to the management of self-access facilities. Their input into evaluating the areas listed in Table 4.2 would

Table 4.2. *Ways in which learners can contribute to evaluation of self-access learning*

Evaluation of:	Comments Sought on:
materials, activities, services	usefulness, appropriateness, quality, quantity, lacunas
goals	range, focus, match/mismatch with personal goals, relationship between self-access and classroom goals
staff	helpfulness, expertise, roles
management	efficiency, style, defects
learning gain	what has been learned (from self-assessment results)
effectiveness	achievement of learning goals, quality and speed of learning, comparisons with other learning contexts (e.g. classroom)
learning strategies	strategies used for self-access learning relationship with strategies used in other contexts

be invaluable. Learners can also contribute to the running of self-access facilities by working in them as assistants. They could be employed (either as volunteers or on a paid basis depending on the philosophy and financial standing of the institution) in a number of roles (see Table 4.3).

Involving learners in managing their learning is not a new idea. It is encapsulated in ideas of learner-centredness (Nunan 1988a) and as long ago as 1983 Littlejohn was giving convincing reasons for encouraging learners 'to take more control over the management of their own study both inside and outside the classroom' (Littlejohn 1983: 595). However, he warned that involving learners in managing their own course should be an incremental process; this is equally true of learners managing self-access. Teachers should not expect too much of their learners initially because past experiences and expectations can make learners unwilling to become involved.

4.7 Training managers

It is not uncommon in educational institutions for teachers to become managers with little or no training in management. This is certainly true of self-access managers. Pedagogical knowledge often has a higher priority than management training. However, the ideal situation is one

Table 4.3. *Roles in which learners can contribute to the running of self-access facilities*

Role	Explanation
Materials organiser	• keeping materials in order • checking for damages or losses and repairing/reporting them • informally monitoring use of materials and reporting back • talking to users and reporting on users' likes/dislikes and needs which are not being met
Materials writers	• working with staff to write new materials • trialling new materials personally • getting other learners to trial new materials and reporting back on their experiences
Buddy	Experienced self-access learners act as mentors to new self-access learners. This could be on a one-to-one or a one-to-many basis depending on the availability and willingness of the mentors.
Demonstrators	demonstrating for other learners: • use of self-access facilities • new materials • study techniques (e.g. note-taking, dictionary use) • practice techniques (e.g. practising pronunciation) • making study plans
Publicists	• making posters • producing a self-access newsletter • advertising electronically through e-mail and newsgroups • sending information to relevant student groups (e.g. students union, or societies' committees)
Members of a self-access learning student society	The self-access staff could help establish a student society focusing on self-access learning. The provision of minimal resources such as a place to meet and refreshments would foster a feeling of belonging among the members. This society could provide valuable input for running a self-access centre.

in which well qualified, experienced teachers with practical experience of self-access work are given management training. There is an increasing number of professionals who meet the pedagogical criteria but sadly there are few who have management training and even fewer who can combine this with management experience.

Holmes and Neilson (1989) are of the firm opinion that training cannot create effective managers but it can contribute. For those who use a standards-based management approach (discussed earlier) Esp (1993: 13) warns that 'some competences cannot be improved significantly by training or development activities'. There are individuals who are undoubtedly natural managers and need little training. However, these are rare and institutions cannot hope for these people to emerge just when they need them. Middlehurst (1995) is of the opinion that failing to train managers amounts to incompetence. One of the recommendations to emerge from the research of Gardner and Miller (1997: 119) was that 'SAC managers should be included in their institutions' staff development programmes'. They found that the managers had mostly gained management expertise by trial and error and by visiting other longer-established SACs in Europe. The institutions were encouraged to provide some specialised training for the managers. The managers themselves welcomed this suggestion. The areas in which self-access managers need training are detailed in Table 4.4. As well as providing initial training for self-access managers, it would be in the interests of institutions to offer them ongoing staff development.

4.8   Evaluation

We discuss methods of evaluation in more detail in Chapter 12. In this section we will deal briefly with the relationship between evaluation and management. Evaluative procedures should be incorporated into the management of self-access facilities from the outset. Managers have two good reasons for implementing evaluative procedures. They are 'justification' and 'improvement'.

4.8.1 Justification

Self-access managers are responsible for the success of their operation. It is in their interests, therefore, to find suitable ways of measuring success. They need to find ways to show the resources (both human and material) are being well used and that results are being achieved. Showing success is a good way of maintaining existing funding. Woolls (1994: 206) reminds us that 'successes should be confirmed rather than assumed'. Success can also be used as a basis for seeking additional funding. It has been suggested (Anderson 1990) that conducting an evaluation in a way administrators favour might help. While it is undoubtedly true that administrators, like everyone, are less likely to be sceptical of a process with which they are comfortable, this cannot be used as an excuse to use 'easy' but meaningless measures. Woolls (1994: 207) observes that 'a major flaw of quantitative measures is that

Table 4.4.   *Areas of management training which would be beneficial to self-access managers*

Training Area	Consisting of:
Management systems	establishing a structure/hierarchy, job descriptions, internal reporting procedures, defining the roles of committees/working groups
Institutional procedures	institutional hierarchy, committee structure, external reporting procedures, procurement procedures
Personnel	hiring and firing, disciplining, praising/rewarding
Financial	budgets, tenders, quotes, accounting
Appraisal	establishing and making public a system of appraisal
Counselling	counselling staff, teaching staff to counsel students
Evaluation	materials, people, systems
Staff development	developing the abilities of self-access staff, running training programs for pedagogical staff, encouraging experimentation by technical staff, providing training opportunities for clerical staff
Negotiation skills	negotiating with self-access staff, teachers, higher level managers
Planning	long-term and short-term development plans, planning for the academic year
Public relations	dealing with visitors, making presentations, representing the institution

administrators place too much emphasis on counting things with little regard to their quality'.

4.8.2 Improvement

Managers need a clear picture of the self-access operation not only to show where they have been successful but also to identify areas which need more input. However, they are under no obligation to release all the results because 'evaluation is a process of deciding what to tell, whom to tell, and why to tell' (Woolls 1994: 214). Some information may be used for internal purposes, working with other self-access staff to improve the materials or services offered to learners. At a later stage, after further evaluation shows an improvement, the information may then be used more publicly to show what has been achieved.

A number of authors consider evaluation as a starting point for innovation (e.g. Kennedy 1988; Raddon and Dix 1989; White 1988) and some also see it as a necessary part of monitoring innovation (e.g. Elliot and Crossley 1994; Kennedy 1988; White et al. 1991). If managers consider themselves not just as maintainers of the status quo but as leaders looking for challenging new approaches as well as greater efficiency and effectiveness, they need to conduct serious evaluations of their self-access operations.

4.9 Summary

In establishing a self-access facility the following management issues need to be considered:

- The model of management
- The method for implementing the model
- The managerial role: management of the status quo or leadership for change
- The duties and responsibilities of the manager
- The manager within the institutional context
- Management of staff
- Management of learners
- Management of resources
- Involving learners in management
- Training managers
- Evaluation of self-access learning, self-access facilities and the manager

4.10 Tasks

1. If you are familiar with a self-access facility decide which model is in use to manage it and the ways in which management is implemented. If not, decide which model you would favour and define the managerial approaches you would use for implementing the model.
2. Think of a group of learners you are familiar with and define ways in which you could involve them in managing a self-access facility.

4.11 For discussion

1. Discuss the management system in an educational context you are familiar with. Explain the process of decision-making.
2. Describe a classroom context with which you are familiar. Say in what ways the management of learners would change if you implemented self-access in the classroom.

Part 2 *Practical perspectives*

5 Learner profiles

5.1 Introduction

In educational contexts it is important to know as much as possible about the learners: their needs, their wants, their learning styles, their beliefs, their attitudes and their abilities. Monitoring learners is relatively easy in classroom-based learning. It is more difficult to achieve in self-access learning because of the individualised nature of the work and because of the reduced level of teacher contact. It might be argued that, in self-access, information about learners is in the private domain of the individuals and that they should be free not to disclose it. We are not suggesting that learners be forced to supply information but that they should be made aware of the benefits of doing so. Learners should be informed of the reasons for collecting information about them and for monitoring their activities. It should be made clear to them how this information will enhance the learning opportunities made available to them through self-access learning.

In this chapter we discuss the collection of information about learners and how this can contribute to enhancing the self-access learning experience. This enhancement is achieved firstly by making the learners individually more aware of their own language profile, and secondly by providing the information teachers need to develop materials and activities directly related to the requirements of the learners.

We suggest the use of learner profiles as an integrated approach to collecting and using information. These profiles are developed for and by individual learners and therefore are of immediate relevance to them. Because the profiles use a standardised format, information can be collected together into a central database from which analyses can be performed of all the self-access learners or selected sub-groups of them (e.g. beginners or part-time students). Such analyses are invaluable for the development of the self-access system, materials and activities. They could also contribute to the measurement of effectiveness (see Chapter 12), and to periodic reports and justifications of funding (see Chapter 4).

Both qualitative and quantitative data can be used in building learner profiles. These profiles can be linked very closely to learner assessments and can be used to record their outcomes. Profiles also have the potential to be used as the basis of assessment procedures. This is an issue which requires careful consideration as it also involves risks (e.g. alienating learners or reducing the usefulness of the awareness raising potential of profiles).

In this chapter we first define learner profiles, then we discuss the goals of using them. Following this, we look at the benefits for students and teachers of using learner profiles. Then we look at what a learner profile contains, how to construct one and how to make it an ongoing, updateable document. Finally, we comment on the issue of who should have access to the information in a learner profile and for what reasons.

5.2 A definition of a learner profile

A learner profile is a collection of information relating to an individual learner (see example in Figure 5.1; also see Section 7.2 for examples of activities for getting learners started on making profiles). Its purpose is to provide a picture of the learner's current development and future potential in terms which relate to self-access learning. The profile will: describe the learner's needs, wants and abilities; record the learner's goals and study plans; document actions taken to fulfil the study plans; and record learning outcomes. These are not new ideas. There is a lot of literature in the field of English language teaching about needs analysis (beginning with Munby 1978). Recording of learners' goals has been debated in the field of self-access learning under the guise of learner contracts (e.g. Dickinson 1987; Or 1994). There is some discussion on the use of study plans in self-access and documenting their success (e.g. Or 1994; Gardner and Miller 1997). Finally, learning outcomes are widely debated in the literature on testing. What is new about the learner profile is an attempt to bring its elements together so they may interact and produce an integrated whole which is of use to both learners and teachers.

5.3 The goals of using learner profiles

There are two major goals in creating profiles of self-access learners. The first is to establish the needs and wants of the learners and the second is to monitor progress. These goals are equally relevant for self-access learners and teachers although their reasons for pursuing the goals are often different (Table 5.1).

LEARNER PROFILE FOR: _____

Commencement Date: _____

To the learner
The contents of this profile are all about you. The purpose of the profile is to give an accurate picture of what you are able to do well and what you need to improve.the contents are not a secret record. You can see them at any time and you can also comment on what is recorded here. You can add whatever you like to this profile and staff in the Self-Access Centre may also add things. You might want to include non-paper items as part of this profile (e.g. a tape recording). That's OK. Just add a note in the relevant section saying where the document is. If you want to discuss your profile take it to your counsellor.

What to put in this profile
The profile is divided into the following sections:

1. Needs-and-wants analysis
   This section records what you *need* and also what you *want* to learn.
2. Contracts
   Here you can state the goals you will aim at during a specific period of time.
3. Study plans
   In this section you keep the detailed plans you make to achieve your goals.
4. Records of learning achievement
   In this section you show your progress. You could use any of the following:
   self assessments, peer assessments, tests, consultants' comments, your views of your progress, your class teachers' views.
5. Reflection
   Here you record your thoughts about the learning methods and materials you have been using and also about your progress.

Remember to keep this profile up to date.

Tabs: Needs & Wants · Contracts · Study Plans · Record of Learning · Reflection

Figure 5.1.   The first page of a learner profile

Table 5.1.   *The goals in establishing learner profiles*

Goal 1: To establish needs and wants

Profiling tool	Staff reasons for pursuing this goal	Learners' reasons for pursuing this goal
Analysis of needs and wants	• to provide the most suitable learning materials and activities for the learners • to raise learners' awareness of their needs and wants • to establish a baseline against which to measure effectiveness of self-access facilities	• to become more aware of needs and wants • to distinguish between needs and wants • to set learning targets • to prioritise targets • to make a study plan

Goal 2: To monitor progress

Profiling tool	Staff reasons for pursuing this goal	Learners' reasons for pursuing this goal
Record of work done	• to monitor use of self-access facilities • to compare needs/wants with actual work undertaken • to measure effectiveness of self-access facilities	• to monitor own input • to compare input with targets • to adjust study plan
Assessments	• to measure learning gain • to compare with learners' targets • to measure the effectiveness of self-access learning	• to monitor learning progress • to adjust learning targets

5.4 The benefits to learners

It should not be assumed that learners are explicitly aware of what they need to be able to do with their target language. A needs analysis will help them *discover* reasons for learning the language and *uncover* areas in which their ability may not be sufficient. It is useful for learners to consciously separate language learning 'wants' from language learning 'needs'. There are many goals they may want to achieve but which they may not actually need. Clearly identifying 'needs' and 'wants' will help learners with the process of prioritisation and in becoming realistic about assigning their own resources (especially time). This may be the first time that learners have had to verbalise the things they need and want to do with their target language.

An assessment of language ability will not be new to most learners. The benefit of considering it as part of the learner profile is that learners are made to think about their ability in relation to their goals. They may not have needed to do this before and it may help them to be realistic in setting their goals. Learners may be unfamiliar with establishing and recording their own learning goals because they may be used to teachers setting goals for them. In using a learner profile, learners have to think about goals, make choices and record them. This encourages learners to take responsibility for their learning. It may also help to heighten their motivation as they will be focusing on meeting their own, self-acknowledged, needs.

In keeping a record of the work they do learners are constantly reminding themselves of their goals and their commitment to achieving those goals. If they are not completing the study plan they have set themselves it will become evident. The responsibility for learning is clearly seen to be with them. In recording the outcomes of their work, learners will see the fruits of their labours. These outcomes can be short-term (like a self-assessment based on a few hours' work) and long-term (like an examination they have been studying for). The main benefit to learners of a learner profile is that in helping them to set goals (and monitor progress towards them) it raises the learners' awareness that responsibility for learning rests with them.

5.5 The benefits to teachers

When their students use learner profiles, teachers, whether in the classroom or the self-access centre (SAC), are better able to facilitate the learning process. They can ensure that the right learning opportunities are made available, they can help learners define their goals realistically, they can advise on ways to monitor progress, and they can assist in assessing outcomes. A further benefit to teachers is that they have access to systematic documentation of self-access learners' goals, how self-access facilities are being used, and what is being achieved. By extracting information across a range of learner profiles teachers are able to build a profile for groups of learners with common characteristics. This information can be very useful for future planning, budgeting, development of self-access materials and activities, research into self-access learning and preparing reports about use of the facilities.

5.6 What a learner profile looks like

There is no fixed physical shape for a learner profile. The paper part of a profile may be a printed booklet with lots of blank spaces for learners to add their own records. Alternatively, it could be a collection of loose sheets of paper which learners and teachers select, reject, adapt and add to as they see fit. The profile may contain other items like audio and video tapes. These would be particularly appropriate, for example, for a self-access learner concentrating on improving oral skills because they could be used to demonstrate improvement, whereas the paper record could only record assessments of improvement. However, the paper records of a profile are probably the most important because they will contain the bulk of the information and they are the most accessible.

Some learners may choose to keep their 'paper part' in digital format. They may then print parts of their profile or send them electronically when they want feedback from peers or teachers. Some learners may choose electronic storage for the entire profile. They might keep their records of work and examples of their writing as word-processed files. Examples of their speaking would be stored as digitised audio or video files. The physical shape of the profile is not important. What is important is that the different elements of the profile are collected together in a way with which the learner is comfortable, and which makes them easily accessible.

The location of learner profiles is also flexible. They may be stored centrally in a SAC or in classrooms. Each student may, for example, be allocated a folder in a filing cabinet. Alternatively, students may be required to keep their own learner profile which they bring with them when they wish to consult teachers, self-access counsellors or peers. Those who use electronic storage may carry the profile with them on floppy disk or store it on a network for easy access.

5.7 Constructing learner profiles

A number of issues need to be considered in constructing a learner profile. The profile should begin with the results of two analyses: first, an analysis of needs and wants which clarifies the learner's targets; second, an analysis of the learner's current abilities which makes clear what the learner is already able to do. The results of these two analyses are used as a basis for setting goals and making a study plan. As the study plan is put into action learning outcomes are recorded. This can feed back into the learner profile as a way of updating it.

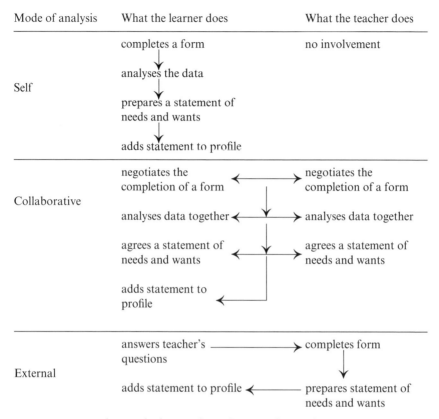

Mode of analysis	What the learner does	What the teacher does

Figure 5.2. Modes in which a needs analysis can be conducted

5.7.1 Needs and wants analysis

Self-access learners could be provided with a needs analysis document. This can be open-ended enough to express learners' perceptions fully but standardised enough to allow for collection of meaningful data. The analysis could be conducted in a variety of ways depending on the context and particularly the maturity level of the learners. Figure 5.2 summarises modes in which an analysis can be conducted.

5.7.2 Analysis of ability

An analysis of ability can be conducted through a formal test or in a number of more flexible self-access ways (these are discussed more fully in Chapter 11 on assessment). Some learners may already have a clear statement of their ability from a recent assessment procedure (e.g. in the classroom or in a public examination). This statement may cover all or

Part 2   Practical perspectives

What I think about my abilities: speaking skills

In the following table comment on your ability with the speaking skills listed. You can also add other speaking skills and comment on them.

Skill	Comments
Social conversations	I make some mistakes but I think I speak well enough not to bore people.
Business conversations	I notice people sometimes get confused about what I am telling them. I need to improve my way of explaining details.
Group discussions	I rarely need to do this but I think I would be OK.
Committee meetings	I don't have any problems.
Tutorials	Not applicable.
One-to-one meetings with a teacher	Not applicable.
Making presentations	This really frightens me. I need lots of practice.
Interviews	It has been a long time since I was interviewed. I don't know how I would do now.
Telephoning	This is OK if I have time to think about what I am going to say in advance. If not I get in a mess.
Talking to children	I need to be nice to my boss' children sometimes but I don't know how to speak to them.

Figure 5.3.   A learner's reflection on speaking skills

some language skills. A preliminary assessment may be imposed as part of a compulsory guidance session when learners first start to use a self-access system (see Figure 4.3 for an example).

Learner profiles can also provide learners with opportunities for reflecting on their abilities. Learners could write statements about their ability to perform certain tasks which they may specify or which may be specified for them (see, for example, Figure 5.3). These statements do not have the same function as test scores. Their purpose is to encourage learners to reflect on their abilities and to be realistic about them. If, for example, there is a mismatch between a learner's test scores and perceived abilities the learner needs to think about why this is so. The process of writing statements of ability is a starting point for considering learning goals.

5.7.3 Setting goals and making a study plan

Learners must set their own goals. They can be helped to clarify goals and to construct goal statements but if they are not the ones that set the goals they may not acknowledge ownership of them. If they do not acknowledge ownership of their goals they will not take responsibility for achieving them.

Once goals are set learners need to establish a study plan. This is their way of committing themselves to a certain amount of work within a certain period of time. When written down the plan will help learners to be realistic about how much time they have available and what they can achieve in that time.

Documents which focus on the setting of goals and sometimes also the commitment of learners' time are often referred to as learner contracts. An example of a learner contract is shown in Figure 5.4 and other examples can be seen in Dickinson (1987), Sheerin (1989) and Or (1994). It is interesting that this stage of preparation for learning is given such a legal term. The documents often have a pseudo-legal look to them being drawn up as an agreement between a student and teacher or self-access counsellor. The documents also try to reinforce the feeling of commitment by requiring the student and sometimes the teacher to sign the contract.

Of course, these documents have no legal validity and are not intended to have. The resemblance to entering into a contract is an attempt to motivate learners and to make them take the process seriously. Perhaps this is effective although it is difficult to see any evidence that signing a learner contract enhances learning in any way. The effect may vary according to the context although it seems that learners will deal with commitment to a learner contract in the same way as they deal with commitment to other study-related work. Thus, hard working students are likely to treat the contract seriously while others are not.

It can be argued that the importance of learner contracts lies in the thinking and discussion that precedes their completion rather than in a semblance of legal formality. Learners who have done the following

CONTRACT FOR SELF-ACCESS LEARNING

NAME: _____

CONTRACT PERIOD: Begins: _____ Ends: _____

1. TIME I WILL SPEND ON SELF-ACCESS LEARNING:

I will study for _____ hours each week/month (delete one)

2. MEETINGS WITH THE SELF-ACCESS COUNSELLOR
During the contract period I will meet with the self-access counsellor as follows:

	Meeting 1	Meeting 2	Meeting 3	Meeting 4	Meeting 5
Time/ Date					

3. OVERALL GOAL FOR THE CONTRACT PERIOD:

My overall goal is: _____

_____

4. STUDY ACTIVITIES/MATERIALS:
To achieve my goal I will do the following things:

ACTIVITY: e.g. writing/ grammar	STUDY MATERIALS: e.g. book/tape/program	REASON: How will this help you?

Signed: _____

Figure 5.4.   An example of a learner contract

things are more likely to pursue their goals regardless of whether they have completed a contract and signed it:

- identified their needs and wants
- considered their own abilities
- set learning goals which genuinely reflect their needs and wants
- considered the time they have available
- made a realistic study plan.

5.7.4 Recording learning outcomes

An important element of a learner profile is the recording of learning outcomes. The following may be recorded:

- results of self-assessments
- results of formal tests
- results of peer assessments
- a self-access counsellor's comments
- the learner's own perceptions of outcomes
- class teachers' perceptions
- examples of learner's best performance (e.g. a piece of written work or a tape of an oral presentation).

5.8 Updating profiles

Profiles are living documents. They need constant updating if they are to be effective. As well as frequently adding data to the record of work done and of learning outcomes, students will want to return periodically to reflect on their statements of needs and wants. These will change over time and should be updated regularly.

Updating learner profiles needs time. If it is perceived to take time away from learning, the profiles may be abandoned (or not introduced at all). To avoid this problem three things need to be done. First, learners must be made aware that profiling does not detract from learning but that on the contrary it is part of the learning process. Second, the administrative aspects of profiling must be made quick and easy. This can be done by providing pro formas which include prompts for much of the information learners may need to record. Finally, where possible, time should be made available. In a taught course this might mean devoting an occasional part of a lesson or a homework session to learner reflection. Time can also be found by making profiles the focus of a language practice task, like a discussion group, an essay or an oral presentation. In a SAC-context learners could be asked to update their profiles as part of a counselling session.

Updating is important because a profile needs to show the current state of a learner's abilities and goals and also how these have developed. This is a useful record to remind learners of what they have achieved and what further goals they are working towards. Having become familiar with the process of maintaining a learner profile, learners may continue to update their profiles once their formal education has ended. This will enable them to continue monitoring their progress as independent language learners.

5.9 Access to information

Learner profiles can provide useful information to teachers and administrators about learners and their behaviour. However, the main function of a profile is to provide learners with opportunities for reflection and record-keeping. Therefore, it is important that they can believe in the confidentiality of the contents of their profile. This is crucial to developing the learner–counsellor relationship that we discuss elsewhere (see Chapter 10). In order to make use of data contained in learner profiles, counsellors need, at the outset, to inform learners of the uses to which this information can be put. One way of using the information in learner profiles is to give feedback to teachers about the use of self-access facilities thus enabling them to improve those facilities. It is important that learners should always feel in complete control of their profiles both in terms of how it is used and what it contains.

5.10 Summary

As a result of using profiles learners will know more about themselves and their abilities, will pursue relevant goals in their learning and will, ultimately, take greater responsibility for their learning. As self-access learning becomes more relevant to individual learners they will become more motivated in their studies. Teachers will have a clearer picture of their students' needs, wants and learning objectives and be better able to assist in achieving those objectives. They will also have insights into how their self-access facilities are used, thus enabling better planning of materials and activities and generally making the provision of self-access learning facilities more effective.

5.11 Tasks

1. Think of a group of learners you are familiar with. Write a document which will help them set goals and establish a study plan. You will need to decide whether to:
   - make the document a form to fill in
   - ask the learners to create their own statements
   - make a statement about the purpose
   - add explanatory notes.
2. Create a learner training worksheet which will raise learners' awareness of the benefits of learner profiles.
3. Design a questionnaire to find out your learners' needs and wants.

5.12 For discussion

1. Discuss how a self-access centre manager could make use of the information contained in learner profiles.
2. In a learning context with which you are familiar discuss the practicalities of implementing a system of learner profiles.
3. Discuss the resistance to learner profiles you might meet in an institution. State where the resistance might come from and how you would deal with it.

6 Materials for self-access language learning

6.1 Introduction

The purpose of this chapter is to discuss ways to build up a stock of self-access language learning materials. We look at different kinds of materials, the sources from which materials can be obtained and issues of materials production. We also discuss the advantages and disadvantages of using different kinds of materials for self-access learning. Our aim is to provide a knowledge base from which educators involved in self-access learning can make informed decisions about the kinds of materials which (1) best suit the language learning needs of their students, (2) are appropriate to the contexts in which the students are learning and (3) fall within institutional budgets of time and money. This chapter provides ideas for obtaining or produc- ing self-access learning materials for all settings from classrooms to dedicated self-access centres (SACs) and for all budgets from those working without additional resources to well-funded, purpose built SACs.

While pedagogical goals and the specific needs of individual learners are the most important factors in considering self-access learning materials, time and money are the most influential factors. In addition to this, every self-access learning context is different. It is not, therefore, relevant to discuss 'the best' way of providing materials or 'the best' source from which to obtain them. There are different ways and different sources. What we discuss in this chapter are the avenues open to those responsible for providing self-access materials. It is up to those providers to decide what is most appropriate for their contexts. We do, however, encourage an eclectic approach because it provides the variety that makes self-access learning more stimulating for learners. In this chapter we look at:

- published language-learning materials
- authentic materials
- specially produced materials
- student contributions to materials.

6.2 Published language-learning materials

6.2.1 Advantages

There are a number of reasons why published language-learning materials are useful in self-access learning (Table 6.1). Purchasing published language-learning materials is a good way of initially building up a stock of self-access materials. It is a quick and easy solution. Decisions about what to purchase can be made by leafing through publishers' catalogues and by canvassing colleagues who between them may have experience of a wide range of course books as well as audio and video tapes. There are some drawbacks to these sources of information. Publishers produce catalogues in order to sell their wares. They tend to give positive descriptions of their materials and are unlikely to point out deficiencies. It is quite common for the label 'self-access edition' or something similar to appear in catalogues. These labels can be misleading as they are applied to a spectrum of publications ranging from those which have truly been written specifically as self-access materials to those which are course books with answer keys at the end. Nevertheless, publishers' catalogues do provide information about materials which are available and the target learners they are intended for. They also provide some indication of which publications contain answer keys.

Relying on the suggestions of colleagues can also have its drawbacks as a way of selecting materials. If the colleagues have no experience of self-access (either as counsellors or learners) they may have some difficulty in visualising how the materials will be used. They may, therefore, recommend published materials which they have found very useful in teacher-directed learning but which would not work well in a self-access context. It should also be remembered that colleagues who teach languages are often those who have a facility for learning languages or who, at the very least, enjoy learning and using languages. While some self-access learners will be in this category it is highly likely that many will not. The materials which appeal to a lover of languages may not appeal to those who want a 'quick fix' for a language-learning problem.

An advantage to suggestions from colleagues is that they are likely to be familiar with the needs and abilities of the learners who will use the self-access materials. They will also have some knowledge of any cultural constraints on the selection of materials for these learners and of the content or materials that are likely to be popular. This 'inside information' is very important in selecting materials.

Table 6.1. *Reasons why published materials are useful in a SAC*

Reason	Comments
Availability	Published materials are listed in publishers' catalogues which also contain information on how to order. In addition, most published material has an ISBN number which means it can be ordered through any reasonable bookshop anywhere in the world.
Cost	Compared to the cost (particularly in teachers' time) of producing materials a published book is very cheap.
Speed	Published materials can be obtained very quickly.
Efficiency	Purchasing published materials dramatically reduces time spent in materials production.
Expertise	If publishers have gone to the trouble and cost of producing a book they want to make sure it will sell. They will, therefore, have made sure that the authors are the right people for the job. The book will also have been reviewed by experts in the field before being accepted for publication.
Track record	Published materials are piloted before being released. By the time they are put to use they have a track record of success.
Quality	Published materials are carefully checked for accuracy. They are unlikely to contain typographical errors which are confusing to learners (especially when there is no teacher present to point out the errors).
Range	• Published materials are already available for all of the language skills. It is possible to purchase course materials for one specific skill, a range of skills or a complete integrated approach. • There are published materials for all of the specialist areas of language learning such as academic writing, English for nursing, tourist language, etc.
Familiarity	Self-access language learners may already be familiar with published materials if they have met them in their language-learning classes. This will make it easier for them to start using the materials.
Specialisation	Some published books contain work that it would be impossible for teachers to produce, like dictionaries, thesauruses, phrase books and grammar books.

Table 6.1 (*contd*)

Reason	Comments
Accessibility	Published works are laid out in a way which provides the user with pathways through the learning material. This makes it easier for them to find what they are looking for and also encourages them to approach their learning in an organised way.
Exposure	By providing learners with the opportunity to try out different published materials learners may decide to continue using a preferred text.
Variety	Published materials are available in a variety of formats and styles. Published materials are also readily available in different media, thus a centre could easily and quickly provide materials for use with audio, video and computer equipment as well as in print format.
Attractiveness	Published materials are attractively presented with text which is well laid out and often with colour images.

6.2.2 Drawbacks

Classroom orientation

Most (but certainly not all) published materials are designed for use with class-sized groups of learners. Activities often require pair work or group work. These are still valid for use in self-access learning but not by learners who choose to work alone.

Teacher direction

Many published materials assume a teacher is present. They frequently contain open-ended activities which enliven a lesson by encouraging students to experiment with the language and which a teacher will guide, control, monitor and/or give feedback on. For self-access learners these activities become meaningless and frustrating.

Lack of answer keys

Not all published materials have answers to the exercises they contain. Publishers are beginning to make concessions to self-access learners by providing answer keys. However, keys for open-ended exercises can only provide suggestions for possible answers.

Quantities

Most published materials, particularly those designed as course books, contain large quantities of learning material. Self-access learners may find difficulty in deciding which parts to use. If the book is written to be followed linearly it may not be possible to use individual sections as stand alone materials.

General appeal

Most published materials are generalised so that they can be marketed to a wide range of learners. As a result, local contexts cannot be included. For commercial reasons controversial topics are often also excluded (if they offend purchasers they will not sell well). This is a drawback because controversial issues and especially those which are sensitive within the learners' context often stimulate greater use of language.

6.2.3 Adapting published materials

There are ways of making published materials more user-friendly for self-access users. It is possible to provide supporting worksheets which guide learners through materials and, where necessary, supply answer keys. The worksheet might also offer advice about how to cope with exercises which were designed for pairs or groups.

Separating books into smaller, more manageable units has been proposed as a way of dealing with the overwhelming quantity of material in a course book. Dickinson (1987) cautiously suggests this, Sheerin (1989) advocates it, Gardner (1995) reports on one way of doing it. However, the copyright implications remain unclear so it is wise to contact the publisher first. Gardner (1993a) describes one attempt to secure a general agreement to split books, videos and audio tapes. Gardner (1995) also describes adding teacher advice directly to the text.

In adapting published materials attention should also be given to the problem of self-access learners using audio-visual materials which were designed for use by a teacher. Learners have difficulty in finding the right part of audiotapes and videotapes. Providing users with a list of counter numbers is a possible solution. Some publishers provide on-screen counters for video materials, e.g. the 'Television English' video-tapes (BBC / The British Council 1985–6). Some researchers have experimented with more accurate but costly and time-consuming methods of accessing sections of videotapes (e.g. Little 1986, Armitage 1992, Gardner 1993b, Gardner 1994, Gardner and Blasco García 1996).

6.3 Authentic materials

6.3.1 Advantages

By authentic materials we mean any text (printed or digital) or tape which was produced for a purpose other than teaching the target language. Little et al. (1989) list three reasons why authentic texts make useful language-learning materials. They feel that the authentic texts are likely to motivate learners, promote acquisition and, if used in sufficient quantities, contribute to language immersion. There is little research evidence to support these statements although they seem logical especially when applied to self-access learning.

Riley (1981, quoted in Dickinson 1987) makes a more practical case for using authentic materials. He argues that learners should use authentic materials related to their professional areas, thus enabling them to channel their language-learning energies in ways that are of direct relevance to their needs. This argument makes sense for instrumentally motivated learners who have a tightly focused reason for learning a language such as a job-related need. However, in self-access language-learning contexts where some or all of the learners have integrative motivation, i.e. they have an interest in the culture and society of the target language, this argument is less valid. In such circumstances focusing learners' attention too tightly might be considered restrictive. Learners should have access to as broad a range of authentic materials as possible.

One way of allowing learners to find their own focus is to encourage them to bring in their own authentic materials. This approach is used successfully for classroom self-access by Dam (1995) but there is no reason why it could not be extended to a SAC. If carefully managed, such a system might also produce a description for other learners of why the text is important/interesting/useful as well as exercises and answer sheets. There are many sources of authentic materials (see Table 6.2).

6.3.2 Drawbacks

There are drawbacks to using authentic materials in their raw form without adaptation or support.

Complexity of language

Authentic materials may potentially make use of any grammatical structure and any vocabulary item in the target language. This is what makes them authentic and therefore of interest to learners. However, it can also make them inaccessible to beginners and elementary learners.

Table 6.2.   *Sources of authentic materials*

Source	Comments
Newspapers	Regular subscriptions give learners access to up-to-date news in their target language. The importance of *current* newspapers is that the learners will be reading the same stories that they see in their mother-tongue newspapers. This will facilitate comprehension and enhance motivation. It should be noted that newspaper subscriptions are relatively expensive for a throw-away resource. Decisions have to be made about whether the cost is justifiable.
Magazines	• Regular subscriptions may build up a regular readership. A range of subject areas will help to meet the needs of a large group of learners. • Up-to-date magazines cater better for the needs of subject specialists who are up-to-date in this field in their own language. However, old magazines donated by colleagues can also meet the needs of less specialist readers who are thirsty for reading materials. • As with newspapers, magazines are a throw away resource although their shelf life is somewhat longer. Where budgets are restricted it may be appropriate to buy occasional issues of magazines which may be of special interest to learners.
User manuals	Manuals from computers, video players and other kinds of equipment provide examples of a very specialist kind of language.
Leaflets and brochures (government departments, travel agencies, banks, etc.)	Free and usually easy to obtain by post, these publications provide information in a wide range of subject areas. They will have motivational value with learners who have professional interests in those areas. They may also be used as sources of information in working on projects.
Foreign mission information (embassies, non-government agencies, etc.)	• Often obtainable all over the world not only in countries using the target language. • As well as providing information about the home country these materials may contain information relating to the host country with which the learners can identify.

Table 6.2. (*contd*)

Source	Comments
International companies	Materials are probably most easily obtained from their headquarters but sometimes also locally. The materials may be subject specific, relating to the companies' products. However, some companies produce materials relating to their policies on animal rights, environmental issues, etc. The companies often invite the public to request these materials.
Airlines	• Airlines are usually geared up to deal with a certain number of languages as well as the language of their base country. Thus they might be able to provide the same document in two or more languages which may facilitate comprehension. • As well as the materials which can be solicited by post or at the airline offices, colleagues who take trips can be encouraged to bring back in-flight magazines.
TV programmes	Copyright laws in many countries prevent copying of programmes from TV. However, sometimes TV stations will give permission for copying programmes they make themselves if it is for educational purposes. In some countries this is already permitted under a licence agreement.
Radio programmes	Copyright laws usually apply as for TV programmes. An advantage of radio programmes is that they are accessible at greater distances than TV programmes. The chance, therefore, of finding something in the target language is greater.
Videos	Movies and documentaries can be purchased on video tape or video disc. These provide a rich source of authentic language. In some cases they provide closed captions (same language sub-titles).
Lectures and speeches	If there is a local source in the target language it is sometimes possible to get permission to video or audio tape these.
Native or near-native speakers	If these are available locally they provide a good source of authentic language. Of course, they cannot be 'stored' in a SAC or classroom but they could be included on a list of suggestions to learners as to how to practise the target language.

Table 6.2. (*contd*)

Source	Comments
Songs	Most learners, whether young or old, are attracted to listening to songs. Some recently established SACs have karaoke rooms which attest to the popularity of learning languages through songs.
Letters	Letters in the target language, or even staff memos, could be posted on a noticeboard for anyone to read. E-mail messages are now proving popular with language learners (see Chapter 10).
Games	There is a large variety of games which are suitable for self-access: Trivial Pursuit and Scrabble, for instance. Learners are attracted to playing games as they de-emphasise learning and place the focus on fun activities.

Learning burden

Authentic materials may contain items (particularly vocabulary) which are of low frequency and of peripheral use to the learner and may never be encountered again.

Acquisition

In learning contexts where authentic target-language materials are not readily available, obtaining them can be time consuming and frustrating.

Pedagogical decisions

A SAC may become overwhelmed with authentic materials. Some selection is required by the staff to decide which materials to make available as they are, which to support with worksheets or further information and which not to keep. In making decisions about authentic materials staff should consider how learners might use the materials, what linguistic knowledge they need, what type of learner training might be needed and what support materials may be required (e.g. dictionaries, grammar reference books, tutors, in-house worksheets). In-house support materials might contain suggestions for using authentic materials or they might contain language-learning exercises designed for use with the authentic materials. Such exercises might be generic and thus useful for a range of materials or they might be specific in order to fully exploit the potential of one piece of authentic material (for a discussion of the differences between specific and generic materials see Section 6.6). In the latter case staff would want to be sure the authentic materials would be used sufficiently to justify the time consuming task of producing the specific support materials.

6.4 Specially produced materials

6.4.1 Advantages

There may be learner needs which cannot be met with the kinds of materials discussed above. In these cases materials must be specially produced. Block (1991) reminds us that in-house materials production allows the inclusion of contexts familiar to the learners. A system has to be established for the production of in-house materials. Miller (1995) suggests a process for this. There are a number of reasons for in-house production of materials (see Table 6.3). Specially produced materials are often enhanced by the inclusion of extracts from authentic sources (e.g. newspapers, subject specialist text books). There are copyright implications to doing this but it is worth pursuing. Miller (1995) suggests how to obtain copyright permission.

6.4.2 Drawbacks

Time

First, producing good materials can be very time consuming. Second, time and effort need to be put into organising and coordinating production efforts. Sheerin (1989) points out that cooperating teachers need to be coordinated and to agree on their goals before beginning.

Quality

If undertaken by novices the results of materials production can be less user-friendly, less useful and less accurate than other sources of materials. In turn, this can have a demoralising effect on learners and staff.

Quantity

Tibbetts (1994) talks about the importance of not being over ambitious in producing materials for self-access. It is important to set realistic goals for materials production; this may, however, limit the amount that can be produced.

Table 6.3.   *Reasons for special production of self-access materials*

Reason	Comments
Specific learning goals	Some self-access language learners may have specific goals, like particular examinations or specific language functions, which are not addressed by other materials.
Learning styles	Learners are individuals. They approach learning in different ways. This diversity of approaches is not always met in available materials.
Culture	Materials which are specially produced can meet the requirements of specific cultures in a way that other materials cannot.
Variety	In-house production allows a large number of small pieces of work with great variety in style and content.
Cross referencing	Materials can make references to other self-access materials.
Pathways	Specially produced materials can include a variety of pathways to suit different learners' needs.
Manageability	Individual pieces of material can be short and thus easily managed.
Motivation	Specially produced materials demonstrate to learners their teachers' interest in helping them.
Cost	In some circumstances in-house production may be cheaper than purchasing published materials, for example when: teacher time has been allocated to it; teachers volunteer to do it; published materials are expensive relative to teacher time; many copies are required; one set of in-house materials replaces the need for a number of published materials.
Teacher development	While engaged in materials production teachers learn more about the needs of self-access learners.
Teacher commitment	When teachers become involved in self-access materials development they may be more committed to the success of self-access learning.
Up-to-date	Materials can be updated on a regular basis so that they are always about current issues.

6.5 Student contributions to materials

6.5.1 Advantages

Self-access learners are an important resource for producing self-access language-learning materials. They can enhance the stock of learning materials in numerous ways (see Table 6.4). Involving learners as a source of materials also provides opportunities for them to become actively involved with the environment in which they are learning. The discussions and negotiations concerning self-access materials can become part of the learning experience.

Learners are the best source of feedback on self-access materials. As users of the materials they can comment on user-friendliness, usefulness and how appropriate materials are. Needs analyses conducted by teachers or learners themselves provide information about learning needs which are not covered by the existing materials and areas where materials exist but the stock needs increasing or updating. Learner input into materials production may either be through co-production with teachers or as sole producers. Learners can also be used as suppliers of authentic materials.

Involving learners in developing self-access materials may result in them feeling a greater commitment to self-access learning. This moves further towards the goal of empowering the learners with more responsibility for their own language learning. For an example of an activity to involve learners in producing materials see Activity 12 in Chapter 7.

6.5.2 Drawbacks

There are also some drawbacks to involving learners in materials production:

Need for teacher guidance

To ensure an acceptable quality in learner-generated materials, teachers need to encourage the learners, and then monitor and edit their work. This results in added workload for the teacher.

Learner time constraints

Although learners may wish to contribute to materials development they may not have enough free time to become involved. This may result in an initial enthusiasm but ultimately a weak response.

Table 6.4.   *Ways in which students can contribute to self-access materials*

Roles	Format
Provider of feedback on materials	• questionnaires at the end of pieces of material • questionnaires about categories of materials • suggestion boxes • self-access club where learners become involved in organising and maintaining self-access facilities
Analyser of needs	• individual student needs analyses • questionnaires about the kinds of materials students would like to have • profiles of typical problems with suggested solutions
Co-producer of materials	• newsletters (using teachers for resources, editing and proof reading) • publicity materials • video documentaries • language games • exercises with answer sheets (following a model provided by a teacher)
Sole producer of materials	• competitions for student developed materials • writing competitions with the entries being used later in the SAC • data from classroom projects • project reports for others to read (with teachers' comments) • visual displays of project findings • assessed essays
Supplier of authentic materials	• old magazines • tourist information brought back from holidays • copies of letters from pen-friends • exchange of Internet addresses for sites with information relevant to, or in, the target language

Learner resentment

Learners may perceive materials development as wholly a teacher's job. If learners are unable to see the purpose of becoming involved they may be unwilling to contribute. Also, they may think that other learners, or they themselves, do not have the linguistic knowledge to produce materials.

Diversity of learner needs

If learner needs are widely diverse they may have problems in producing materials for each other, e.g. exercises produced by Spanish-speaking learners to focus on their pronunciation problems in English would not be of much use to Cantonese-speaking learners.

6.6 A note about generic materials

In the different categories of materials we have discussed in this chapter we have referred mostly to materials which have a specific language-learning content, that is, materials which have instructions, exercises and often answer sheets aimed at learning or practising specific language items. In all of the materials categories there is also a place for generic materials, that is, materials which aim at providing language-learning procedures which learners can use many times, varying the content for themselves. Generic materials can focus on very specific skills but they do not specify language items. Both specific and generic materials make useful contributions to self-access learning. The former provide teacher-like support for self-access learning, the latter encourage learners to find their own ways of learning and provide an assisted path towards autonomy. A clearer idea of the differences between specific and generic materials can be gained by comparing the example materials in Figures 6.1 and 6.2.

Generic materials are, perhaps, a little harder to write than specific materials because they need to be flexible enough to cover a range of possible uses and possible users. This is probably easier when the materials writers know the intended users of the materials and what facilities and opportunities they have available. It may be for this reason that there are few examples of published generic materials.

6.6.1 Advantages

Cost effective materials development

Writing good language learning materials is costly because it is time consuming. One generic worksheet could provide learners with as much language work as a whole series of specific worksheets. Simply because fewer generic materials are required they are less costly to produce.

Relevance to learners

Learners can customise generic materials to their own contexts; in this way, they will be learning language which is relevant to their own needs and wants.

Vocabulary in academic texts (1)

The following passage is taken from *Symbols of America* by Richard O. Dent (1988, p53).

INSTRUCTIONS:

1. As you read the passage pay particular attention to the underlined words.
2. In the box at the end of the text try to explain the words. The first one is done for you.
3. When you have finished check your answers on the back of this sheet.

Mickey Mouse is a well loved <u>symbol</u> of the greatness of America. He represents a long <u>carefree</u> era when everything in the world has gone well for the most <u>prosperous</u> nation on earth. He <u>symbolises</u> the prosperity of Americans throughout a period when they have dominated the world both economically and politically.

It is significant that a <u>creature</u> often viewed in other countries as a pest to be <u>eradicated</u> can rise in the United States of America to become a movie star and a household name. This symbolizes <u>the American dream</u> where everyone (including apparently rodents and quite possibly many other non-human personalities) can expect <u>freedom of speech, freedom of actions</u> and freedom to make an honest living. It is important to note in this context that the rise to fame and/or riches of an <u>underdog</u> has long been a popular theme in the <u>folk lore</u> of western countries in general but of America in particular.

Not content to make a hero out of one rodent, the American public has also <u>idolised</u> Mickey's partner Minnie. It is interesting to note that Mickey and Minnie frequently unlike human courtship bel

Words	Explanation
Symbol	A thing which represents something or someone
Carefree	
Prosperous	
Symbolises	
Creature	
Eradicated	

ANSWER KEY:

Words	Explanation
Symbol	A thing which represents something or someone
Carefree	Without any worries
Prosperous	Rich, well off
Symbolises	Represents
Creature	A living being
Eradicated	

Figure 6.1.   Specific self-access worksheet

Vocabulary in academic texts (2)

Select a short passage from a text book you need to read for your studies. It could be a chapter or even one section of a chapter.

Before you begin reading make a table something like the following one in your notebook. The first line here is just an example to show you how to fill it in. Make sure you leave lots of space for writing your comments.

WORD	WHAT I THINK IT MEANS	NOTES AFTER CHECKING
Eradicate	Kill	The dictionary says: "Get rid of" Ling Ling (in my class) says that the way to get rid of a mouse is to kill it so I'm right but for some things you don't have to kill e.g. to eradicate cheating.

INSTRUCTIONS:

1. Read the passage and list any words you do not understand.
2. Try to explain what each of the words means.
3. When you have finished check your answers. You could do this in one or more of the following ways (these are in priority order):
   a) Look in a dictionary (you might need a specialist dictionary).
   b) Check with classmates.
   c) Ask a consultant in the Self-Access Centre.
   d) Ask the teacher who recommended the text book (only use this option for words you really can't find out about in other ways).

Figure 6.2. Generic self-access worksheet

Life-long learning

Generic materials show learners procedures which they can continue to use long after they have finished with formal education. If learners choose they can continue informal language learning for as long as they wish.

Responsibility, independence and autonomy

Generic materials require learners to take more responsibility for their language learning activities. They need to select the language content to which they will apply the generic procedures. They need to reflect on their learning and make decisions about whether to continue using, to adapt or to change procedures. In this way learners are encouraged to become independent of their teachers and may eventually become fully autonomous learners.

6.6.2 Drawbacks

Lack of precision

Generic materials do not provide precise answer keys or feedback to learners, although they can provide suggestions about how to check answers. Some learners may find this disconcerting.

DIY

Generic worksheets may appear to be somewhat like a do-it-yourself kit. There are instructions and suggestions but learners have to find their own learning content. Learners may recognise their own lack of expertise which could lead to a loss of face validity, especially with learners who are not very independent.

Learner workload

Generic materials demand more of learners than other kinds of materials. They need to find content, they need to learn how to apply a procedure, they need to find their own ways of checking their performance and they need to reflect on what they have done and learned in order to make decisions about further uses of the materials. Some learners would undoubtedly prefer the quicker option of specific materials.

Teacher absence

All the materials we have described in this chapter are for self-access learning and are therefore assumed to be for use independent of a teacher. Nevertheless, most self-access materials have the clearly distinguishable 'controlling' hand of a teacher in them. They are teaching by remote control. Generic materials have far less control built into them. This can be frightening for teacher-dependent learners and can even make relatively independent learners anxious until they become used to it.

6.7 Stocking a self-access centre

No single category of self-access materials will satisfy all the needs of the learners in a SAC. Each has advantages and drawbacks. The solution is to take an eclectic approach. On opening a SAC, providing published materials is quick and convenient. As the SAC matures and user-needs become apparent this stock can be filled out with adapted or purpose-written materials. It may also be necessary to weed out some of the early materials if they are found not to be useful or not to be used much. Before purchasing, adapting or designing any self-access materials some practical and pedagogical questions need to be asked (see Tables 6.5 and 6.6).

6.8 Knowing how good your materials are

Materials – whether adapted, developed or purchased, whether new or old – should be constantly open to evaluation. Feedback can be collected in a number of ways (which are not mutually exclusive). New materials can be trialled with willing self-access learners. In-house materials can contain a request for feedback. Published materials can have a request attached to them (e.g. a sticker on the cover). Generic feedback forms can be made available for use with any materials alongside a drop-off box. A more general suggestions box will collect feedback on materials along with other things. Another form of materials evaluation is the rate at which take-away materials (e.g. worksheets and information sheets) disappear. This form of evaluation also occurs for materials which are not intended to be taken away. While conducting one of the case studies in this book, we were informed that 'our most reliable feedback, alas, comes from which materials disappear from the centre and are never returned' (Felicity O'Dell, personal communication).

Regular staff–student sessions to discuss self-access learning facilities will also uncover some feedback on materials. Introductory sessions for particular kinds of materials (e.g. software for computer-assisted language learning: CALLware) can also be used to obtain feedback. Learners can be asked to form their own groups for self-access

Table 6.5.   *Practical questions to ask about self-access materials*

Aspect	Questions
People power	• Can the people involved with self-access do the job (purchasing, adaptations, productions)? • If not, can they be trained (or train themselves)? • Are there other colleagues who can help? • Can enthusiasm be maintained?
Cost	• How much is this going to cost (estimate)? • How much money is available?
Life span	• How durable are the materials? • Will in-house materials last as long as published materials? • Do materials need to be laminated?
Copyright	• Will there be copyright problems with the proposed way of using the materials? • How can copyright problems be resolved? • Do the people involved with self-access understand the copyright situation?
Access	• How will users access the materials (over the counter, off the shelves)? • Will materials be separated by media (e.g. video, audio, print) or will they be available as packages (e.g. video plus book)?
Storage	• What system of storage can be used? • Is special storage furniture needed?
Technology	• What kinds of technology do the materials need? • Are suitable staff available to cope with technology demands?

evaluation; in these groups they would look at the materials, among other things.

6.9 Implications for self-access materials development

The above discussion of different features of self-access materials raises a number of fundamental questions that should be asked before purchasing, adapting or developing materials. In many contexts the awareness which comes from answering these questions will lead

Table 6.6. *Pedagogical questions to ask about self-access materials*

The 'Published materials' column contains questions you should ask before buying materials. The 'In-house materials' column contains questions you need to ask yourself when planning to write materials (including support for authentic materials). If you are planning to adapt materials you will need to use questions from both columns.

Aspect	Organisational issues	Published materials	In-house materials

Language level	• At which language levels do you need materials?
	• What are your short-term and long-term goals? (e.g. start with introducing intermediate level materials and add upper-intermediate materials later)
		• What level(s) is aimed at?
		• If this is from a series, are different levels available which meet your long-term organisational needs?
			• What level(s) are you producing materials for?
			• Are you planning several pieces of material?
			• If yes:
			  – Are they at different levels?
			  – Must they be used in a particular order or are they stand-alone?

Skills	• Which skills areas do you need to target? • What are the short-term and long-term goals? (e.g. start by buying general listening materials and later produce in-house materials to meet specific needs based on learners' feedback)	• What are the skills areas that are targeted? • Do these materials meet your organisational goals?	• What skills areas will you target? • Will the materials meet your organisational goals?
Objectives	• What learning objectives do you want to pursue for materials in the above level and skills category?	• What are the objectives of this piece of material?	• What are you trying to achieve with this piece of material?

Table 6.6. (*contd*)

Aspect	Organisational issues	Published materials	In-house materials
Length of activity	• How long will learners be able to spend using self-access materials? This may be governed by external factors like timetables. • How long will learners want to spend on an individual activity? • Do different groups of learners have different amounts of time available and different attention spans?	• How much time would learners need to complete a unit of work in these materials? • How long would an individual activity take?	• How will you fit your materials to suit the available time of your learners? • How long will you make your activities? • Will you vary time required according to learning level, specific target groups or some other factor?
Language of instructions	• Do you have a policy on the use of mother tongue in materials? • Will instructions always be in the target language, always in the mother tongue or will the choice of language be appropriate to the level of the materials?	• What language is used for giving instructions in the materials?	• What language will you use for giving instructions in the materials? • Will you vary the language according to the learning level?
Pathways	• Do your learners need help using materials? • Do you want to provide different groups of learners with different ways through the materials?	• Are learners guided through the materials?	• Will you guide learners? How? • Will you provide multiple pathways to accommodate different groups of learners?
Technology	• Are your learners familiar with technology?	• Do the materials indicate clearly when to use technology (e.g.	• How will you indicate when to use technology?

Table 6.6. (*contd*)

Aspect	Organisational issues	Published materials	In-house materials
	• Will using technology aid or hinder learning? (e.g. through unfamiliarity) This will probably vary for different kinds of technology.	tape recorder, computer, video)? • Do you have the right kind(s) of technology? • Is the technology available and working correctly enough of the time to prevent user frustration? • Will you need to provide additional technological instruction and/or support to your learners?	• Are you going to focus on technology which will be easily available to your learners? • Will the learners be familiar with the technology? • If no: – How will you help them cope? – Who will provide support?
Assessment	• Do you want to provide assessment opportunities? • Is monitoring achievement important? • Do you want assessment to be separate from materials or be integrated into them? • Do you want assessment to be recorded, not recorded or optionally recorded?	• Do the materials provide assessment opportunities? • How are learners given feedback? • Do the materials meet your organisational needs?	• Do you intend to provide assessment opportunities? • If yes: – How will the assessment be conducted? – How will you provide feedback? – How will you meet the organisational needs?

Table 6.6. (*contd*)

Aspect	Organisational issues	Published materials	In-house materials
Evaluation	• Do you want to evaluate the materials? • What is the purpose of evaluation? • Do you prefer evaluation to be separate from materials or integrated into them?	• Do the materials provide evaluation opportunities? • Does the evaluation meet your organisational needs?	• Do you intend to provide evaluation opportunities? • If yes: – What kind of evaluative feedback will be invited (e.g. user-friendliness, usefulness)? – How will evaluation be recorded?
Progression	• Do you want your self-access materials to make suggestions to students about what to do next?	• Do the materials suggest what to do next? • Do the suggestions vary according to outcomes from the current materials? • If the materials refer to other published materials, do you have them? If not, are you willing to buy them?	• Will the learners be shown what to do next once they have completed a piece of work? • If yes: – How will you do it? – Will your suggestions vary according to outcomes? – How prescriptive are you planning to be? – Will you refer to published materials? – Do you have those materials?

teachers to consider developing their own self-access materials. Table 6.6 helps materials writers plan a systematic approach for in-house materials production and helps them identify areas in which materials are needed. Figure 6.3 provides a checklist for use once writers have an idea for materials development. It acts as a guide to help them think about goals, what they are trying to achieve with this material and how to implement their ideas. The relative importance of the questions on the checklist will depend on the context; for example, questions relating to technology become unimportant with self-access materials which do not make use of technology.

6.9.1 Producing self-access materials

There are advantages to using a set format for producing self-access materials. Once the format has been established it becomes easier and

Table 6.7. *Suggested format for a coversheet*

Section	The stock of materials should be broken into sections which are meaningful to users. This division will make materials easier to locate. Possible sections might be Reading, Writing, Listening, Speaking, Vocabulary, Grammar, Paralinguistic communication, Self-assessment, Learner training. In a large collection smaller divisions may be used, e.g. Reading for pleasure, Academic reading, Speed reading.
Title	Titles for individual pieces of material will aid identification by students and staff (e.g. it might be confusing if the material only has a catalogue number such as FEN-X-412–001). Well-chosen titles may also aid browsers in making a choice (e.g. excuses for being late).
Level	Some materials can only be used for one level but where possible they should be written to cover multiple levels. This may be achieved by providing different worksheets or sections on a worksheet which are oriented to specific levels. Specifying a level will help learners identify materials which are suitable for them.
Aims	The aims of the material must be clearly stated in a way that the learner can understand them.
Activity time	State the estimated time for completion of the activity. This will vary somewhat depending on the speed at which individuals work but will give the learners some idea of what to aim for.

Developing an idea for self-access materials development

First answer yes or no to the following questions:

	Yes	No
Self-access versus teacher-direction Will the learners be able to manage your materials without a teacher?	☐	☐
Would the materials be more effective under teacher direction?	☐	☐
Will teachers agree to use certain activities in the classroom which will help their learners exploit your materials in the SAC?	☐	☐
Pedagogical support Can the materials be developed so that they are stand alone?	☐	☐
Will the materials include some kind of assistance?	☐	☐
Will the learners need human help (e.g. a counsellor)?	☐	☐
Rewards Will the material be credit bearing?	☐	☐
If yes, is the link between classroom activities and the materials made clear?	☐	☐
If no, can learners be motivated to use the materials?	☐	☐
Interactions Will the materials require learner-to-learner interaction?	☐	☐
If yes, will the learners cooperate with each other?	☐	☐
Will this material create a noise-level problem?	☐	☐
Will individuals as well as pairs/groups be able to use the materials?	☐	☐
If there is no interaction will learners learn anything?	☐	☐
Technology Will the necessary technology be available?	☐	☐
Will all learners know how to use the technology?	☐	☐
If the technology breaks down will learners still be able to learn?	☐	☐
Publicity Will your materials be publicised?	☐	☐

Figure 6.3.   Checklist for developing an idea for self-access materials development

Monitoring		
Will use of the materials be monitored?	❑	❑
Will feedback be collected from learners?	❑	❑
Flexibility		
Can the materials be used for a variety of purposes?	❑	❑
Will materials suggest a variety of pathways?	❑	❑
Will the materials make learners aware of individualisation?	❑	❑
Assessment		
Will learners have access to an answer sheet?	❑	❑
Will learners be able to cheat?	❑	❑
Does cheating matter in your context?	❑	❑
Which of the following will be included:		
self-assessment	❑	❑
peer-assessment	❑	❑
teacher-assessment	❑	❑
a combination of the above	❑	❑
none of the above	❑	❑

Now go back and look at each of your answers and ask yourself the questions 'Why?' or 'How?' as appropriate.

Figure 6.3. (contd)

quicker to write to that format. If the learners become familiar with the format they will be able to use the worksheets more efficiently. The drawback to a set format is that it may not accommodate all kinds of development and that users may become bored with the lack of variety.

A suitable format is to use a coversheet which contains information about the contents of the material and its objectives (see Table 6.7). Attached to the coversheet should be any other information and worksheets that the learners require to complete the activity.

6.10 Summary

In this chapter we have suggested that there are a variety of sources of self-access learning materials (published, in-house prepared, student contributions and authentic). Materials from each of these sources have advantages and disadvantages in terms of time, money, availability and suitability (cultural and pedagogical). We recommend an eclectic approach collecting anything available which may be of use to self-access learners. In fact, learners often think of innovative uses for materials.

6.11 Tasks

1. Look at any published text book. Choose one section of it. Prepare a coversheet and any necessary worksheets to adapt the section for self-access use.
2. Develop a classroom task the result of which is student-generated material for self-access use.
3. Review Section 6.6, then design a generic worksheet to accompany a section of a newspaper (e.g. the front page, sports section, TV page).

6.12 For discussion

1. Choose one of the following groups of language learners, or think of your own learners:
   - 11-year-old primary school class, monolingual, no funds available
   - 16–19-year-old summer school students, multi-lingual, limited resources, a library available
   - secretaries, adult learners, monolingual, limited time available for language improvement
   You have one month in which to produce or obtain self-access materials for them. What would you do?
2. If you were the manager of a self-access centre and your budget were sufficient to either: (a) hire one member of staff for six months, or (b) purchase published materials, what would you do? Why?
3. Before writing self-access materials how can you find out about your learners' needs?
4. Select one type of self-access system from the typology in Chapter 3. Discuss ways in which you would expect the stock of materials to change as the system matures?

7 Self-access activities

7.1 Introduction

In Chapter 6 we looked specifically at the production of materials for self-access language learning (SALL). In addition to good materials, self-access needs to offer activities which stimulate language learning. In this chapter, we focus on self-access activities which are easy to arrange and carry out. We look at activities for learners working on their own, in pairs or in small groups with some support. The activities we describe are grouped according to level: beginners, intermediate and advanced. We begin by outlining some activities which learners may engage in before they start self-access learning. Then, we briefly discuss some innovative activities that may be used in SALL (Section 7.3). In the final section we offer some suggestions for activities which a wider range of learners can participate in (Section 7.4).

In this chapter we only offer a small selection of activities. We would, however, direct the reader to the many other suggestions for self-access activities in Sheerin (1989) and Gardner and Miller (1996). In Section 7.2 (Getting started) we illustrate each activity using the format for materials production that we suggest in Chapter 6. In our activities we use English as the language for instruction and for the activity; in some learning situations, however, it may be necessary to prepare 'Getting started' activities in the mother tongue. Even at higher levels some parts of the activity sheets may be prepared in the mother tongue. These are issues for individual self-access management teams to decide. In Section 7.3 we briefly describe a number of activities. The purpose of this section is to stimulate teachers to develop innovative activities which meet the needs of their learners. Finally, a number of commonly used activities which are suitable for large groups of learners of different levels and ages are described in Section 7.4.

7.2 Getting started

The following activities illustrate some learner support tasks which prepare learners for work in SALL. The first activity helps learners identify their language abilities and difficulties: what they can do and what they have difficulty doing in the L2. The second activity is a learning contract which encourages the learners to take responsibility for their learning. The third activity is a study plan. This helps learners to organise and monitor their learning. The three activities together require learners to prioritise their language-learning activities.

The example activity worksheets below (Activity 1–3) may be made available as loose-leaf worksheets, or they can be bound into small workbooks which learners can personalise. In either case, learners will need to consult and revise these documents over a period of time. The documents could be distributed to learners by their classroom teacher, or as part of a SAC orientation meeting and may form part of the learner's profile (see Chapter 5). The documents should also be easily accessible for drop-in casual users of SACs.

7.2.1 Language ability

Activity 1a: Language ability (beginner)

Section:	Before you start
Title:	What can I do?
Level:	Beginner
Mode of working:	Individual
Aims:	To think about what you can do in English and what you would like to be able to do
Activity time:	10 minutes
What you need:	Copy of the blank 'What can I do?' list.

What can I do?

Name: _____ Date: _____

Use the following key to complete the table below.

I am very good at this   = ✓✓✓
I am quite good at this   = ✓✓
I am OK at this   = ✓
I need to practise this more = ✳
I am quite weak at this   = ✗

Reading . . . . ❏
Listening . . . . ❏
Writing . . . . ❏
Vocabulary . . . . ❏
Using English to play games . . . . ❏

Activity 1b: Language ability (intermediate)

Section:	Before you start
Title:	Language ability?
Level:	Intermediate
Mode of working:	Individual
Aims:	To think about what you can do in English and what you would like to be able to do
Activity time:	10 minutes
What you need:	Copy of the blank 'Language ability' list

Language ability
This worksheet contains the main areas of language ability. Consider your own abilities and use the key to make a profile of yourself.

KEY: I can do this well   = ✓✓
       I can do this quite well   = ✓
       I can't do this very well   = ✗
       I need to be able to do this better = ✳
       I don't need to be able to do this = ⊗

Listening
General conversation with native speaker   ❏
General conversation with non-native speaker   ❏
Lectures   ❏
Seminar   ❏
Telephone conversations   ❏
TV/radio   ❏
Songs   ❏
Others   ❏

Speaking
General conversation with native speaker   ❏
General conversation with non-native speaker   ❏
Interaction in seminars   ❏
Shopping   ❏
Telephone conversations   ❏
Business meetings   ❏
Others   ❏

Reading
Newspapers and magazines   ❏
Novels   ❏
Academic texts   ❏
Instruction manuals   ❏
Memorandums and office documents   ❏

Others	❐
Writing	
Academic papers	❐
Creative writing	❐
Formal letters	❐
Informal letters	❐
Minutes	❐
Reports and proposals	❐

7.2.2 Learner contracts

Activity 2a: Learner contracts (beginner)

Section:	Before you start
Title:	Learning contract
Level:	Beginner
Mode of working:	Individual
Aims:	To think about what you want to do in self-access
Activity time:	10 minutes
What you need:	Copy of the blank contract

My learning contract

Name: _____

From: _____ to _____ (date) I will practise the following. Tick the relevant boxes.

☐ Read a story book
☐ Listen to something in English
☐ Write a short story
☐ Learn some new words
☐ Play games using English
☐ Complete worksheets

Signature: _____ Date: _____

Activity 2b: Learner contracts (intermediate)

Section:	Before you start
Title:	Learning contract
Level:	Intermediate
Mode of working:	Individual
Aims:	To think about what you want to do in self-access
Activity time:	10 minutes
What you need:	Copy of the blank contract

Learner contract

Refer back to the worksheet you completed on your language ability. From the list make a selection of language skills and sub-skills you would like to work on in self-access. Remember to consider how much time you will be able to spend on self-access each week, and do not be overly ambitious. You can re-plan your learning contract at any time with the help of a consultant.

Time I have available to work on self-access each week = _____ hours.

I plan to do self-access work during the following times each week:

	morning – from/to	afternoon – from/to	evening – from/to
Monday			
Tuesday			
Wednesday			
Thursday			
Friday			
Saturday			
Sunday			

I plan to achieve the following in the coming month:

Goal	Number of hours I will spend doing this	Reason why I want to do this

Signed: _____ Date: _____

7.2.3 Study plan

Activity 3a: Study plan (beginner)

Section:	Before you start
Title:	Learning plan
Level:	Beginner
Mode of working:	Individual
Aims:	To think about what you will do in self-access today
Activity time:	10 minutes
What you need:	Copy of the blank learning plan

Planning your work

Choose what you are going to do in self-access today from the following:

Reading .... ❑
Listening .... ❑
Writing .... ❑
Vocabulary .... ❑
Using English to play games .... ❑

After you have finished your activity, tick how well you did it and record this in your self-access learner log.

I am very happy with my performance today   ❑
My performance today was OK   ❑
I think I can do better   ❑

Name: _____ Date: _____

Activity 3b: Study plan (intermediate)

Section:	Before you start
Title:	Learning plan
Level:	Intermediate
Mode of working:	Individual
Aims:	To think about what you want to do in self-access today
Activity time:	10 minutes
What you need:	Copy of the blank contract

Learning plan

Name: _____ Date: _____

Time I plan to spend on self-access: _____

Refer to your learner contract before you make your plan.

Today I plan to do the following:

Goal	Time on activity
1. _____	_____
2. _____	_____
3. _____	_____

After you have finished your work complete the second section of this plan.

Reflection: Consider the work you did today, write a few words to remind yourself of your performance or anything you need to consider in your future self-access work.

Goal 1:
Goal 2:
Goal 3:

7.3 Ideas for self-access activities

There are many different types of activities which can be done in self-access mode: reading a book, listening to a tape, doing a grammar exercise, for instance. Below we describe what we consider a selection of interesting activities. These will stimulate teachers to become imaginative in planning activities for their learners. We have arranged the activities according to whether they can be done individually, with a partner or in a group. For each of these there is an example at beginner, intermediate and advanced level.

7.3.1 Individual activities

Activity 4: Word tree (beginner – young learners)

Level:	Beginner (young learners)
Title:	A word tree
Aim:	To encourage learners to develop their vocabulary
Resources:	Notice board (or wall space), outline of a word tree (see Figure 7.1)

On a notice board somewhere in the classroom or SAC make an outline of a tree. At the end of each branch space should be left for a word or phrase. Place a topic above the tree and a notice encouraging students to add words at the end of each branch which match the topic. Students can increase their vocabulary on different topics by reading the tree (Figure 7.1). Each week clean off the words and change the topic of the tree.

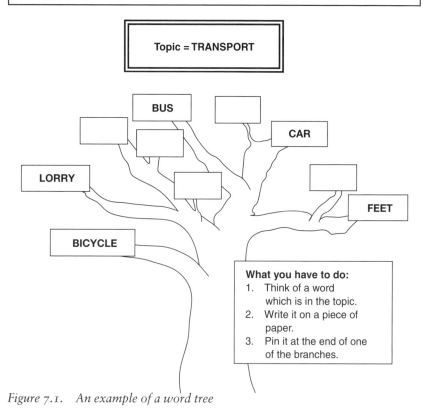

Figure 7.1.   An example of a word tree

Activity 5: Learner participation in self-access administration (intermediate)

Level:	Intermediate
Title:	SAC monitors
Aim:	To encourage learners to become involved in their SAC
Resources:	Badges with 'Monitor' and the learners' names. Advert seeking volunteers

Put up an advert on the SAC notice board seeking volunteer monitors. That is, learners who are prepared to help out in the SAC for certain periods of time each week (1–2 hours). Once a group of monitors has been identified, allocate duty hours when they should go to the SAC and give them manageable tasks to be performed during their duty hours. For example, tidy up book shelves, help to cut and paste worksheets, answer questions from other SAC users about materials, decorate walls, and keep the notice board up to date. The monitors should be given a badge to identify them to other users and staff and they should be encouraged to use only English when in the SAC. This monitoring can also take place in a classroom during designated self-access activity time.

Activity 6: Building up pathways through learning materials (advanced)

Level:	Advanced
Title:	Cross-reference hunt
Aim:	To build up pathways for self-access learning materials with the help of the learners themselves
Resources:	Information sheet explaining what pathways are. Decorated shoe box

Provide an information sheet for learners explaining that one way to make use of a SAC is by identifying pathways through difference sources of material. As dedicated SACs often have large amounts of materials this task of cross-referencing is difficult and time-consuming for staff. Encourage learners to keep a record of any pathways they think are useful for themselves and other language learners to know about. These pathways can be in terms of language structure, topic, level, etc. Ask learners to write down what the materials are, where they can be found and what the connection is. Place a decorated shoe box somewhere in the SAC and encourage learners to provide this feedback as a service to the staff and their fellow students.

7.3.2 Pair activities

Activity 7: Familiarising learners with a SAC

Level:	Beginner
Title:	I know, you know
Aim:	To find out as much as you can about the SAC
Resources:	Short SAC quiz

Provide a short quiz sheet about the SAC (see Chapter 9). Learners do the quiz on their own. Then, they find a partner to compare their answers with. The pair should try to talk in English, but they may have to use their mother tongue also. The aim of the activity is to find out who knows more about the SAC. If there are gaps in their joint knowledge, they can go together to find the answers. Learners can sit in the SAC and try to find out things about the SAC or materials in it which they did not already know about.

Activity 8: Developing oral descriptive skills (intermediate)

Level:	Intermediate
Title:	Record and listen
Aim:	To develop good oral descriptive skills
Resources:	Instruction sheet. A bank of interesting photographs, a tape recorder, paper and pencil

Learners work in pairs to practise their descriptive abilities. Learner A looks at a photograph for 1 minute. The tape recorder is then turned on and Learner A tries to describe the picture for 2–3 minutes. After this the tape is rewound, both learners listen to the description and transcribe what learner A said. They discuss how the description could be improved, and Learner A records a second description of the same photograph. The learners then listen to both descriptions to see if there is an improvement. The procedure can be repeated as many times as the learners wish. The learners then reverse roles and begin again with a different picture.

Adapted from: Dwyer 1996

Activity 9: Conversational exchanges

Level:	Intermediate
Title:	Conversational exchange
Aim:	To encourage learners to help each other learn a language
Resources:	Notice board

On a notice board provide a section marked 'Conversational exchanges'. Provide a brief description of the purpose of the activity, e.g. 'To meet up with someone who speaks a language you are learning and who wants to learn your mother tongue'. Students use the notice board to find a partner; for example, someone who speaks Arabic may want to exchange language lessons with someone who speaks French. Learners can provide some brief information about themselves and a contact number. The students can then meet up on a casual basis to help each other with their conversational skills (see Chapter 10 for more information about conversational exchanges).

7.3.3 Group activities

Activity 10: A puppet theatre

Level:	Beginner (young learners)
Title:	The puppet theatre
Aim:	To encourage reading and listening to a story in English
Resources:	A puppet theatre (see Figure 7.2). A selection of easy story books

Set up a puppet theatre in a corner of the classroom or the SAC (Figure 7.2). Next to the theatre provide a range of easy reading books suitable for the level of your learners. Inform the learners that if they wish they can put on a puppet performance. One or two learners can read out loud the story while another one or two can operate the puppets to correspond to the story. Any other learners can sit and watch.

Figure 7.2. A puppet theatre

Activity 11: Oral presentation skills

Level:	Intermediate
Title:	Prepare to present
Aim:	To practise oral presentation skills
Resources:	Camcorder. Monitor. A quiet area in the SAC

Each learner in the group prepares a presentation. This can be done in the SAC, in class or at home. In a quiet area of the SAC (preferably in a free room or a video room) the learners videorecord their presentations. Afterwards they view the presentations together and make comments on how well the topic was presented, and the effectiveness of the speaker's pronunciation, intonation and non-oral aspects of the presentation.

Activity 12: Learner materials development

Level:	Advanced
Title:	Material production
Aim:	To involve learners in developing self-access materials in English
Resources:	Access to all the materials development resources available

Arrange learners into small groups according to their interests in developing some self-access materials e.g. listening, speaking, psycholinguistics, etc. Provide the groups with some samples of existing self-access materials, and guidelines on the format to use (see Chapter 6, Materials). Learners then arrange times when they can get together to produce materials. They need to prepare the materials, pilot them, then meet with a teacher to discuss what they have produced.

7.3.4 Comments and caveats

In Activities 4, 7 and 10 for beginners the focus is very much on manageable tasks which the learners might enjoy doing. The emphasis, at this level, should be on fun, especially with young learners. At this stage learners can be offered opportunities to explore the new language and find out what they are able to do in it. In each of the activities 4, 7 and 10 possibilities to go further than the description of the activity are offered. For example, in the word tree learners might be encouraged to keep a learners' log (see Chapter 5), in which they can record the words from the tree. Competitions might be arranged once a month to see who knows the most words from the trees. In Activity 7, after completing the task, the learners may compile their own quiz and give it to their classmates to complete. And in Activity 10 learners may think up their own stories to perform in the target language. These could be simplified versions of folk stories the learners know in their mother tongue.

The intermediate activities described in Activities 5, 8 and 11 show how learners with more language skills can be encouraged to practise and analyse their language abilities. In Activity 5, by helping in the SAC, learners get to use the second language in an authentic setting: communicating with the staff. By asking the learners to use the target language with each other for administrative purposes – finding out where materials are kept, for example – learners are given what may be their only chance to use the language outside of the classroom. In Activities 8 and 11 the focus is squarely on analysing the learners' abilities with the target language. In each activity the learners are encouraged to help each other become language users. Once the learners become familiar with the idea of using each other as language resources another avenue for their language development opens up.

In the examples of activities for advanced learners there is another shift in focus. Now learners not only have to take responsibility for their own language learning, but also pass on what they have learnt to others. Activities 6, 9 and 12 all deal with encouraging the advanced learners to produce something for others. In Activity 6, conversational exchanges, learners must help someone learn their mother tongue. This helps learners think about what they want to say in the target language and how they use their mother tongue to talk about such things. A useful activity here is for the learners to have a fifteen-minute discussion in one language then stop and have exactly the same conversation in the other language. Activity 12 deals with material production. Once learners have a good grasp of the target language they can be a useful source for finding out what other learners might want to do in SALL and the types of problems the learners have in using the materials. Some of the topics chosen by students may be very different from what a staff member would prepare, and having a learner's perspective on instructional language can lead to greater efficiency in getting learners started on materials.

7.4 General activities in a self-access centre

The SAC's primary function should be as a facility for learners to use as they like in order to improve their language skills. However, the facility can be used in other ways for several reasons:

- A dynamic SAC constantly needs to change its focus depending on the learners' changing needs.
- Some learners like to use SACs for more relaxed language learning.
- Administrators like to see a facility being well used.
- SACs need innovative management in order to be attractive to the learners.

The activities we describe in Section 7.3 have specific focuses in terms of language skills and levels. The following ideas are for activities which encourage joint participation of a diverse range of learners. The advantage of such activities are:

- Learners of different levels help each other.
- Motivation of lower level learners is enhanced.
- Learners are introduced to new areas of learning.
- Groups provide a less threatening environment for experimenting with new activities.
- There are more opportunities to develop effective learning strategies.

- Learners see their peers using learning strategies which they may choose to try.
- Creating a more enjoyable atmosphere may encourage learners to take a greater part in their language learning.

7.4.1 Workshops

A series of short 1–2 hour workshops can be offered. They should cover language skills which learners require or request. The purpose of the workshops is to stimulate discussion on specific topics which learners want to know about and to guide learners in ways they can practise or develop their skills. Examples of topics for workshops are creative writing, pronunciation, speed reading, writing a resume, using dictionaries and public speaking.

7.4.2 English club

Many institutions establish an English club as a way of encouraging more natural use of the language in a non-classroom setting. This type of club could be situated in the SAC with a specific time-slot each week or month. Members of the English Club may also be encouraged to volunteer to help run the SAC (see Activity 5 above).

7.4.3 TV viewing

Many learners who go to a SAC which has televisions spend some (or a lot) of their time watching TV. Their justification for this is that they want to relax and try to enjoy listening to the language. SACs should cater to this group of learners by providing comfortable chairs and a section of the SAC where language learning for entertainment purposes can be enjoyed. In addition to this, the SAC may consider showing satellite news programmes at set times. Learners can then drop into the SAC to watch ten minutes of the news in English.

7.4.4 Native-speaker contacts

Where learners do not have access to speakers of the target language in the institute, it may be possible to invite guests in to talk with the learners. These native speakers may be encouraged to wander around the SAC and chat to learners to find out what they are doing, why they are learning the language, or just chat socially with the learners. If possible, these volunteers could be encouraged to visit the SAC on a regular basis and their visits could be announced on the notice board.

7.5 Summary

In this chapter we have tried to illustrate some of the activities for learners in SALL. We believe that some form of planning is essential to prepare learners to make good use of facilities. We also believe that teachers should be imaginative in the types of activity they offer their learners. Furthermore, dedicated SACs must be used to their full potential by providing general as well as specific language-learning activities for the learners.

7.6 Tasks

1. Prepare a language-ability sheet (see Activity 1) for a group of learners you are familiar with.
2. Prepare a learner contract for advanced learners (see Activity 2).
3. Choose an activity from Activities 4–9 in this chapter. Prepare the information sheet you give learners to explain the activity.
4. Make a list of workshops you think your learners would like to attend. Prepare the advertising poster to accompany the workshops.

7.7 For discussion

1. Do you think that planning for SALL activities should be undertaken solely by the learner? Why?
2. How easy or difficult would it be to set up the activities outlined in Activities 4–9 in this chapter in a situation you are familiar with?
3. Do you think that there are some learning activities which would be best done in class?
4. Discuss the value of the general activities in Section 7.4.

8 Physical settings and resourcing

8.1 Introduction

The physical settings, equipment and furniture used with self-access language learning (SALL) have an important role in instilling and maintaining learner motivation. Regardless of where SALL takes place some consideration to the management of the physical settings and resources needs to be made. Decisions may be at the level of rearranging classroom furniture, or at the level of designing purpose built self-access centres. This chapter deals with the learning environments which teachers have some control over, e.g. classrooms, libraries, or self-access centres. In each of these situations different people have a part to play in developing and maintaining the SALL environment. Table 8.1 shows who is involved in each setting. Apart from who is involved, each SALL environment needs basic equipment and/or furniture. Table 8.2 illustrates what may be considered essential for each system of self-access.

8.2 The classroom

As has already been mentioned (Chapter 1), much self-access language work can, and does, take place in the classroom. This is the simplest setting where students can be introduced to self-access work and, as can be seen from Table 8.1, there are fewer stakeholders involved in preparing for such work. The main parties involved here are the teacher and the students. Much of Dam's work (see for example Dam 1995)

Table 8.1. *People involved in preparing the physical setting for SALL*

Classroom	Library	Self-access centre
Teacher	Teachers	Teachers
Students	Students	Students
	Librarian	Librarian
	Principal	Principal
		Technician
		Clerical Staff

Table 8.2.   *Self-access systems and the essential equipment and furniture needed*

System	Essential equipment/furniture
Telephone sales	Telephone Computer (connection with Internet services)
Mobile shop	Trolley Boxes containing materials Tape-recorders
Market stall	Cupboard Desks Boxes containing materials Tape-recorders
Bring and buy	Desks
Postal sales	Room/office from which materials can be prepared and sent out to learners.
Boutique	Whatever is needed to support the specialist materials and activities of the SAC.
Video rental shop	Video machines TVs Headphones Chairs
Technology shop	Audio tape-recorders Video-players (tape and possibly videodisc) TVs Computers (equipped for multimedia) Headphones Desks and chairs
Catalogue shop	Hardcopy of catalogue or on-line catalogue Computer Storage space for materials Check-out desk
Fast-food restaurant	Equipment and furniture to facilitate easy access and intensive study, e.g. study carrels
Games arcade	A selection of language games. Cupboards and/or shelving to keep the games.
Discount store	Boxes, filing cupboard or shelves (depends on where the discount store is: in a classroom or in a dedicated centre)
Supermarket	Lots of display space to facilitate browsing.
Cash and carry	Photocopier Storage space for multiple copies of materials
Department store	A wide range of equipment and furniture to support the resources of a number of boutique systems within the SAC.

illustrates how students can be involved in classroom based self-access work. In terms of the typology set out in Chapter 3, the most appropriate SAC systems for a classroom context are:

- Mobile shop
- Market stall
- Bring and buy
- Cash and carry.

Self-access language learning in the classroom needs to be easy to organise and must involve the students as 'owners' of the facilities, rather than simply users. In organising SALL work in the class the teacher needs to be able to turn the classroom into a different type of setting quickly and easily so that the students can feel freer to organise their learning in other ways. For example, a speaking corner can be made by partitioning off a corner of the class with desks; an individual listening section can be made by backing desks onto a wall. Figure 8.1 shows how a traditional style classroom can be turned into a self-access environment.

Of course, chaos can result if the organisation of rearranging the classroom is not properly supervised and the teacher should try out small rearrangements of furniture first before embarking on any major changes to the students' learning environment. Classrooms in older schools may have fixed desks. Not much rearranging can be done here, so a more creative solution to changing the students' mind-set is needed. In this situation it may be possible to use coloured plastic tape to section off the classroom into different skill areas. For example, blue for speaking section, green for listening section. The teacher's desk and the front of the classroom could also be used for activities.

The reorganisation of the classroom can become a part of the negotiation for creating a SALL environment between the teacher and the students. If, after initial discussions about what they want to learn and how they want to learn it, the teacher then involves the students in decisions about how to rearrange the classroom, the students may feel that they have a stronger investment in what is happening in their language learning. This feeling of ownership can be encouraged by asking the students to bring items into the class which might contribute towards their language learning. Things like old magazines their parents might have; a holiday brochure in the target language; audio or video tapes of students interviewing their family members in the target language; and stories students write as part of their regular language class. Anything that is student generated and is of a reasonable standard should go into the materials for SALL in the classroom setting.

In considering establishing SALL in the classroom, the reader should look at the sections Mobile shop, Market stall, Bring and buy, and Cash and carry in Table 8.1 to see what types of furniture and equipment

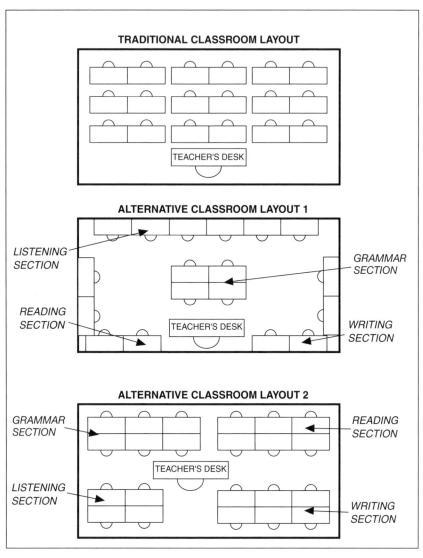

Figure 8.1.   Classroom arrangements for self-access work

might be required. The following are a few comments on the essential equipment and furniture for SALL in classroom settings:

Cupboard. One large cupboard in the classroom can be designated as the SALL cupboard. All the material related to this type of work can then be kept together so that the students know where to go when they want to do SALL work.

Boxes. Open-top boxes (any shape or size) can be used for storing materials together. These boxes can be removed from the cupboard at the appropriate time and laid out around the classroom so that all the students have easy access to them. Many low-cost self-access centres rely on this type of filing system, and it proves very effective.

Desks. Simply by reorganising the desks in the classroom the teacher can create a listening section, a reading section, a writing section, a speaking section and so on. Table-top signs for each location help maintain a focus for each skill.

Trolley. A trolley allows the SALL material to be moved between classrooms. In some institutions, it is the teachers and not the learners who change rooms. Therefore a 'mobile shop' system (with a trolley) allows teachers to take the SALL materials with them as they move from classroom to classroom.

8.3 Library

School libraries can often accommodate a small section designated specifically for SALL. However, more people become involved in preparing the physical setting (Table 8.2). First, the school principal and librarian need to be consulted so that they agree to give a certain amount of library space over to SALL. The teacher may need to prepare a good argument and perhaps even demonstrate how much the students enjoy and benefit from SALL activities. This can be done by inviting the principal and librarian into the classroom when the students are using SALL materials. Once agreement to allocate space in the library has been obtained, the next task is sectioning off a part of the library for SALL work. Simple partitions or existing book-shelves may suffice. Some of the types of SAC which work best in library situations are:

- Boutique
- Video rental shop
- Discount store
- Cash and carry.

The equipment needed for success here is similar to that used in a dedicated self-access centre and will be described in detail in the next section. In addition to establishing the physical setting in the library a few other points need to be noted. SALL work in the school library is only successful with the cooperation of the librarian. Rules need to be worked out in advance with the students and in consultation with the librarian. However, if the students perceive their language learning as an extension of regular library studies, they may be disinclined to participate or use the facilities. The SALL area of the library needs to be seen as a different type of learning environment – similar to changing the classroom setting described in the previous section. Before setting up a SALL section in the library many things need to be discussed with the teacher, librarian and students; for example:

- Can the SALL section have a 'noisy' area where students can practise their speaking skills or other activities which require them to make a noise?
- Can students borrow the SALL materials from the library or must they use materials in the library?
- When can students make use of the SALL materials – at any time, or during specific times when other library users may not be there?
- Can student-generated materials be held in the library?
- What type of coding system will be used with the SALL materials? Will it be the same as the library system or different?
- Will including SALL materials in the library increase the librarian's workload? Can a student users' committee be formed to assist the librarian in tidying up materials or supervising other users?
- Will a separate budget be used for purchasing SALL materials, or will this come out of the established library budget?
- Who will make decisions about what to buy for the SALL section in the library: the teachers, librarian, students or all three parties?

Once the major decisions about the type of system, responsibilities and funding have been taken, a SALL section in the library can be set up. Some important considerations for the success of SALL within a library are:

- Do not disrupt the regular library service.
- Maintain the librarian's cooperation and good-will.
- Opt for a small dedicated section of the library rather than integrating SALL materials within existing sections of the library.
- Involve the students at an early stage in developing materials for SALL.
- Link some classroom-based work to SALL materials, for example, set a homework task that will require students to go to the library and use the SALL materials.
- Designate a time when classes can go to the library to use SALL materials.

The amount of equipment specifically for SALL work in the library will depend on an institution's finances. In some situations it will be possible to buy new equipment specifically for SALL work. In other situations, it may be necessary to beg or borrow equipment and then adapt the equipment to suit the needs of the students using the library for self-access work.

8.4 Self-access centres

Dedicated self-access centres (SACs) are usually funded in two ways: start-up funding and recurrent funding. The start-up funding is intended to get the centres ready for use. All major items of equipment and furniture are purchased with this money. It is essential to plan a centre before using the start-up fund in order to make the best use of this one-off finding. During the planning stage it is wise to call on the expertise of others (see Table 8.1).

The recurrent funding is the yearly amount given to maintain the centre. The following are some of the recurrent expenses to consider:

- salaries
- heating/air-conditioning/lighting
- maintenance
- repair costs for machinery
- cost of updating hardware
- materials
- replacement of damaged/lost materials
- stationery
- cleaning services
- up-keep of fixtures/fittings
- staff development.

For dedicated SACs the following systems work well:

- Boutique
- Video rental shop
- Technology shop
- Supermarket
- Cash and carry
- Department store.

8.4.1 Space

Most SAC managers are allocated space by the institution, and there is usually little leeway for discussion or petitioning for specific amounts of space. However, it is useful to know how much space has been allocated, and how many learners can be accommodated. Table 8.3 shows a range of self-access centres, the areas they have for their centres and the number of learners each centre can accommodate.

Table 8.3.   *Area and number of learners that can be accommodated in a variety of SACs*

Self-access centre	Area (m²)	No. of learners
Self-Access Area, British Council, Bangkok	80	78
The Resource Centre, Chulalongkorn University, Bangkok	800	102
The Resource Centre, British Council, Kuala Lumpur	300	92
Hong Kong Bank Regional Training Centre	100	26
The Language Resource Centre, Hong Kong University	140	43
The Self-Access Centre, City University of Hong Kong	258	86
The Independent Learning Centre, Chinese University of Hong Kong	300	100
The Self-Access Centre, University of Science and Technology, Hong Kong	300	60
The Self-Access Centre, Sekolah Rendah Kebangsaan (L) Methodist Primary School, Kuala Lumpur	56	40
The Self-Access Centre, Sekolah Menengah Wangsa Maju 2 Secondary School, Kuala Lumpur	135	40
The Learning Centre, Eurocentres, Cambridge, UK	300	100

Sources: Miller 1992; Pemberton 1992; personal communication with self-access teachers

As Table 8.3 illustrates, a considerably large area is needed for a dedicated SAC. From the table, though, two centres stand out. The Resource Centre of Chulalongkorn University is very spacious, while the Self-Access Area of the British Council in Bangkok is cramped. Whereas the former is a self-access centre in its own right, the latter is part of the library. Riley (1993) suggests that an area of 1.7m² per student is a basis on which to calculate the space required for a self-access centre. However, Riley also notes that this recommendation of 1.7m² does not include non-user spaces, a reception area, a technician's cupboard, staff offices or space which might be occupied by equipment.

$$\frac{\left(\text{Fixed space}\right) - \left(\begin{array}{l}\text{Equipment space, Activity} \\ \text{areas, Materials storage,} \\ \text{Staff space, Dead space}^*\end{array}\right)}{\left(\text{Personal space}\right)} = \begin{array}{l}\text{Number of potential} \\ \text{learners at any one time}\end{array}$$

* Dead space = aisles, doorways, emergency exits

Figure 8.2. Formula for calculating the number of users for a fixed space

$$\left(\begin{array}{l}\text{Personal} \\ \text{Space}\end{array} \times \begin{array}{l}\text{Potential number} \\ \text{of learners at any} \\ \text{one time}\end{array}\right) + \left(\begin{array}{l}\text{Equipment space, Activity} \\ \text{areas, Materials storage,} \\ \text{Staff space, Dead space}^*\end{array}\right) = \begin{array}{l}\text{Space} \\ \text{needed}\end{array}$$

* Dead space = aisles, doorways, emergency exits

Figure 8.3.   Formula for calculating the space required for a fixed number of users

In establishing a SAC teachers may be allocated a fixed space or be invited to negotiate for a space. In the former situation teachers will need to calculate how many learners they can accommodate (see Figure 8.2). In the latter situation teachers will need to calculate the space required on the basis of the number of learners they wish to accommodate (see Figure 8.3). In either case it will be necessary to establish what is an acceptable personal space per learner (this may vary for different cultures). In addition to allocating space for learners, it is important to calculate the space required to accommodate equipment, staff, materials and special areas. A list of the types of areas and rooms a SAC might have are shown in Table 8.4.

8.4.2 Before planning a SAC

Before planning a SAC the manager needs to become as well-informed as possible. This can be achieved by reading the literature (for discussions on planning and setting-up SACs see Dickinson 1987; Sheerin 1989; Little 1989; Chin 1991; Miller 1992; McCall 1992; Riley 1993; Gardner and Miller 1994; McDevitt 1996), conducting a needs analysis (see Chapter 5), determining which system to adopt (see Chapter 3) and visiting as many SACs as possible. Visiting established SACs will provide an insight into the problems and pitfalls encountered by others and has become an essential part of the SAC manager's self-training because, as we have seen in Chapter 4, there are very few formal training opportunities for SAC managers. There are other

Table 8.4.   *Possible areas and rooms in a SAC*

Areas	Rooms
Reception	Manager's office
Leisure reading area	Store room
Audio booths	Consultation room
Teacher consultation desk	CALL laboratory
Video booths	Karaoke practice room
Computer booths	Multi-purpose room
Writing area	Seminar room
Reading area	Technician's workshop
Catalogues	
Worksheets	
Shelves	
Dictionaries	
Storage area for student records / learner profiles	
Talking area	
Quiet area	
Lobby	

sources of inspiration for the SAC planning team. The shopping environment provides many ideas that can be transferred to the SAC (Table 8.5).

8.4.3 Furniture

Furniture plays an important role in creating an image for a SAC. Many types of furniture can be used (see McCall 1992). Furniture catalogues are a good source for ideas. They provide illustrations of different types of furniture with their specifications which assist in planning. In many instances, SACs have to make use of existing institutional furniture. Advanced planning ensures the quality and appropriateness of used furniture and it is important that the SAC does not become a dumping ground for institutional cast-offs.

Seats. A combination of seats and seating arrangements should be considered. All the seats should be sturdy enough to stand up to frequent use. It is recommended to have bucket seats for desk work, swivel seats for computer work, and soft sofas for leisure reading and TV viewing.

Table 8.5.   *The shopping environment as a source of inspiration when planning a SAC*

Shops	SACs
Special offers placed near the door.	New materials should be displayed near entrance.
Items which customers buy regularly are placed on middle shelves.	Popular materials should be easily accessible.
During festivals (e.g. Christmas) there are special displays and special offers.	Materials related to festivals could be advertised and displayed together during festivals.
Workers are trained to be responsive to customers' needs in a polite and friendly manner.	SAC workers need to respond to learners' needs in a positive and encouraging way.
Management hierarchy ensures that customers can direct complaints and comments to higher authorities.	The management hierarchy should be clear to SAC users so they know where to direct comments and requests.
Customers can assess the quality of goods before buying.	Aims of materials should be clearly stated.
Customers can seek advice from shop assistants about suitability of products for their individual needs.	SACs should provide counselling services.
Products often carry guarantees. Dissatisfied customers can be recompensed.	SACs should provide avenues for students to give feedback on the quality of materials and services. SACs should have a policy of responding to student feedback.
Late night shopping is a response to shoppers' schedules.	SACs should be open at times which suit learners.
Benefits for regular customers, e.g. discounts for club members, invitations to special promotions.	SACs could form user groups and reward regular users with field trips, parties, etc.
Comfortable shopping environments, e.g. air-conditioning, mood music, decor.	SACs should be comfortable and inviting environments for study.
Fashionable products which customers want to buy.	SACs need to have modern materials and up-to-date technology.
Security systems prevent theft.	Security systems will keep materials in the SAC thus making them available to all users.

Desks. In deciding on the type of desks for a SAC, consideration should be given to space, budget and the self-access system being developed. It is desirable to have a mixture of work-desks for writing, partitioned desks for private study, computer desks, and low tables (coffee tables) for the leisure areas.

Shelves. Shelves can be used for storage and display. Those used for storing books should have moveable shelves to allow flexibility. Low-level shelves are useful as partitions and give the impression of space. Magazines are best housed on front-facing display shelves where the current issue can be seen and back issues can be stored inside. Carousel shelving can be considered for audio and video tapes.

Cupboards. Cupboards are essential for office use in the SAC. Also, many SACs use open cupboards as hanging shelves for special materials.

Filing cabinets. Filing cabinets are essential for office use and, if well labelled, they can also be used for student worksheets in the SAC. A large number of materials can then be housed in a small area.

Screens. Light-weight moveable screens, like shelving, can be used as partitions. They allow for flexibility and can be used to quickly section off areas for specific purposes, for example, as a speaking corner.

Other pieces of furniture which are useful to have in a SAC are: notice boards (both wall mounted and moveable), racks for newspapers, umbrellas and coats, and bag storage if you do not want learners to take their bags into the centre.

8.4.4 Equipment

Some technical equipment is usually included in a SAC. Many dedicated SACs have a wide range of technical equipment including computers, satellite TV, and laser-disc players. Before ordering any equipment for the SAC the manager should consult a technician, and, if possible, other SAC managers to find out what is available on the market and how well used different equipment is. It can be attractive to go for high-end technology to dazzle learners and impress visitors, for example interactive computer programs. However, these may also dazzle the staff and be of little or no use if they go wrong, especially if there is no one to support the technology. SACs should be equipped with technology that the staff can work with, or staff should be trained to a level where they feel comfortable with the technology. Some points to consider when planning technology for a SAC are:

- where technical support will come from
- how staff will be trained to use the technology
- how technology literate the staff are
- whether the learners are technology literate
- whether equipment can be tried and tested before purchase
- whether the technology is for impressing visitors or for pedagogical purposes
- whether there is sufficient funding for software
- whether there is sufficient space to house the technology
- the impact the technology will have on the SAC environment
- the power requirements
- whether there are local restrictions on accessing externally generated media (e.g. satellite broadcasts and Internet connections)
- durability of the equipment
- budget for repairing/replacing damaged or worn out equipment
- predicting usage rates of types of technology and adjusting the purchasing ratio accordingly.

The following are some of the most popular types of technology found in SACs:

Audio-recorders. There should be a selection of audio-recorders in the SAC. Learners can work on their own to develop pronunciation skills, in which case they will need to make use of an audio-recorder by themselves. They may also wish to do task-listening with other learners, in which case a spider network system is recommended. Some SACs also have personal stereos for loan so that students can listen to a tape in any part of the SAC.

Computers. There are three major uses of computers for language learning work. (The term CALL, for computer-assisted language learning, is often used in this context.) First, there is a large number of computer programs specifically designed for language learning. Second, word-processing is being used increasingly to improve writing skills. Third, accessing the Internet has become an important activity contributing to language development. Computers, therefore, are a popular feature of high-tech SACs. If computers are to be used in a SAC it is essential that pedagogical and technical support are available to facilitate use and keep up with the rapid pace of innovations.

Multimedia has become an important addition to CALL software. It offers TV-quality moving video, stereo quality sound, speech recording and recognition, and high quality images. Until recently there have been risks of incompatibility between multimedia software and hardware. Fortunately, standards have emerged for multimedia hardware and newer operating systems have also contributed to smoothing the way.

Computer hardware must be updated relatively frequently if students are to be offered access to the latest software. A common piece of advice for those buying computer hardware is to buy the newest and fastest technology available. Those who are able to follow this advice will be relatively safe from the compatibility problems that those struggling with older equipment will be facing until it is finally upgraded.

CD drives have become an important attribute of multimedia and, therefore, merit a special mention. CDs are often used to distribute multimedia software which is too large to be stored on floppy disks. The transfer rate, or speed, of CD drives has been increasing. Faster CD drives allows faster loading of data. This means programs respond faster to users and, in particular, faster loading improves the quality of multimedia video. Most CD drives can play CD-ROMS (e.g. multimedia) and most can also play audio CDs (music) and VCDs (movies). CD drives cannot play DVDs which conform to a more recent standard and which are destined to replace CDs because of their greater capacity and quality of images.

In the past multimedia has also used laserdiscs (LD) which are able to display higher quality and larger video images than CD-ROMs. However, LD equipment is expensive and cumbersome, and the discs themselves are less robust than CDs. In addition, authoring software does not always provide a reliable interface between LD technology and modern computers which makes the use of LDs frustrating for teachers who want to produce their own multimedia materials. For all these reasons there is little modern multimedia software which uses LDs; however, in some parts of the world they are popular as a medium for viewing video (see below).

Videotape players. Many modern language textbooks come with a video package for language practice, and viewing video movies is also considered a worthwhile SALL activity. Therefore, it is useful to have videotape players for learners to use in the SAC. There is a wide range of machines available on the market but simple play-back machines are the most suitable for SACs. They are easy to operate and if something does go wrong with them they are less expensive to repair. The size of the monitor on which the video is displayed will depend on the distance from which it will be viewed. Individual users working in a booth will require a small screen, whereas group viewers will require a large screen. Consideration will also need to be given to audio equipment to be provided with video playback systems. A series of decisions needs to be made (see Figure 8.4).

Laserdisc players. Most films are now available on laserdisc (LD) as well as videotape. The quality of the picture is consistently high and the LDs are more durable than video tapes. Sound quality from LDs is of a higher standard than that of videotapes. This benefits language learners because it facilitates listening.

Closed caption decoders. Most laserdiscs and many videotapes have the option to use a target-language sub-title system (closed caption) so that students can listen and read the dialogue at the same time. In order to make use of this facility an extra piece of equipment called a closed caption decoder needs to be added between the video player and the TV. Some modern TVs are now incorporating decoders.

Satellite TV. Satellite TV dramatically increases learners' exposure to the target language. An important feature of satellite TV is that it broadcasts up-to-the minute news which users can cross reference with the news stories they have seen at home in their own language. Many learners also welcome the opportunity to learn a language by watching TV in a relaxed manner. SACs can now have satellite TV running all day long. By connecting the TV to a spider headphone system several learners can watch the programme without disturbing others.

Camcorders. A dedicated SAC can either partition off a section or have a separate room where learners can make videos of themselves in the target language. This is a good way of preparing for a formal presentation or of doing diagnostic pronunciation work. Camcorders are simple to operate and are not expensive. Providing camcorders also offers the opportunity to run learner training sessions in the target language on making videos. This has proved popular in classrooms (see Armanet and Obese-jecty 1981).

Karaoke machines. Learning a language through music has always been a popular activity. Now, with the use of a karaoke machine, learners can entertain themselves and practise the language. If a karaoke machine is purchased, a separate and fairly well sound-proofed room is also needed.

Photocopy machine. In SACs which do not allow learners to borrow books or which laminate their worksheets, managers should consider installing a photocopy machine for learners to use. A simple pay device can be fitted by the photocopy hire company and the machine can be used by learners for a small fee.

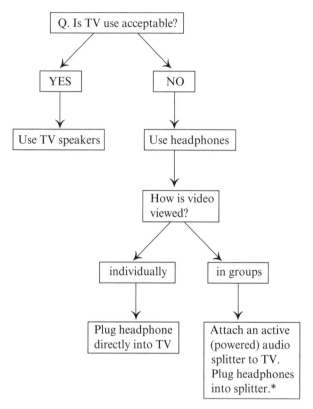

*Note: Using a passive audio splitter will result in loss of volume and degeneration of sound quality.

Figure 8.4.   The process of decision-making for providing audio feedback with video players

8.5 Summary

Self-access learning can take place anywhere. In controlled environments such as classrooms, libraries or dedicated SACs many different people become involved. Each of the stakeholders has a part to play in decisions about the type and amount of equipment and furniture needed. Classroom self-access is the easiest to plan and resource and it has fewer participant stakeholders. Library self-access relies to a large extent on how SALL can be integrated into the existing environment, and the cooperation of the librarian is essential. Dedicated SACs are the most difficult to plan and equip. The time and effort of a large number of people are required for the successful development of a self-access centre.

8.6 Tasks

1. Design a floor plan for the rearrangement of your classroom so as to make it an environment for SALL.
2. Make a list of rules to give to your students for when they work at SALL in the library.
3. Look at Table 8.4. Design your ideal SAC. What equipment and furniture would you include for your learners? Why?

8.7 For discussion

1. Consider the implications of integrating SALL in a library in your school. Look at the questions in Section 8.3. How would you answer them?
2. Discuss ways in which you and your students could raise funds for SALL equipment.
3. With reference to the shopping environment in Table 8.5, what other sources of inspiration could you use in developing self-access?

9 From teacher-directed to self-access learning

9.1 Introduction

In this chapter we examine how teachers can introduce their students to self-access learning. It is important for teachers to begin a process of sensitisation to self-access, including learner training, where many students feel most secure, i.e. in the classroom. By discussing and demonstrating self-access approaches to language learning, the teacher can encourage students to move towards independent learning. This independent learning may include using a self-access centre (SAC). In situations where there are dedicated SACs it can be difficult for teachers or students to see the links between what happens in the classroom and in the SAC. Gardner and Miller (1997), for example, found that teachers and students either saw no link or a very weak link between their classroom-based learning and the work they did in their SACs. This scenario may be represented as shown in Figure 9.1.

Crabbe (1993: 444) believes that autonomous learning 'needs to become a reference point for *all* classroom procedure'. In order for this to happen he maintains that there must be an interface between 'public domain' learning, that is, learning which is based on shared classroom activities and 'private domain' learning, that is, personal learning behaviour. In Figure 9.1 the focus is on public-domain learning with little or no reference to the students' private-domain learning. We share Crabbe's view that these two domains of learning should be integrated. It is for that reason that in this chapter we propose a closer relationship between self-access learning and classroom based learning as illustrated in Figure 9.2.

This chapter is divided into three sections: Getting started in self-access, Designing and implementing self-access learning, and Reflecting on self-access. We briefly review some of the literature in these areas and exemplify how teachers may go about implementing self-access learning in the classroom.

Figure 9.1. *Two common relationships between the SAC and the classroom*

Figure 9.2. *Two proposed relationships between self-access and classroom-based learning*

9.2 Getting started in self-access learning

9.2.1 Learning styles

Learning styles are the ways learners like or dislike learning a language. Many of these likes and dislikes are unconscious approaches to language learning which, when recognised, can help learners become aware of their language learning potential. Ellis and Sinclair (1987) suggest that learners should be helped to become aware of their learning styles and that 'the teacher plays an instrumental role in helping the learner learn how to learn' (Ellis and Sinclair: 167). In preparing learner training materials / activities which sensitise learners to their learning styles, Ellis and Sinclair point out several constraints and considerations:

1. Teachers have to consider how much *time* is available in class for such training and that the time spent on such activities is perceived by learners as well spent.
2. Learner training of learning styles may be affected by the students' *level of awareness* about their language learning. As most advanced learners are already aware about effective learning strategies, learners at post-elementary and low-intermediate level may benefit most from knowledge about themselves as language learners.
3. The language level of learner training materials / activities should be at an *appropriate level*, and the tasks accessible to the learners so that they appreciate the relevance and importance of the training.

4. There should be some *outcome* from the learner training so that the learners see the tasks as helpful to their language learning.

Adapted from: Ellis and Sinclair 1987: 168

Ellis and Sinclair illustrate these concepts well in their book *Learning to Learn English* (1989). Nunan (1996) gives an example of the type of activity which could take place in class to sensitise learners to their learning styles (see Classroom Activity 1). The activity is based on Willing's work (1989) which is the result of extensive research in this area (see, for example, Willing 1988).

9.2.2 Learning strategies

After discussing with learners their learning styles and how these might affect the way they learn a language, teachers can begin to explore specific learning strategies with them. A learning strategy is 'a specific mental procedure for gathering, processing, associating, categorizing, rehearsing and retrieving information or patterned skills' (Willing 1988: 7). Stern's (1975) seminal work laid some of the foundations for investigating learners' strategies. Stern lists 10 main strategy groups. The labelling of these groups is simplified by Grenfell (1994). Grenfell's labels and Stern's concepts of the strategies are shown in Table 9.1.

In implementing the Flexible Learning Project in London secondary schools, Grenfell (1994) talks about the difference between what he terms 'communicative strategies' and 'learner strategies'. According to Grenfell the former are more difficult to teach as:

• they are less under conscious control
• they are more determined by personality
• spontaneous speech is generally irregular.

Source: Grenfell 1994: 10

Learner strategies, on the other hand are easier to teach as they:

• can be systematically explained
• are less dependent on real-life situations
• are less personality dependent
• are essentially behavioural strategies that learners can make themselves do
• are not necessarily involved in spontaneous speech.

Source: Grenfell 1994: 10

It seems that some of Stern's strategies (e.g. empathetic, communicative and internalisation strategies) may be more difficult to teach than others (e.g. planning, semantic and monitoring strategies) and the teacher should be aware of this. In describing the Flexible Learning Project,

Classroom Activity 1.   Learning styles

HOW DO YOU LIKE TO LEARN?

For each of the following types score yourself 0, 1, 2, or 3 in the brackets to show how you like to learn best.

0 = no   1 = occasionally   2 = usually   3 = yes

Type 1
I like to learn by watching and listening to native speakers.   [   ]
I like to learn by talking to friends in English.   [   ]
At home, I like to learn by watching TV and/or videotapes in English.   [   ]
I like to learn by using English out of class.   [   ]
I like to learn English words by hearing them.   [   ]
I like to learn by having conversations.   [   ]
                                                            Total   [   ]

Type 2
I like the teacher to explain everything to us.   [   ]
I want to write everything in my notebook.   [   ]
I like to have my own textbook.   [   ]
In class, I like to learn by reading.   [   ]
I like to study grammar.   [   ]
I like to learn English words by seeing them.   [   ]
                                                            Total   [   ]

Type 3
In class, I like to learn by playing games.   [   ]
In class, I like to learn by looking at pictures, films and videotapes.   [   ]
I like to learn English by talking in pairs.   [   ]
At home, I like to learn by using audiotapes.   [   ]
In class, I like to listen to and use audiotapes.   [   ]
I like to go out with the class and practise English.   [   ]
                                                            Total   [   ]

Type 4
I like to study grammar.   [   ]
At home, I like to learn by studying English books.   [   ]
I like to study English by myself (alone).   [   ]
I like the teacher to let me find my mistakes.   [   ]
I like the teacher to give us problems to work on.   [   ]
At home, I like to learn by reading newspapers.   [   ]
                                                            Total   [   ]

Add up your score for each section and put the number in the Total box. The highest total shows what kind of learner you are.

Continued

Look at the descriptions below:

Type 1: If you have a high score in this section, you are probably a good communicator. You enjoy interacting with people and using the English you have learned in a natural way.

Type 2: If you have a high score in this section, you probably enjoy learning English in class. You like the teacher to lead you through learning the language.

Type 3: If you have a high score in this section, you probably enjoy learning English by examples. You like learning with other people and you see learning a language as fun.

Type 4: If you have a high score in this section, you probably like learning English by studying it in detail. You like to work by yourself and find out how to use the language on your own.

- You may find that you do not fit neatly into any one of the above categories. If so, write out the statements that are most true for you, then try to write a description of yourself as a language learner.

- Look at the items you have scored with 0. Can you explain why you do not like doing these activities?
- What do you do in place of these activities? Discuss your thoughts with a partner, other group members, or your teacher.

After: Nunan 1996: 4–5

Grenfell says that pupils were allowed the freedom to work on tasks that interested them. However, it soon became clear that they needed support to guide them through the tasks, and 'to operate within the framework of lessons' (Grenfell 1994: 8). In essence, the students had to learn how to learn first before they could work independently of the teacher. This requires a degree of personal competence which Sharkey (1995: 18) defines as 'students' well-informed awareness of their personal learning process coupled with skills enabling them to be in command of that learning process: learning not by accident but through awareness and conscious decision-making'.

One way in which to raise students' consciousness about specific learning strategies is to describe and discuss strategies they might use in a task. They can then choose the strategies they want to use to complete a task. It is also important to discuss the usefulness of the strategy employed after completion of the task. Classroom Activity 2 is an example of how students approaching a reading text might be made

Table 9.1.   *Ten learner strategies*

Grenfell's Label (Grenfell 1994)	Stern's Concept (after Stern 1975)
1. Planning strategy	Strategies which learners choose to adopt to complete tasks and/or communicate with others. These are the strategies language learners use in preference to others which they may know about but which they decide not to use.
2. Active strategy	Strategies which learners use to take responsibility for their learning when they actively seek out learning opportunities.
3. Empathetic strategy	Strategies which learners use to relax when using the target language. These are usually situations when learners are able to accept ambiguity and tolerate making mistakes in their attempt to learn the new language.
4. Formal strategy	Strategies which rely on learners using their first language as a reference system and which allow learners to understand how the new language system works.
5. Experimental strategy	Strategies which allow learners to discover things about the target language and form rules for themselves.
6. Semantic strategy	Strategies which enable the learner to understand meaning in the target language as fully as possible.
7. Practice strategy	Strategies which learners use to practise using the target language as much as possible.
8. Communication strategy	Strategies which engage learners in authentic use of the target language and which are not practice based situations.
9. Monitoring strategy	Strategies which allow learners to monitor their language learning themselves.
10. Internalisation strategy	Strategies which allow learners to begin thinking in the target language without constant reference to their first languages.

Classroom Activity 2.   Reading strategies

Instructions

Before reading the text look at the following reading strategies. Decide:

(a) Which strategies you have used before. Put a tick next to them.
(b) Which strategies you have not used before. Put a cross next to them.
(c) Underline two or three strategies you would like to use today. Discuss your decisions with a partner.

After the lesson you will be asked to reflect on your choice of reading strategies.

Strategies to use before reading

- Relaxing for a moment before reading the text.
- Thinking about the topic, e.g. what do you already know about this topic?
- Looking at the headings and sub-headings, e.g. what do they tell you about the text?
- Looking at any pictures, diagrams, charts, e.g. how do they help you?
- Looking at the length of the text, e.g. how long do you expect to spend reading it?

Strategies to use while reading

- Considering what you already know about the topic as you read, e.g. how does this help you make sense of the text?
- Trying to guess the meaning of new vocabulary, e.g. look at the sentence structure to help you understand the vocabulary.
- Ignoring new vocabulary, e.g. try to understand the text as a whole unit.
- Reading each paragraph carefully, e.g. try to get a main point from each paragraph.
- Looking at the pictures, diagrams, charts while reading the text.
- Highlighting the main points in the text as you read.
- Looking for vocabulary specifically related to the topic.

Strategies to use after reading

- Considering how the text made you feel. Happy, sad, annoyed, amused?
- Writing a one paragraph summary of the main points of the text.
- Considering any new information you gained by reading the text and how this relates to what you already know.
- Attempting to draw some diagrams or charts if there are none in the text.
- Checking some of the difficult vocabulary with another student.
- Discussing what you have read with someone.

Reflections

Now think about the reading strategies you have just used.
Why did you choose these strategies?
Were they helpful? Why / why not?
If you had to read a similar text, which strategies would you choose? Why?

---

aware of some reading strategies; it uses several of the strategy categories outlined by Oxford (1990).

Oxford gives extensive lists of the types of strategy learners may employ when learning a language. She categorises them into direct and indirect strategies. Direct strategies include:

- memory strategies – creating mental linkages, applying images and sounds, reviewing well, and employing action
- cognitive strategies – practising, receiving and sending messages, analysing and reasoning, and creating structure for input and output
- compensation strategies – guessing intelligently and overcoming limitations in speaking and writing.

Indirect strategies include:

- metacognitive strategies – centring learning, arranging and planning learning, and evaluating learning
- affective strategies – lowering anxiety, encouraging yourself, taking your emotional temperature
- social strategies – asking questions, cooperating with others, empathising with others.

There are dozens of learning strategies learners might use, some of which will already be part of students' learning repertoires. As part of everyday teaching, teachers can discuss with their students ways of approaching tasks. Oxford (1990) suggests strategy search games which encourage students to think about different types of learning strategies within a given context. Having discussed with students different learning strategies, Oxford suggests language tasks similar to those in Classroom Activity 3. In this activity learners are invited to consider both the cognitive strategies and metacognitive strategies which they might use. Cognitive strategies are techniques the learners employ to try and complete the task, e.g. guessing the words. Metacognitive strategies are the discussions students have with their peers about the task, e.g. 'Has anyone been in this situation before?', 'Was it an easy or difficult situation to deal with?' (for a comprehensive discussion about cognitive and metacognitive strategies see Flavell 1979; Victori Blaya 1996).

9.3 Designing and implementing self-access learning

9.3.1 Classroom activities

By helping students to think about what they are doing in the language classroom, teachers encourage them to become more involved in SALL. Therefore, teachers' responsibilities go beyond that of being informers,

Classroom Activity 3.   Learning strategies

Instructions

In groups, look at the situations below. First, consider if you have been in a similar situation and what you did. Then, think of how you would go about dealing with the present situation. Discuss your ideas.

Situation 1:   *What's in the news?*

You are a foreign student in Britain. You want to read the newspapers to (a) improve your English, and (b) find out what is in the news. However, every time you try to read the paper you get stuck with lots of unfamiliar words. What strategies do you need to use?

Situation 2:   *Tourist*

You have joined a tour of the city of Cambridge. There are many different nationalities on the bus and the tour leader is giving the tour in English. She has given you a map of the tour and is now talking about the interesting things in the city. However, you are having some difficulty understanding her. What strategies should you use?

Situation 3:   *Project writing*

You have joined an academic writing class and have to work with a group to present a project on pollution. You have to present the project orally and as a written assignment. In your group, each person has to contribute an equal share. What strategies do you need to use?

Situation 4:   *Party time*

You have been invited to a party by a group of your English friends. You know that this is a good opportunity to meet people and use your English, but you are afraid of making a fool of yourself. What strategies should you use?

---

organisers, monitors and evaluators; they also become stimulators of thinking about ways to learn and ways to apply learning.

Lamb (1996) describes a secondary school in England where pupils were required to learn a foreign language: German, French or Japanese. He states that the language-learning outcomes of the pupils had never been good, as measured by the GCSE examination results. The motivation of the pupils to take part in lessons was also poor. It was therefore decided to encourage pupils to take more responsibility for their learning, in particular the planning, monitoring and evaluation of their progress. The teachers continued to teach the core units of the courses, but the pupils were then asked to use self-access materials to extend and consolidate their learning in ways they found useful and interesting. As a result of this approach Lamb states the following benefits:

- Pupils enjoy setting their own pace.
- Pupils enjoy making informed choices about their needs according to their ability, being able to work on what they want, when they want.
- Pupils feel they work as well or even better when they have responsibility for their own learning.
- Pupils' organisational skills improve once they become accustomed to working in this manner.
- Pupils are able to draw on skills from other curriculum areas.
- Pupils develop skills of self-assessment: 'I can mark my own work and see for myself where I went wrong'.
- Pupils are motivated to seek help if unsure, thus increasing the efficiency of their work in relation to progress achieved.

(Lamb 1996: 112)

Thomson (1992) describes a language course which encouraged beginner-level students of Japanese to become more independent of their teacher. The overall goal of the course was to 'create, administer, and summarise the results of a questionnaire interview' (Thomson 1992: 528) in Japanese. Thomson states that even in the fourth week of a beginners course the 'concept of communication, learner-centred, process-oriented and self-directed learning is not unrealistic' (p531). It is interesting to look at the five activities these beginner students were asked to do during the course and the objectives for the activities (Table 9.2). The objectives are divided into those dealing with aspects of learning the language, and those dealing with learning how to learn.

The activities outlined in Table 9.2 illustrate how a teacher can plan to give low-level language learners some responsibility for their learning. This approach can be incorporated by all teachers into their lesson planning as a way of maintaining links between their lessons and self-access learning.

9.3.2 Project work

Project work can be used in the classroom for a variety of reasons, some of which are listed below:

- It encourages cooperation between peers.
- It encourages students to focus not only on language skills, but also on how they manage their learning.

Table 9.2.   *Activities designed to help learners take control of their learning*

Teacher role:	Monitor, facilitator, resource person, commentator and evaluator.
Learner role:	Support group member, discussion participant, questionnaire writer, interview partner, report writer, resource person, and one's own self.
Setting:	Own classroom, other classrooms / group work, pair work.
Key to kinds of objectives:	a = language-skill objectives b = learning-skill objectives

Kind of objective	Activity

Activity 1 – Create a Japanese adjective list

a/b	to create a list of adjectives of one's own choice
a	to understand the existence of and difference between Na-adjectives and I-adjectives in Japanese
a	to understand that English adjectives are not always expressed in adjectives in Japanese
a/b	to familiarise oneself with the use of a dictionary
b	to understand that one does not have to limit oneself to the vocabulary in the textbook
b	to use the instructor as a resource person
b	to collaborate with peers in creating a piece of work

Activity 2 – Creating a Japanese language study questionnaire

a	to understand the interview procedure
a/b	to ask descriptive questions of one's choice
a	to read and write down questions in Hirhana and Katakana syllabaries
b	to use peers as well as instructors as a resource
b	to collaborate with peers to create a piece of work

Activity 3 – Interviewing peers

a	to familiarise oneself with the interview and with interview procedures
a	to ask and answer descriptive questions
a	to write down answers
b	to use the instructors and peers as a checking mechanism to assess and clarify the questionnaire

Table 9.2. (*contd*)

	Activity 4 – Interviewing unfamiliar people
b	to get used to taking the initiative in meeting new people using the new language
a	to ask descriptive questions and write down answers
a/b	to answer unfamiliar questions asked by the students from other groups true to your feelings
a/b	to start and complete the activity entirely in the target language
b	to collaborate with the interview partner to have a successful interview
b	to view the instructor as a facilitator

	Activity 5 – Discuss and report the interview results
a	to report to the class one's findings from the interview
a/b	to collaborate with peers to create a written report
a	to write a report using as much Japanese as the class can produce
b	to share one's feelings from the interview experience
b	to use the instructor as a commentator and evaluator

After: Thomson 1992

- It integrates the language skills.
- It allows for students who are strong in one area but weak in others to contribute.
- It creates real-life links with students' experiences outside the classroom.
- It sometimes calls on students to use their specialist subject knowledge (EAP/ESP* students in particular), or think in the target language about their other subjects (in primary or secondary schools).
- Students may use skills other than language skills to communicate (drawings, constructing models).
- It takes the focus off the teacher and puts it on the task at hand.

Although a project may be started in class, students could use self-access facilities and libraries to continue their work; they can also look for materials, ideas and information outside the institution. In this way classroom-based learning can be linked with a self-access centre and with the uncontrolled learning environment.

Project work with low-language-level students

Veado et al. (1993) write of introducing young learners (8–11 year olds) to self-access learning. They suggest that the best way of introducing

* EAP: English for academic purposes; ESP: English for specific purposes.

learners to the materials in a SAC is by class teachers assigning exercises or projects which need to be completed in the SAC. They make several interesting points about self-access work with young learners:

- Competitions are a must.
- Self-correction works very well, but the children need to show the completed task to an adult for praise and recognition.
- Young learners are not concerned about the grading of materials. They want to do everything. If the task is too difficult they ask for help.
- Different children mature at different rates. They do not all develop the ability to learn at the same time.

(adapted from Veado et al. 1993: 64)

The above points are equally applicable to project work with young learners and the following might be added:

- The language level of the task must be considered; if it is too difficult for the children they will give up.
- Projects need to be in manageable units as children need to see what they have achieved fairly quickly.
- The project should be fun and involve activities other than language-related tasks (drawing, painting etc.).
- A combination of mother-tongue and target-language projects should be considered.
- Other important people in a child's life, e.g. parents, should be invited to view the projects.
- Projects should become a regular part of the language-learning experience so that children become accustomed to the concept of finding things out for themselves.

By combining some of the above points teachers can develop projects for young learners which are interesting and are meaningful contributions towards the child's language learning experience. Classroom Activity 4 is an example of teacher's notes for a low-language-level project

Project work with intermediate-language-level students

In discussing issues about adult learners, Rendon (1995: 43) states that a 'series of small activities leading to a major classroom project fosters group sharing and negotiation and establishes a significant framework for individual learning'. This concept may also be applied to intermediate language learners (many of whom will also be adults).

Project work at intermediate level can often be related to classroom work. Content is given priority in projects and teachers have to focus

Classroom Activity 4.   A low-language level project

A Vocabulary Project

Objectives:
Language – vocabulary development
Learning – pupils find ways to learn new vocabulary inside or outside of the classroom

Stage 1 – Arrange the pupils into groups of four or five. Write several topics on the board (this can be done in the mother tongue) and ask each group to choose one topic. Explain to the pupils that at the end of the week each group is going to design a poster with drawings or pictures of any words they have found which they can associate with the topic.

Stage 2 – Each day remind pupils of their topic and ask them how they are finding new words: from their family members, dictionaries, ask teachers in the school, go to the library and find a book on the topic. Also remind pupils to cut out any pictures from magazines they have at home which relate to the topic.

Stage 3 – At the end of the week give each group a large sheet of paper. On the top of the paper tell the pupils to write their topic. Then, together they must decorate the poster with drawings, pictures or words that relate to their topic.

Stage 4 – Once the posters have been completed, ask each group to show them to their classmates and try to say the words. They might want to explain in the mother tongue what some of the words in the target language mean.

Stage 5 – Display the posters on the wall for another week and when possible refer to them during lessons.

---

their teaching on the specific skills which the project demands (North 1990). Depending on the type of project, these skills will vary. For example, North (1990: 222–3) refers to four different types of project each of which would require different skills (Table 9.3).

Apart from the specific content of the projects, the teacher may also want to include some input sessions in class time, e.g. how to use visuals when giving a talk, signalling stages in a talk, and non-verbal behaviour (e.g. eye-contact), and how this affects the message.

McGowan (1989), in a study of intermediate language level students in a university, identified reasons for establishing project work. Those which may be widely applicable are summarised below:

- For students who may have reached a plateau in their language learning, a project might liven up their learning experience.
- Projects often encourage students to have direct contact with native speakers by asking for information or interviewing them.

Table 9.3. *Types of project requiring different types of skills*

Type of project	Examples of the types of skills needed
Community project	preparing questionnaires (written or spoken), interviews, letter-writing
Case studies	dealing with authentic texts, problem-solving discussions, role-play
Practical projects	designing/building a model, carrying out an experiment, designing a computer program
Library projects	extensive and intensive reading, referencing skills

Adapted from: North 1990

- Projects allow students to consolidate and integrate their language skills.
- Students may already be familiar with their peers and so be willing to cooperate.

Adapted from: McGowan 1989: 57

To these points can be added:

- Students may already be familiar with group-work activities in the class and see a project as an extension of this.
- Students at this level may wish to *display* their language ability rather than be tested on it.
- Different students have different strengths as language learners and projects help them complement their individual styles and may lead to peer teaching.

Classroom Activity 5 is an example of an intermediate-language-level project where the aim is to help learners work cooperatively in preparing a project of general interest to them. At intermediate level students are often eager to receive some feedback on their presentations. Some time should be set aside after all the presentations have been completed for teacher, peer and self-evaluation (see Stage 4 of Classroom Activity 5).

Project work with high-language-level students

Armanet and Obese-jecty (1981) describe a university situation in France in which the learners had a lack of interest in the traditional course on offer and this resulted in growing absenteeism. The problem seemed to lie in the fact that their students had already been through 10

Classroom Activity 5.   A general project

A General Project

Objectives:
Language – integrated language skills
Learning – learners work cooperatively to prepare an oral presentation

Stage 1 – Inform students that they are going to prepare a project for the end of the term. Have students form groups of three or four. In their groups they should brainstorm a topic which interests all the group members. The teacher might give some suggestions, e.g. survival rules for living in a foreign city, special foods from around the world, feasts and festivals in different countries, caring for our environment, teenagers' problems and how to solve them.

Stage 2 – After deciding on the topic for their project, the students should work in their groups to decide how they are going to collect the information. Tasks should be assigned to each member of the group – one member collects pamphlets, another conducts some interviews, a third visits the library/SAC to get more background information.

Stage 3 – During the rest of the term the students should make arrangements to meet out of class to work on their project. They should collect and share information for their project.

Stage 4 – Presentation format. This stage can be done in class. The group meets with the teacher to explain what they are going to present. Then, perhaps with the teacher, they decide on the best way to present the project: straight oral delivery, role-play, class quiz, etc. While the teacher discusses the presentation with each group in turn the other groups can continue working on their project outlines in class.

Stage 5 – At the end of the term each group presents their project to the rest of the class. Depending on the level of students, these presentations can be from 5 minutes to 30 minutes long. The presentations can form part of the oral assessment for the students. The students may also be encouraged to do a peer or self-assessment on their project.

---

years of 'traditional' teaching in school and their needs and wants as university students had changed. In order to meet these new, and unknown, needs and wants Armanet and Obese-jecty decided to offer a different learning experience to their students. Using the terminology developed by Thomson (1992) it can be seen that the learning skill objective was to get their students to find out more about the research activities in their university, while the language objectives were to be able to describe their university environment, describe architectural space, describe scientific experiments, and to acquire better pronunciation. The students had to make a presentation at the end of the term and produce a film of their project, with commentary in English. Armanet and Obese-jecty (1981: 27) found that 'after a preliminary familiarisation period of several weeks, the student groups attain an intensive rhythm of work in which the help of the teacher is needed less and less'. Other examples of project work with high-language level students can be found in Pang (1994) and Ho and Crookall (1995). An example of an outline for an academic project which can be run as part of a course on academic English is given in Classroom Activity 6.

Projects may not work well with all students. Before beginning project work it may be useful to discuss with the students how they would like to approach the project: whether they prefer to work in a group, in pairs or individually. If the students have already considered their individual learning styles they may know how they like to work. Alternatively, a learning style questionnaire as suggested by Willing (1989), and adapted by Nunan (1996) (see Classroom Activity 1), could be used. An adaptation of such a questionnaire might include who to work with, how to share the workload, how to collect information, what pace to work at, and how to use the information. Kinsella (1996) used such a questionnaire with her students at the start of their project work. By considering *how* they prefer to work before starting the project, students can make better decisions about their work.

9.3.3 Timetabled self-access

Self-access periods can be timetabled into the normal work routine of a class. In this way the connections between classroom-based learning and self-access learning become clearer to students and teachers. This practice is currently used in many secondary schools in Malaysia. Of those schools which have a SAC one of the five English lessons each week (one period) is spent in the SAC. The English teacher goes with the class to the SAC and the students have to complete several worksheets (related to their class work) before they are allowed to do other activities, such as computer games, puppet shows, reading for pleasure, etc. Because the teacher is present, and because the students are completing their self-access work in a formal class period, students have no problem linking their self-access work with what happens in class.

Gierse (1993) writes about how an independent language school (Cultura Inglesa de Sao Paulo) in Brazil linked their Open Learning Centre (OLC) with classroom based lessons. She states that linking the OLC to classroom work helped motivate the learners who were of different ages, levels and backgrounds. It also created closer involve-

Classroom Activity 6.   A high-level academic project

A General Project

Language Objectives:

1. to follow the conventions for writing a technical report such as simple description, functional description, process description, comparisons, summarising, writing about graphics.
2. to develop oral skills for meetings (agreeing, disagreeing, interrupting, concluding) and presentations (introduction of topic, presentation of data, summarising, concluding).

Learning Objectives:

1. to work cooperatively in a group.
2. to take responsibility for identifying a product to investigate.
3. to work outside of classtime to collect information about a product.

In the first lesson students are asked to form groups of three or four to work together for the rest of the semester on a project. The aim of the project is to investigate a manufactured product and report the findings as both a written report and as an oral presentation. The groups decide for themselves what product to investigate. Some examples of products are, an alarm clock, a table lamp, a shaver, a Walkman. Once a group has decided on their product, they must each find a different model of the same product to investigate. Therefore, if the group of four decides to investigate a table lamp they should have four different lamps to look at. The students are encouraged to find a product that is not too difficult to write about.

The following stages are an outline of the contents of a course in academic English. The students have to apply what they learn in class to their projects.

Stage 1 – Introduction to project: students form groups and decide on the product they will investigate.

Stage 2 – Simple description: groups talk about and write about a simple product, e.g. things about the house.

Stage 3 – Functional descriptions: students discuss and write about how things work.

Stage 4 – Process descriptions: students discuss and draw diagrams about how things are made.

Stage 5 – The language of meetings: students learn about the language for interrupting and asking for more information. They prepare an agenda for a meeting.

Continued

Stage 6 – Briefing report: students present to each other what they have found out about their products.

Stage 7 – Comparisons: students compare similar products and make comparisons.

Stage 8 – Summarising information: students write clear summaries of technical information.

Stage 9 – Using graphics in writing: students look at the differences between presenting graphics orally and writing about them.

Stage 10 – Putting together a project: students learn about layout, formatting and editing.

Stage 11 – The language of presentation: students learn about introductions, staging, involving the audience, summarising and making conclusions.

Stage 12 – Oral presentation: each group presents its project to the class.

---

ment between teachers and their learners. Gierse (1993: 57) found that learners' involvement with SALL 'increased gradually as a direct result of having a system of scheduled class sessions' in the SAC. In the context described by Gierse the beginning point for introducing learners to the SAC was a quiz which 'proved highly successful' (p58). Classroom Activities 7 and 8 show examples of simple quizzes which can be used for discussion and reflection in class about a self-access centre.

9.4 Reflecting on self-access

9.4.1 Encouraging learner reflection

Once learners have begun using self-access as part of their language learning experience, they must be encouraged to engage in a process of reflection on their learning. This can be done in a number of ways: as an integral part of each self-access activity (example Classroom Activity 1), as an independent activity to record the learners' experiences and attitudes to them (see Section 9.4.2), as part of assessment of learning in self-access (see Chapter 11), as part of the process of evaluating the usefulness of self-access (see Chapter 12).

Classroom Activity 7.   A low-language-level self-access quiz

---

Self-Access Quiz

Find out where the Self-Access Centre is. Go there and find the answers to the following questions. Bring your completed quiz to the next lesson.

1. Where is the Self-Access Centre? (use next to, near, above)

    _____

2. When is the Self-Access Centre open?

    _____

3. Who is in charge of the Self-Access Centre?

    _____

4. What can you borrow from the Self-Access Centre?

    _____

5. How many of these things are in the SAC?

tape-recorders	☐
TVs	☐
video-tapes	☐
desks	☐
chairs	☐
books (!)	☐

6. Find the following materials and write their details below:

Catalogue no.	Title	Listening/Speaking Reading/Writing
L–ELM–003		
W–ADV–014		
S–INT–010		
R–ELM–024		

9.4.2 Learner logs

A major belief among students is that it is their teacher's responsibility to assess and take responsibility for their language learning (see Chapter 3). We have suggested in Chapter 5 that establishing learner profiles encourages learners to change their beliefs. Myers (1990: 83) states that teachers 'need to provide learners with ongoing opportunities to reflect upon and articulate *what* it is they're learning, *why* they're learning it, and *how* the learning is helping them to acquire new information,

Classroom Activity 8.   A high-language-level self-access quiz

---

TEST YOUR KNOWLEDGE

Tick true (T) or false (F) after the statements below then go to the SAC and check your answers. Be prepared to talk about your answers at the next lesson.

		T	F
1.	I can choose to study materials that fit my interests and needs.	☐	☐
2.	I have to come to the centre for a fixed period of time.	☐	☐
3.	I should keep a record of the work I have to do in the centre.	☐	☐
4.	The work I have done will be corrected and will be assessed by a teacher.	☐	☐
5.	The counsellor on duty in the Self-Access Centre will instruct me what to study.	☐	☐
6.	Self-access learning means that I must always work on my own.	☐	☐
7.	I can use materials outside the centre for my self-access study.	☐	☐
8.	Not everyone is capable of self-access learning.	☐	☐
9.	Self-access learning means that I should be fully responsible for my own learning.	☐	☐
10.	I should take over all the work traditionally given to a language teacher in my self-access learning.	☐	☐

Adapted from: a worksheet at the Hong Kong University of Science and Technology's Self-Access Centre.

strategies, and skills'. Myers suggests that one way in which to do this is to encourage students to keep a learner log or diary. A log is a factual account of what happened. A diary is a personal account and may include feelings and emotions. Classroom Activity 9 shows what a log may look like.

After an initial discussion about keeping track of learning, and a brainstorming session about useful categories, learners might want to design their own learner logs. Each one could be different and reflect individual concerns. Learner logs can be personal documents which only the learner sees, or can be shared with the teacher for comments and responses. Learners may choose to use their logs (or extracts from them) as part of their portfolio assessment (see Chapter 11). Carroll (1994) lists reasons why keeping a journal (combining a log and a diary) is useful to language learners:

- Courses can be improved by being more responsive to student needs.
- Learners' awareness of their learning needs increases, and both teachers and learners improve their self-evaluation skills.
- Learners are empowered by participating in the research, enhancing learning outcomes.
- The practice of regular reflective writing is in its own way a powerful language learning activity.
- Journals provide valuable data for research into the language-learning process

(Carroll 1994: 19)

Reflection is a crucial element in SALL. By keeping a written account of their work and their reflection on it, learners gain deeper insights into their learning processes and preferred learning styles. A number of studies support this view; for example, Carroll (1994: 21) finds that students who keep journals 'progress towards a more autonomous way of learning'.

Classroom Activity 9. A learner log

Learner Log

Week: _____ Lesson: _____ Time: _____

What did we do in the lesson?

_____

_____

Why did we do it?

_____

_____

How did you learn?

_____

_____

9.5 Summary

In order to encourage students to move from teacher-directed to self-directed learning, teachers have to relinquish their views of themselves as the centres of power in language classrooms. In this chapter we have demonstrated a need for teachers to move the centre of focus in the classroom from themselves to their students by allowing students to experience responsibility for their learning. As a result of taking responsibility they gain a deeper sense of achievement in their learning. This will enhance students' motivation to continue self-access language learning thus moving towards greater autonomy in their learning.

9.6 Tasks

1. Look at Classroom Activity 1. Think about yourself as a language learner and complete the form. Does it fit with your own views of yourself as a language learner?
2. Prepare a listening strategies checklist for listening to the news. You could use a similar format to the reading strategies checklist in Classroom Activity 2.
3. Design a lesson plan which shows learning skills objectives as well as language skills objectives.
4. Design a project for your students which will make them focus on one of the following language skills:
   - describing places
   - comparing products
   - reporting events.

9.7 For discussion

1. Think about a group of language learners you are familiar with. Do they have any common preferred learning styles? How do you know this?
2. Consider the same group of students as in discussion question 1. Are there any typical learning strategies they use? Why does this group use these strategies?
3. Have you used project work in class? What type of project was it? What were some of the problems you encountered?
4. Look at the following entry from a learner's diary. Discuss ways in which the teacher may respond to the learner.

Week 8   Lesson: The future   Date: Wed 10 Sept   Time: 2pm

I quite like lesson but somtimes I get bit boring because the teacher speeks too fast and I not catch everything. Also I need to think about topic and not enough time to do everything. My ability is not good in learning English and I don't know enough words to understand everything. I like the class and I like do the pair work with my friend she help me a lot know topic.

10 Counselling

10.1 Introduction

Teachers' roles in self-access are different from their traditional teaching roles. Riley (1997: 121) maintains that 'in almost all forms of counselling, it is found necessary and worthwhile to spell out the roles'. These new roles need to be clearly defined in a way which teachers and learners can relate to. Teachers who work in self-access have a variety of different roles (see Chapter 1). In this chapter we outline the roles of counsellors. Counsellors' roles in self-access are often confused because of the variety of titles used to describe their work in the literature: e.g. consultant, facilitator, helper and advisor. 'Counsellor', we feel, sums up the focus of the new roles a teacher has to adopt when working in self-access. It may not always be easy to make the many and substantial changes required to become an effective counsellor. This chapter looks at some of the requirements of a good counsellor and how a teacher can be helped to become one. We discuss some of the management considerations in selecting and coordinating counsellors, outline some of the practical aspects of counselling, and examine some aids to help counsellors when interacting with students. We also suggest types of training that can help teachers become effective counsellors. Finally, we look at some alternative counselling techniques.

10.2 Classroom teachers and self-access counsellors

10.2.1 Classroom teachers

Teachers usually react to a group of learners in a unified, structured manner. They prepare language lessons based around a syllabus and the learning needs of a class. They use off-the-shelf language courses and are able to adjust their teaching level to suit their students. They are able to respond to specific requests for information within the confines of what is being taught. They have a specific register and teaching techniques which aid the class in following the lesson. Teachers often make use of 'display' type questions in their lessons (questions to which the teacher already knows the answer). They have set goals, as have their students, and usually it is easy to test the effectiveness of teaching and learning by means of language tests. Teaching takes place within the classroom environment and during a specified period of time.

10.2.2 Self-access counsellors

Self-access counsellors usually counsel one learner at a time. The manner in which counselling takes place can be determined by the counsellor or the learner. Counsellors need to be prepared to give advice, offer suggestions, or answer questions for information on a variety of levels from the same or different learners. Each learner may have different learning or personal goals and it is not always easy for counsellors to follow through to see if these goals have been achieved. Counsellors have to guide the learners through an array of materials and new technologies. Counsellors most often use 'referential' type questions in the counselling sessions (questions to which the counsellor does not already know the answer). Counselling may take place in a variety of settings: the classroom, the SAC, the cafeteria or a walk around campus, and may occur at different times and for different durations. Table 10.1 shows some of the main differences between the roles of traditional classroom teachers and self-access counsellors.

Teachers' roles in the classroom have been changing as they have adopted learner-centred methodologies. These encourage teachers to relinquish their traditional roles as controllers of students' learning. However, teachers have not always found it easy to fully implement their new roles. Nunan (1987), for example, found that even in what are considered situations of communicative language teaching (CLT), well qualified and enthusiastic teachers used a register of teaching which is reminiscent of 'traditional' teaching methods. Nunan showed, through analysing teacher/student discourse patterns of a CLT class, that (1) there were a large number of drill-like conversations between the teacher and students; (2) the teacher most often used the initiate/ response/follow-up (IRF) pattern; (3) 'display' type questions were used more than 'referential' type questions; (4) a main focus of the teaching was error correction and grammatical explanation; and (5) it was the teachers who decided who should speak and when. Nunan also maintains that 'there are comparatively few opportunities for genuine communicative language use in second-language classrooms' (Nunan 1987: 141). He shows the difficulties teachers have experienced in attempting to change their roles in the classroom when using a different methodology from their previous methods. The change of roles teachers have to undergo when counselling language learning is an even more dramatic one.

Table 10.1.   *Some differences between the roles of traditional classroom teachers and self-access counsellors*

Teachers	Counsellors
The term 'students' is used.	The term 'learners' is used.
Teachers are seen as *leaders* of students.	Counsellors are seen as *collaborators* with learners about their language learning.
There is a *pre-determined syllabus*.	There is a *negotiated* and *flexible pathway*.
Teachers teach their students from a *prescribed textbook*.	Counsellors orientate learners to an *array of materials*.
Teachers are *assessors* of students.	Counsellors discuss with learners different ways to *self-monitor* their progress.
Teachers are *instructors/organisers*.	Counsellors are *reflective listeners*.
Teachers use a variety of *teaching aids* (board, overhead projector, video).	Counsellors *demonstrate* to learners how they can use materials and equipment.
Teachers *monitor a whole class* and look for *common language problems*.	Counsellors discuss on a *one-to-one* basis *individual language problems*.
Teachers *give feedback* on learning tasks.	Counsellors *encourage learners to reflect* on the outcomes of the language learning tasks.

Kelly (1996: 94) states that 'Counselling is essentially a form of therapeutic dialogue that enables an individual to manage a problem'. If this is true, counsellors cannot be successful in achieving such a dialogue by relying on their teaching techniques and classroom management strategies. Kelly suggests a range of skills language counsellors need. She divides these into macro-skills (Table 10.2) and micro-skills (Table 10.3).

As can be seen from Kelly's micro-skills and macro-skills, the work of language counsellors is complex and goes far beyond the type of teacher–student dialogues commonly found even in CLT situations. Counselling requires teachers to make significant shifts in their attitudes and perceptions of the teacher–student relationship, and requires training and guidance.

Table 10.2.　*Macro-skills of language counselling*

Skills	Description	Purpose
Initiating	Introducing new directions and options	To promote learner focus and reduce uncertainty
Goal-setting	Helping the learner to formulate specific goals and objectives	To enable the learner to focus on a manageable goal
Guiding	Offering advice and information, direction and ideas; suggesting (sic)	To help the learner develop alternative strategies
Modelling	Demonstrating target behaviour	To provide examples of knowledge and skills that the learner desires
Supporting	Providing encouragement and reinforcement	To help the learner persist; create trust; acknowledge and encourage effort
Giving feedback	Expressing a constructive reaction to the learner's efforts	To assist the learner's self-awareness and capacity for self appraisal
Evaluating	Appraising the learner's process and achievement	To acknowledge the significance of the learner's effort and achievement
Linking	Connecting the learner's goals and tasks to wider issues	To help establish the relevance and value of the learner's project
Concluding	Bringing a sequence of work to a conclusion	To help the learner establish boundaries and define achievement

Adapted from: Kelly 1996: 95

10.3 Managing counsellors

Managers of self-access centres (SAC) need to decide the level of counselling they can practically provide for their learners. Releasing teachers from teaching and administration duties to become counsellors is often considered as an expensive luxury. However, counselling can reduce problems caused by unsuccessful and discontented students

Table 10.3. *Micro-skills of language counselling*

Skills	Description	Purpose
Attending	Giving the learner your undivided attention	To show respect and interest; to focus on the person
Restating	Repeating in your own words what the learner says	To check your understanding and confirm the learner's meaning
Paraphrasing	Simplifying the learner's statements by focusing on the essence of the message	To clarify the message and to sort out conflicting or confused meanings
Summarising	Bringing together the main elements of the message	To create focus and direction
Questioning	Using open questions to encourage self-exploration	To elicit and stimulate learner disclosure and self-definition
Interpreting	Offering explanations for learner experiences	To provide new perspectives; to help self-understanding
Reflecting feelings	Surfacing the emotional content of learner statements	To show that the whole person has been understood
Empathising	Identifying with the learner's experience and perception	To create a bond of shared understanding
Confronting	Surfacing discrepancies and contradictions in the learner's communication	To deepen self-awareness, particularly of self-defeating behaviour

Adapted from: Kelly 1996: 96

which are often costly in the long term. Bailly (1995) suggests that the efficacy of a SAC relies on expert, competent and available (i.e. easily accessible) counsellors. Gremmo (1995) also argues that counsellors are central to self-access learning. If an institution is prepared to spend a large amount of money on establishing a SAC, it should also provide the human support to allow it to function well.

Decisions about whether to use full-time or part-time counsellors (discussed in Chapter 4) have implications for the type of training required by teachers. Other management decisions focus on: suitability of staff for counselling duties, when and where to make counsellors available, the importance for SAC staff to keep in touch with each other, and the importance for them to keep their manager informed.

10.3.1 *Suitability of staff*

As we have indicated above (Section 10.2.2), teachers may have difficulties in changing their roles from teaching to counselling. In order to assess the suitability of potential counsellors the manager must try to find out what a teacher is like to work with (from colleagues), and the type of relationship the teacher usually has with students, e.g. strict and authoritarian, or open and friendly. The teacher should be invited to a short interview to discuss such things as philosophies toward teaching, perceptions of students and perceptions of the role of a counsellor. The manager should be wary of teachers who see work in self-access as an 'easy option', or as a way to reduce their teaching load.

10.3.2 *Timetabling counselling*

Counsellors have to be available at times when learners want to see them. We recommend two types of counselling: appointments and drop-ins. A schedule for when learners can talk with a counsellor should be displayed, and the learners should be made aware of how to make an appointment. With full-time staff, one or two hours per day for each staff member may be set aside for counselling. For part-time staff a rota may be useful to decide who has counselling duties and who works on other tasks. Staff who have been allocated counselling duties can, when they do not have appointments, initiate conversations with learners who are in the SAC. This is sometimes referred to as the 'pain at the party' type of counselling (Barnett 1995).

As a way to encourage learners to speak to a counsellor we suggest that before beginning to use the SAC for the first time learners have to have a counselling session. Only after this would the learner be allowed to use the centre. In this way the purpose of counselling can be explained and its benefits can be demonstrated. Also learners will become familiar with at least one counsellor who they might approach again. Where learners are obliged to participate in self-access learning they can be timetabled for counselling sessions by their teacher (who might also be their counsellor).

10.3.3 *Where to counsel*

In some SACs a counsellor's desk is placed in a prominent position in the room. Learners can then see if anyone is on counselling duty and if they are free to talk. In other SACs a private room is made available for counselling. This may make it easier to engage learners in conversation about their language learning because they know that no one is listening in to their conversation. SAC managers need to consider where to put the counsellors so that they can be seen, but also so that the learners receiving counselling have some privacy.

10.3.4 Meetings

There are two main reasons for having regular counsellors meetings. First, it encourages professional dialogue. Counsellors can exchange views and support each other. New counsellors will benefit from feedback from more experienced counsellors. Second, meetings are an opportunity to keep management informed about counselling activities.

10.4 Practical skills for working in a SAC

Being able to direct learners to appropriate areas in the SAC and/or demonstrate how equipment works may not be considered, by some, to be 'real' counselling work. However, the notion of 'trust' and 'approachability' are central to the work of a good counsellor. If learners trust the person they ask practical advice from, they may return at a later stage to discuss other aspects of their learning.

An important role of a SAC counsellor is to help learners find and use the materials and equipment in their SAC. O'Dell (1992) describes ways in which this role is made easier through the development of counselling materials. SACs may carry a huge volume of materials and equipment. It is the *volume* which can create a challenge for counsellors to have a comprehensive knowledge of their SAC's materials and facilities. It seems reasonable that a large number of initial questions from learners using a SAC, especially new users, will focus on understanding the system, how to find things and how to operate equipment. They might ask questions like 'How do I find out what's available on business English?', 'Where can I find a good pronunciation book?' and 'How do I start this computer program?'. Questions about learner training and language improvement will come later when the learners become comfortable using the SAC. If the counsellor can demonstrate an adequate knowledge to assist with the initial questions there is a strong possibility that learners will return for language counselling. On the other hand, if the counsellor lacks the practical skills to assist with the initial questions learners may be unlikely to return and the opportunity to go further with language counselling may be lost.

Reference guides are a useful tool which counsellors can use to help learners. They should contain lists of materials held in the SAC with useful notes and descriptions (see Figure 10.1). The guides should be regularly updated with counsellors' comments as to their usefulness for

Speaking/ Pronunciation Title	L	TB	K	T	Supplementary	Content	Comments
Headway Pronunciation Cat #: Pron/3 Location: Pronunciation shelf	E PI I UI	✓	✓	✗	Cassettes (12)	sound contrasts to intonation	• good communicative activities • use with Headway coursebook • not systematic • emphasis on segmentals • lists sections of interest to different nationalities
Sounds English Cat #: Pron/2 Location: Pronunciation shelf	I	✗	✓	✗	none	mainly minimal pairs	• intro. for independent learners • lang. chart for 15 lang groups • traditional layout • no self-correction • not systematic
Elements of Pronunciation Cat #: Pron/7 Location: Pronunciation shelf	I to A	✗	✗	✗	Cassettes (4)	clusters linking weak forms, word and sentence stress	• humorous classification • natural dialogues • well organised • very culture bound • vocab. level advanced • not holistic
Ship or Sheep Cat #: pron/1 Location: Pronunciation shelf	E to I	✗	✓	✗	Cassettes	minimal pairs	• list of likely errors by nationalities • diagnostic test • clear layout • no sensitisation • no self-correction • no free production • vocab. distracts

Key: TB = Teacher's Book, K = Answer Key, T = Tests, L = level, E = Elementary, PI = Pre-intermediate, I = Intermediate, UI = Upper intermediate, A = Advanced.

Figure 10.1.   Example of notes on materials for counsellors
Adapted from: Rogerson-Revell and Miller 1994: 100

specific groups of learners. Quick guides to high-tech resources could also be prepared. These would contain short descriptions, comments on usefulness and comments on technical issues. For example, guides to Internet resources for specific areas of language learning, guides to using spell-checkers in word processors and guides to using camcorders.

New counsellors should attend training sessions about the materials and technology in the SAC. When new technology or computer programs are introduced into the SAC, training sessions should be arranged for all counsellors. These sessions should be brief and may become part of the regular timetable of counsellors. In this way specialist knowledge about the materials can be passed on easily and counsellors will feel confident in handling materials with learners. Short, expert training sessions will quickly allow counsellors in the SAC to cope with relatively large amounts of materials and equipment which may be constantly changing.

Clerical staff and student helpers may also be used for giving practical information to learners. However, as noted above, when counsellors give practical information they may encourage learners to return later for more in-depth language counselling. Clerical staff and student helpers who give practical information also need training. Some of the advantages to using clerical staff are that:

- it frees the counsellor for more language-based counselling
- clerical staff may be more familiar with the day-to-day running of the SAC and know when new materials have arrived and where to locate them
- it expands the role of the clerical staff and may make them more committed to the success of the SAC.

Some of the advantages of using student helpers are that:

- other learners may feel more comfortable approaching their peers
- it encourages students to become more involved in the SAC
- student helpers may identify problem areas not noticed by counsellors or clerical staff
- student users, by seeing their peers play a role in the SAC, may feel a greater sense of commitment to the centre.

10.5 Counsellor training

Harding and Tealby (1981) state that for counselling to be efficient it needs to be relevant to learners and that learners' needs are constantly changing as they redefine their objectives and reassess their achievements. Therefore, counselling is not a static technique that can be learned and then applied. Staff development in counselling needs to be an ongoing process. In this section we offer advice and suggestions about workshops and training which may help teachers to become better counsellors. The workshops are based on worksheets which prompt discussion. They are planned to last between 15 and 30 minutes. Prior to the workshop a staff notice may be displayed advertising the workshop and suggesting areas the counsellors may wish to consider before attending.

Workshop 1.   Orientation

Pre-workshop notice

Topic: *Finding your way around the SAC*
Time: *9am, January 23rd*
Place: *Room Y7604*

To think about: *As you work in the SAC record the questions you are most often asked by learners and bring these to the training session.*

Worksheet

STAFF DEVELOPMENT WORKSHOP

Topic: Finding your way around the SAC

Look at the following student questions and statements and discuss how you would answer them:

- Can I listen to the tape for this book?
- Where is the reading section?
- What book can I use to practise my listening?
- I've finished all the green easy readers, what should I do now?
- There are not any video booths free.
- Can I take this tape home and return it tomorrow?
- I need someone to check this essay for me.
- Someone has cut adverts out of the newspaper.
- The tape for this book is not on the shelf.
- Actually, I want to practise my German.
- Where's the toilet?

Part 2 Practical perspectives

Workshop 2. Dealing with technical problems

Pre-workshop notice

> **Topic:** Technical problems
> **Time:** 9am, February 11th
> **Place:** Room Y7604
>
> **To think about:** While working in the SAC look out for technical problems you have to deal with. Keep a note of them and bring your notes to the training session for us all to discuss.

Worksheet

> # STAFF DEVELOPMENT WORKSHOP
>
> **Topic: Technical problems**
>
> *Look at the following situations and discuss how you would handle them:*
>
> - A student is reading a dialogue from a listening textbook without the tape. The SAC holds the audio tape for this book.
> - A student wants to write an essay using a word processor but does not know how to access the program.
> - While using a program on the computer it crashes. The learner asks for your help.
> - Several students would like to record their conversation. The SAC is busy but quiet, the students feel self-conscious about making a noise.
> - An audio tape has got stuck in a tape-recorder.
> - The programme guide for satellite TV states that it is time for the BBC news in English. Several learners are watching a soccer match and do not want to change the channel.
> - Two students are watching a movie together and chatting at the same time about the movie. Other students have complained about the noise.
> - The photocopier has been jammed (again!) by the same student who now complains that she is losing her money by using the machine.

Workshop 3. Developing counselling skills

Pre-workshop notice

> **Topic:** Developing counselling skills
> **Time:** 9am, February 25th
> **Place:** Room Y7604
>
> **To think about:** Reflect on your classroom teaching and SAC work closely over the next week. Think about any differences and similarities.

Worksheet

STAFF DEVELOPMENT WORKSHOP

Topic: Developing counselling skills

With a partner, discuss the following:

- List the differences between being a classroom teacher and a self-access counsellor.
- What makes a good teacher?
- What makes a good counsellor?
- List the differences between learning in the classroom and in self-access.
- What makes a good student in the class?
- What makes a good self-access learner?

Workshop 4.   What makes a good counsellor?

Pre-workshop notice

Topic: *What makes a good counsellor?*
Time: *9am, March 3rd*
Place: *Room Y7604*

To think about: *What type of personal characteristics do you have to have to work as a SAC counsellor?*

Worksheet

STAFF DEVELOPMENT WORKSHOP

Topic: What makes a good counsellor?

Look at the following personality traits. On a scale of 1 to 10 (10 being 'that's me', and 1 being 'that's definitely not me'), rate yourself:

- tactful
- empathetic
- patient
- relaxed
- creative
- flexible
- pragmatic
- sensitive

- encouraging
- non-judgmental
- approachable
- enthusiastic
- perceptive
- objective
- realistic
- open-minded

How did you arrive at your rating? Can you give any personal examples of situations you have been in, in the SAC, when you have used these personality traits?

Part 2   Practical perspectives

Note: This worksheet is based on a session Christine Heuring conducted at the Hong Kong Polytechnic University, Hong Kong

Workshop 5.   Conversations with learners: role plays

Pre-workshop notice

Topic: *Dialogue building*
Time: *9am, March 15th*
Place: *Room Y7604*

To think about: *Consider any conversations you have had with SAC learners in the past few weeks. Who initiated the conversation? What did you talk about? Was it easy or difficult to keep the conversation going?*

Worksheet

STAFF DEVELOPMENT WORKSHOP

Topic: Dialogue building

Two staff members will role-play a first counselling session.

Learner's role: You know that your speaking and listening skills are not very good. A classmate told you that there is a lot of material in the SAC which might help you but you don't know where to begin. You are very shy. A counsellor has approached you and asked if you want help. You are nervous about speaking to this stranger. Try to get the counsellor to tell you what you should do to improve your listening and speaking without actually saying very much.

Counsellor's role: You notice a new student in the SAC who has come in alone and is browsing around. Although the learner has not asked for help you sense that some is needed. Have a chat with the learner

Take five minutes to think about your roles and then act out the situations. Other counsellors watch and make suggestions later as to the effectiveness of the conversation.

Workshop 6.   Dealing with general problems

Pre-workshop notice

Topic: *Problems, problems, problems*
Time: *9am, March 28th*
Place: *Room Y7604*

To think about: *If you come across any difficult situation in the SAC, make a note to discuss this problem at the training session.*

Worksheet

STAFF DEVELOPMENT WORKSHOP

Topic: **Problems, problems, problems**

How would you deal with the following difficult situations?

- In your first counselling session you feel that the learner does not like you and is being unresponsive.
- A learner demands a study plan from you saying that it is your job to provide one.
- A learner has been recommended to attend the SAC to improve reading skills. The learner is not happy at having been recommended. Also, the learner does not know what reading skills to improve.
- Everything seems to be going fine with the counselling session, then the learner breaks down in tears.
- A learner has been caught trying to take a video out of the centre.
- A learner keeps on bringing you assignments to proof-read even though you have made it clear that this is not your job.
- You don't get on with one of the other counsellors in the SAC.

10.6 Effective counselling

There are certain aspects that Kelly (undated) outlines and we elaborate on here, which counsellors should be aware of while counselling. These are:

Confidence
   Both learners and counsellors need to reduce their anxiety levels and work together to make counselling effective. If learners are confident that they can get help from counsellors, and counsellors are confident that they can offer learners advice, then the sessions will have a better chance of success.

Comfort
   Feeling comfortable about a counselling session is closely connected with confidence. Comfort will arise from familiarity with counselling and with the new interaction patterns between counsellors and learners. Both parties need to feel comfortable about a counselling session for it to be effective.

Student/Teacher relationship
   As learners and counsellors begin to feel comfortable about their new roles, the quality of their relationship may also change. Counsellors may be seen less as 'teachers' and more as 'helpers'.

One problem that may occur is that counsellors may also be teachers of learners they are counselling. This may require more sensitivity to their changing roles.

Tolerance of errors
As part of their changing roles both learners and counsellors, need to be prepared for an increase in, and tolerance of, errors in learners' language. Counselling sessions should be an opportunity for both learners and counsellors to meet and exchange ideas free from the stress of the classroom environment. The objectives for self-access learning may be very different from teacher-directed learning, so the learning conventions and expectations may also need to change.

Self-awareness
By the end of each counselling session, learners should be more aware of their learning situation, and their learning aims. Similarly, counsellors should be aware of students' development.

10.7 Non-counselling duties

As we have outlined above, the work of counsellors is wide ranging and can vary depending on the learners they are dealing with. As much as counsellors wish to develop their roles as helpers to their learners there are certain extra duties they should avoid. These duties fall into three categories: (1) they can be an inefficient use of counsellors' time, (2) they may be jobs which language counsellors are not trained to do or (3) they may be tasks which contradict the aims of counselling. We give examples in the following sections.

10.7.1 Inefficient use of counsellors' time

Examples of roles which would be an inefficient use of counsellors' time are:

Solver of administrative problems
Learners frequently encounter administrative problems such as timetable clashes, financial difficulties and unsuitable accommodation. While counsellors need to be sympathetic to these problems and may suggest where the learners can go for advice, they should try to keep the focus of their sessions firmly on language counselling.

Clerical officer
A certain amount of clerical work may be required of a counsellor, especially if clerical staff are not available. However, this

type of work should be kept to a minimum otherwise it can prevent counsellors from performing their counselling duties.

Cleaner
While helping to tidy up is a reasonable activity, cleaning operations should be done by other staff. It is inefficient for a counsellor's time to be spent cleaning up and in some cultures it may result in a loss of respect for the counsellor.

10.7.2 Jobs for which counsellors may not be qualified

Examples of roles for which counsellors may not be qualified are:

Technician
Most counsellors have basic technical knowledge about the equipment because they need to help learners with simple problems. However, main problems with the equipment are better dealt with by qualified technicians. Counsellors can help in identifying the equipment problems for the technicians.

Social-worker
Sometimes there is a fine line between counselling a learner about their language learning and listening to them talking about their personal problems. Learners' life problems often have an effect on their studies. When learners demonstrate that they have psychological problems it is more appropriate to suggest that they seek professional advice.

10.7.3 Activities which contradict the aims of counselling

Examples of activities which contradict the aims of counselling are:

Proof-reading
Some learners will try to bring their essays or assignments to the counselling session and expect the counsellor to correct them. Counsellors should avoid this. Providing a proof-reading service will not help the learner to become a better writer. One solution is for counsellors to look at a piece of writing with a learner to identify some obvious areas of weakness. The purpose of the session should be to enable the learner to develop his or her own proof-reading skills.

This problem is often made more difficult to deal with because the learners who come looking for a proof-reading service have left things too late for any kind of learning process to be practicable. They are looking for a quick fix. In such situations counsellors may find it difficult to be hard hearted and refuse help. Once the immediate problem has been solved (either by being hard hearted or helping) it is important for counsellors to consider how a learner managed to get to this point without being helped. The answer will vary according to the context but if it lies in inadequate provision being made for learners then, at the very least, the counsellor needs to make this situation known. Counsellors may also work together to pre-empt the problem by providing appropriate resources for learners (e.g. self-study materials, writing workshops or checklists for common writing errors). In this case it is important to advertise to learners not only the existence of the resources but also the consequences of not using them.

One-to-one teaching

Counsellors should avoid being used as private teachers by learners. When this appears to be happening counsellors should refer learners to self-access materials and invite them to make a further appointment for counselling. It should be made clear that at the next appointment the learner will be expected to report on progress and discuss study plans. Counsellors may find it difficult to end a counselling session which has turned into a private lesson, especially when no other students are waiting to be counselled. In the long term the best solution to this problem is to make the counselling so popular that there is always a queue.

Providing study-plans

Study planning is an important part of the self-access experience. Learners should be made aware of the different ways they can plan their study. However, the learners themselves must select an appropriate planning method and implement it. The counsellors should act as advisers but avoid becoming the planners.

10.8 Alternative counselling

We have mostly discussed counselling from the point of view of face-to-face contact with one learner at a time. Now, we will talk about some alternative counselling situations. These include: using e-mail messages, learner logs and diaries, learner-groups, and conversational exchanges. Each of these provides counselling in different ways.

10.8.1 E-mail messages

The use of electronic mail is becoming more widespread with the introduction of computers into schools and universities. Little (1996) states that there are a number of projects making use of e-mail which bring language students into contact with their peers in the target language community. These contacts 'strengthen the bi-directional relation between language learning and language use' (Little 1996: 217) and also promote learner autonomy as part of a larger process of intercultural communication. Gardner (1992) reports on cultural exchanges between geographically disparate groups. These e-mail exchanges of a 'pen-pal' nature can contribute to the counselling process. Kroonenberg (1994) reports on using e-mail with her 14–15-year-old students. In this monolingual environment, one of the benefits she reports is that 'computer-literate classmates enthusiastically volunteered to be instructors' (Kroonenberg 1994: 24) to their classmates. This created a support system for students who were unsure what to do.

E-mail messages can become one of the counsellor's tools. Hoffman (1993), in a study in which he used e-mail to interact with his own students, found it a medium which complements other forms of teacher–student interaction. Through the use of e-mail he found his relationship with his students changed significantly.

We suggest a number of reasons why e-mail should be used as a counselling tool:

- Shy learners are more likely to use e-mail than face-to-face consultations.
- E-mail gives students a *real* reason for writing, i.e. to get help.
- The learners can communicate with a counsellor whenever they feel like it, or whenever they need help.
- Counselling can be done at any time.
- Counselling can be done from a distance.
- Frequently asked questions can be dealt with using standard prepared responses.
- The counsellor can keep a record of learners' questions and problems and check back on them if needed.

10.8.2 Learner journals

In Chapter 5 we suggested that learners should keep a record of their work. A learner journal may fulfil this function. It can be used in two ways. First, it may be used as an aid to the counselling sessions. The counsellor and the learner may look over the journal and discuss issues about the learner's learning. Second, it can be used to obtain written comments from the counsellor when the student does not want face-to-face contact. There are a variety of ways in which learners can keep a journal (see Chapter 7). Learners are often recommended to keep a record of their work in the SAC. One part of a journal is a learner's log which is a record of events. Simmons (1996) implies that learners' logs should attempt to go beyond simple record keeping of what has been learned. Conversely, Martyn (1994: 76) has shown that when logs are too 'complex or cognitively demanding' they may demotivate students and teachers. Journals are a useful learning tool but their use should not be enforced in a way that becomes a burden to the learners or to teachers.

10.8.3 Learner-groups

Learner-groups can take on different functions. Farmer (1994) describes a situation in which his learners had difficulty in using a SAC. This was because:

1. the learners had no foundation on which to develop their autonomous learning as they had been used to a traditional approach to language learning at secondary school
2. the learners lacked confidence in using English and hence lacked motivation to improve their language skills.

The learners, therefore, did not want to use the SAC as individual learners. In response to this situation the SAC adopted a different approach. Learners were grouped together and allocated a tutor who monitored their work. In such a situation the learners were able to obtain some direction, from the tutor, when they wanted it. They were, however, also able to develop their language skills in a situation they felt more secure with, i.e. their peer group. Esch (1996) describes a different situation in which it is impracticable for students to learn together. In her institution the SAC offers over 60 different languages. During learner training courses learner groups talk about learning. The aim here 'is to help them learn to learn, not to learn a particular language' (Esch 1996: 42). Both learner-groups of Farmer and Esch above offer counselling to the student but in different ways. This is illustrated in Table 10.4.

10.8.4 Conversational exchanges

Dickinson (1987) illustrates a number of situations in which learners are paired up to exchange languages. Voller and Pickard (1996) describe these exchanges as having two different approaches: (1) *mutual* learning, a situation where both learners are learning the other's language and hence both benefit from the exchange or an (2) *expert-informant* situation where one person acts as a surrogate teacher. Although Voller and Pickard describe what appears to be a one-way process, the 'expert' also benefits from the interaction. The benefit may

Table 10.4. *How learner groups can function in different ways*

In the situation described by Farmer (1994)	In the situation described by Esch (1996)
Learners may have common language problems which they can discuss.	Learners find problems common to many different languages and may not feel so overwhelmed with their own personal language-learning problems.
Learners can use their mother tongue to feel more at ease with their attempts at autonomy.	Learners have to use their mother tongue to discuss the issues which may give them more confidence in talking about their styles and strategies.
Friendships develop between the learners and this offers even more support to their language learning.	Learners may find someone in the group who has already mastered the target language and receive encouragement from that learner.
As a tutor is assigned to each group, the group always knows who to go to for assistance. This offers some psychological support if the group 'loses its way'.	Learners may feel less inclined to ask for tutor support as they are all learning different languages. They may decide to support themselves.
Although the learning takes place in the SAC, it is somewhat structured – all the learners in the group have to meet at the same time each week.	Learners can meet anywhere for their group activities to work.
This type of independent learning can act as a first step towards greater learner autonomy.	
	Many different styles and strategies emerge by discussing the issues in a group.

not be in linguistic terms but can take the form of learning about culture, having a friend or having a good feeling about helping. The most important point about a conversational exchange is that it is an informal, non-academic approach to language learning.

'Tandem learning' as described by Lewis et al. (1996) has similar characteristics to conversational exchanges. It has the following three premises:

- each person benefits from taking part in the language exchange
- a basic principle of autonomy is upheld in that the learners take responsibility for the learning process
- the participants of the interaction are members of different cultural groups and so cultural exchanges are also part of the learning experience.

Lewis et al. describe tandem learning at the University of Sheffield where the following pairings were available: French/English, German/English, Italian/English and Spanish/English. In this situation learners were able to take part in face-to-face interactions where the learners met for at least one hour per week to talk with each other, or in e-mail exchanges with two or more learners communicating. During the face-to-face interactions the learners 'clearly took charge of large areas of their learning' (Lewis et al. 1996: 110) and feedback on the activity indicated 'a high level of satisfaction' (ibid.). Learners who took part in the e-mail tandem learning increased their confidence in their writing skills, increased their cultural awareness, had access to authentic language and received some corrections on their writing from their partners.

The pairing-up of learners to exchange languages needs some administration and control. This is to ensure that the pairings are suitable and that there is something for the learners to begin talking about. This administration can best be done by a counsellor in a SAC. The SAC can also be used as the meeting point for the exchanges. Participants need to supply personal information such as in Figure 10.2. Material can be made available to help start conversations, for example a list of topics for to talk about (Figure 10.3), or a specially prepared worksheet (Figure 10.4).

There are various reasons why learners should be encouraged to use conversational exchanges.

- They help learners develop their oral/aural skills.
- They provide learners with help in other language related areas (e.g. reading, writing).
- They help build up learners' confidence in using the language.
- They assist learners to learn more about cultural contexts.
- They aid in developing friendships.

10.8.5 Monitoring alternative counselling

In looking at what we have described as alternative counselling we have illustrated ways in which to support learners in their language learning. Although these alternatives broaden the support for learners, they do not replace the services of a trained counsellor. The counsellors' roles

The Learner
• name
• age
• sex
• where the learner lives
• where the learner would like to meet
• best time to meet
• mother tongue
• other languages the learner can speak
• target language
• interests
The Desired Partner
• age
• sex
• interests
• native or non-native speaker

Figure 10.2. *Information that conversational-exchange participants need to specify*

should include monitoring the use and success of alternative counselling activities.

10.9 Summary

In this chapter we have looked at some of the differences in roles between language teachers and self-access counsellors, and have shown that for teachers to become effective counsellors they must adjust their perceptions of their learners and their own approach to helping them with their language learning. This shift in attitudes and manner of interactions between teachers and learners may not be easy for everyone to achieve. Therefore, counsellors should be selected from those

---

Worksheet: Conversation topics for a first conversation

When you first meet your conversational-exchange partner you will need to exchange some information about each other. Below is a list of topics you might want to discuss:

- Yourself
- Your family
- Your childhood
- Hobbies
- Your country
- Language learning
- The environment
- Prejudices
- Superstitions
- Politics
- Countries you have visited
- Favourite holiday places
- Famous people in your country
- Food in your country
- Festivals in your country
- Sports
- The weather
- Films
- Books
- Jobs you have/have had
- Your future

Figure 10.3.   A worksheet to help start conversational-exchange partners talking

teachers who are willing to adapt themselves to the special demands of counselling.

Training sessions need to deal with all aspects of a counsellor's work. This can range from practical issues about how equipment works, to more specialised counselling skills like reflective listening. Counsellors must also be aware of the need to encourage learners to take responsibility for their own learning. We have suggested here that teachers need training to become effective counsellors. This can be done through workshops. At the end of the chapter we discuss some alternative counselling ideas and suggest that those who work in a SAC should try to promote innovative ways which encourage student interaction as a way of developing their independent language-learning skills.

Worksheet: Conversation exchange 1: Festivals in your country

This worksheet suggests some aspects of a topic that you and your partner might want to talk about. You can adapt it as much as you like.

- Describe a main festival in your country.
- When is it?
- Is it a new festival or an old one?
- Who celebrates it (everyone or only some people)?
- Why does it happen?
- What preparations are necessary?
- How do people dress on that day?
- What do people do?
- Do you eat anything special?
- Do you go anywhere special?
- How long does the festival last?
- Do you enjoy the festival?
- Can you celebrate it anywhere in the world?

Figure 10.4. An example of a conversational-exchange worksheet

10.10 Tasks

1. Make a list of questions learners have asked you while working in a SAC. Or, make a list of the types of questions you would expect to be asked.
2. Prepare a Staff Development Workshop for one of the following: coping with learners who are resistant to self-access; helping learners plan for self-access; learning styles; characteristics of being a good reflective listener.
3. Write a conversational exchange worksheet for one of the topics in Figure 10.3.

10.11 For discussion

1. How do teachers' and counsellors' different roles affect their relationships with learners (see Table 10.1)?
2. Look at the macro- and micro-counselling skills in Tables 10.2 and 10.3. Which of these skills can be used in classroom environments? How easy or difficult would it be to use these skills as part of classroom teaching?

3. Discuss the types of non-counselling duties which you might be asked to perform in a SAC. Which of these duties would you be prepared to do?
4. How can a counsellor support alternative counselling activities (see Section 10.8)?

11 Assessment in self-access learning

11.1 Introduction

In this chapter we look at ways of assessing self-access learning and the purposes to which these assessments can be put. We suggest that assessments need to become an integral part of self-access work even though many of them may be very small scale and not credit-earning in an institutional sense. Holec (1980: 21) refers to self-assessment as 'an integral part of the learning'. This is echoed by Tudor (1996: 162) who sees it as 'central to the active and reflective involvement of learners' and by Thomson (1996: 88) who shows that self-assessment procedures 'involve learners to a much higher degree in learning than any pre-scribed learning'. Holec also showed that 'all learners practise self-evaluation of one kind or another' (Holec 1985: 151). Thomson, while agreeing with this suggests that although learners self-assess internally 'they are seldom aware of it' (Thomson 1996: 85).

We begin the chapter by looking at the purposes of self-access assessment. Then we look at kinds of assessments, considering differences in assessments prepared by teachers and learners, as well as differences between specific and generic assessments. Next we discuss the content of assessments. We also look at the ways in which assessments can be administered; considering assessments by external agents (teachers, SAC staff or qualification-awarding bodies), assessments conducted by learners (self-assessments and peer-assessments) and collaborative assessments conducted through negotiations between teachers and learners. Finally, we look at how the results from assessments can be used. We consider the important role assessments play in helping learners reflect on their learning and make decisions about their future learning. We also discuss the uses teachers and self-access managers can make of assessment results.

11.2 Purposes of assessment

The assessment of self-access learning may depend on the personal choices of the individual learner or the requirements of an institution.

Where learners have total autonomy, choices over whether to assess, what to assess, when to assess and how to assess will be their own. In contexts where learners are involved in self-access learning as part of an organised programme there may be assessment requirements. The requirements may have enough flexibility to allow learners to make choices about modes of assessment (e.g. peer-assessment or self-assessment) or they may be very rigid.

Results of assessments of self-access learners may be useful to SAC managers to show what is being achieved by learners in their centres, although it must be acknowledged that the contributions of SALL can rarely be completely isolated from other contributions to language learning like classroom learning. Nevertheless, evidence of learning gain can be used to justify the provision of self-access resources. This may fulfil an administrative need; however, it should never be considered as a primary purpose of self-access assessment. The primary purpose should be to provide information about the achievements of learners both in terms of absolute ability at any given time and in terms of improvement over a period of study.

Assessments serve a number of purposes for self-access learners (Table 11.1). Assessments are essential to learners as a way of evaluating the effectiveness of self-access learning as a personal tool. Self-access is a new approach to studying for many learners and lacks the traditional system of feedback on achievement inherent in teacher-led education. Assessments, even on a small scale, can provide learners with feedback on how they are doing and may lead them to reassess their approach or to motivate them to further study. Assessments can also be seen as useful language practice and practice for taking examinations.

11.3 Kinds of assessment

There are five main kinds of assessment suitable for use in a self-access context. These are: teacher-prepared assessments, generic assessments, collaborative assessments, learner-prepared assessments and portfolio assessments. We discuss each of these in greater detail below and they are summarised in Table 11.2.

Table 11.1. *Purposes which assessments serve for self-access learners*

Purpose	Comment
Confidence building	Assessments at the right level at which learners can succeed will boost their self-confidence.
Evidence of learning gain	Assessments based on a period of study will demonstrate what has been achieved during that period. These can be used to satisfy institutional requirements as well as providing personal satisfaction.
Assurance	Assessments provide learners with evidence that they are engaged in 'serious' study and remind them that they have 'respectable' goals towards which they are working.
Motivation	Successful assessments motivate learners to do more. Unsuccessful assessments motivate learners to change their study plans and/or seek help.
Opportunity for reflection	After completing an assessment learners should be encouraged to reflect on their progress, their goals and their study plan. This may result in learners reconfirming their approach and moving on to the next stage. Alternatively, it may result in a reassessment of their approach with consequent changes. In either case the reflection will have had a positive effect as it will have led learners to take greater control of their learning and to be responsible for it.
Practice	Assessments can be used individually by learners as a way of practising language skills. They may use the same assessment a number of times until they feel confident with their ability. Learners may also use self-assessments as a way of preparing for external assessments (e.g. public examinations).

11.3.1 Teacher-prepared assessments

In this category we include not only in-house prepared materials but also published materials. In-house materials include assessments (e.g. Figure 11.1) accompanied by answer sheets (e.g. Figure 11.2) which have been specifically prepared for self-access use. Published materials

Table 11.2.   *Kinds of assessment and the uses to which they can be put*

Kind of assessment	Criteria for assessment created by:	Content selected by:	Possible uses
Teacher-prepared	Teacher	Teacher	external assessment, self-assessment, peer-assessment
Generic	Teacher	Learner	self-assessment, peer-assessment, external assessment
Collaborative	Negotiation between teacher and learner	Teacher	external assessment
Learner-prepared	Learner	Learner	self-assessment, peer-assessment
Portfolio	Teacher and learner	Learner	external assessment

include text books and test materials, for example, 'Ship or Sheep' (Baker 1981) and 'Cambridge Key English Test 1' (Cambridge 1997). Self-access assessments in this category resemble classroom-administered tests but the ways in which they are used may be different. Learners have greater choice over how to use them and what to do with the results; for example, they can select which parts of the assessments to do. Learners would choose to make use of these assessments at appropriate stages in their learning.

Teacher-prepared assessments might be designed to be administered and marked by a teacher. Alternatively, they could be designed as self-assessments which are self administered and self marked. The difference in these approaches may reflect the purpose to which the assessment is to be put and may also reflect the philosophy of the institution. The pros and cons of administration are discussed more fully in Section 11.5.

11.3.2 Generic assessments

As an alternative, or a supplement, to producing a set of prepared assessments, teachers may produce help sheets which explain to learners how they can construct their own assessment procedures (e.g.

Self-assessment of grammar
Sheet 6: Agreement between verbs and nouns

Before you start
1. You can review the way verbs change in the Present Tense. Look in your text book or in a grammar book (for example English Grammar in Use by Raymond Murphy: Units 1, 2, 3 and 4).

2. If you want to see how quickly you can do this test make sure you record your starting time.

The test
Section A: Select one correct answer for each gap.

1. He _____ to school every day of the week.
   (a) go   (b) going   (c) goes   (d) is

2. All the computers, including the one in his office, _____ correctly.
   (a) work   (b) works   (c) can   (d) are

3. _____ Alex and the other boys like swimming?
   (a) Are   (b) Does   (c) Is   (d) Do

Section B: Correct any errors you find in the following text:

Most of the people in my class likes swimming. Each of us go swimming quite often although Harry, a friend of mine, don't go at all. He is afraid of water and think he might drown. He can't even swim. That's quite dangerous because one day he may find himself in a situation where they needs to swim. Those of us who swim regularly is very good at swimming but we still wants to improve. We all plan to take a swimming test at the end of the year.

After the test
1. If you were timing yourself, how long did it take?
   10 to 15 minutes would be about right.

2. Check your answers with the answer sheet. Give yourself a score out of 10.
   How did you do? Are you happy with your score?

3. If you did well on Section A but not on Section B why is that?
   It might mean you know the rules but are not good at applying them. If that is true, what are you going to do about it?

Figure 11.1. Example of a teacher-prepared assessment

Figure 11.3. For further examples of generic assessments see Gardner 1996). Generic assessments must contain the following information:

- the purpose of the assessment
- the benefit to the learner
- the procedure for conducting the assessment
- the procedure for marking the assessment
- a suggested marking scale
- a choice of follow-up actions based on the score achieved.

In addition, learners can be encouraged to think of ways to adapt the assessment to make it suitable for their individual needs. So, for example, in the case of Figure 11.3, learners may focus on assessing their ability to understand specific vocabulary items rather than general listening comprehension. If teachers get learners to report back on adaptations they have made, a bank of new assessment materials can quickly be built up.

Self-assessment of grammar
Sheet 6: ANSWERS

Before the test
If you look at this sheet before the test you won't know how good you are.

After the test
Here are the answers:
Section 1:
1. He _____**goes**_____ to school every day of the week.

2. All the computers, including the one in his office, ___**work**____ correctly.

3. ___**Do**_____ Alex and the other boys like swimming?

Most of the people in my class **like** swimming. Each of us **goes** swimming quite

often although Harry, a friend of mine, **doesn't** go at all. He is afraid of water and

thinks he might drown. He can't even swim. That's quite dangerous because one

day he may find himself in a situation where **he** needs to swim. Those of us who

swim regularly **are** very good at swimming but we still **want** to improve. We all

plan to take a swimming test at the end of the year.

Figure 11.2.   Example of an answer sheet for a teacher-prepared assessment

---

Self-assessment of listening comprehension

PURPOSE: To test your ability to listen to news programmes.
BENEFIT: To help you think about your listening ability and what to do next.

This sheet describes a way in which you can make up your own test and then use it to test yourself. You might need to adapt the method to suit your needs. Be creative.

Before the test
Make sure you have access to English language radio or TV.

The test
1. Listen to a news programme in English. Make notes about the main story.
2. Later (probably the next day) get a newspaper and check how much of the story you understood (see notes 1 & 2).

Scoring
1. Give yourself a mark out of 10 for the main points.
2. Give yourself another mark out of 10 for details.

After the test
How well did you do? Are you happy with your score?
If you scored well on the main points but not on detail, what does that mean? Perhaps it indicates you are not so good at listening for long periods. Listening to the news regularly might help you improve.

NOTES:
1. The newspaper you use can be in your own language as you are using it to check information not language; however, if you can get one in English that would be an added bonus.
2. Occasionally you might find the story you took notes on is not repeated in the newspaper (perhaps because another, more important story developed overnight). That's a pity but you will still have been practising your English.
3. Newspaper reports are often different from TV or radio reports. They are often longer, contain more details and sometimes disagree about the facts.

Figure 11.3.   Example of a generic self-assessment

11.3.3 Collaborative assessments

Assessment can be undertaken through collaboration between teachers and learners. Collaboration can be restricted to production of assessments or to their administration; alternatively collaboration can extend to both production and administration. The content of collaborative assessments is similar to the other kinds of assessment discussed in this

Preparing your own self-assessment

PURPOSE: To make a test for yourself.
BENEFIT: *You* decide what to test and *you* choose how to mark it.

Making the test
1. What do you want the test to be about?

   (a) Skill area (e.g. reading, listening): _____

   (b) Specific area (e.g. reading books, newspapers): _____

2. What are you going to use as the test material? (e.g. a newspaper report, a TV programme, a presentation you make):

   _____

3. Does the test have to be completed in a fixed time? If yes, how long? _____

4. What do you have to do during the test? _____

   _____

   _____

Making the marking scheme

1. What is the maximum mark for the test? _____

2. Describe how you will award yourself marks: _____

   _____

3. Now say how many marks are needed to achieve the following:

   ____ marks = excellent   ____ marks = good   ____ marks = average

   ____ marks = fair   ____ marks = poor

4. How many marks do you expect to get? _____

After the test
1. Ask yourself the following questions:
   • How well did you do?
   • Are you happy with your score? If not, why not?
   • Are you going to make another self-test?

2. Would your test be useful for other students? If yes, why not ask your friends to try it. Also, why not give this sheet (or a copy of it) to your teacher or self-access counsellor. They might be able to make it available to lots of students.

Figure 11.4.   Example of a learner-prepared self-assessment worksheet

section. They differ only in the ways of producing and administering them.

11.3.4 Learner-prepared assessments

Learners can develop their own methods of self-assessment then administer and score the assessments themselves. These assessments can take the form of self- or peer-assessments. Learners may need some initial guidance in doing this but once started it will become increasingly easy for them to find new ways of assessing themselves. One way in which this could work is illustrated in Figure 11.4. Perhaps learner-prepared assessments should be seen as the ultimate form of generic assessments.

An example of a learner-prepared assessment is reported by Miller and Ng (1996) who observed groups of students writing and conducting oral tests for each other. When students' assessments of each other were compared with those made by their teachers, a high level of correlation was found. However, it was concluded that to be successful, the participants must be highly proficient, of similar abilities, and familiar with each other's abilities.

Teachers or self-access managers might want to keep a record of the most successful learner-prepared assessments and make them available to other learners (with the authors' permission). As well as providing variety for learners there are two good, time-related, reasons for doing this. First, a bank of assessment opportunities could be built without demanding enormous input from teachers. Second, as Dickinson (1987) points out, self-assessment takes some of the assessment burden away from teachers. This is important because teachers' time can then be spent in other ways (e.g. materials production, counselling and management).

11.3.5 Portfolio assessments

Learners may decide, or perhaps be required, to keep a portfolio of their work for assessment. Learners use their portfolio to collect evidence of their achievements over a period of time and thus present for assessment what they consider to be the best picture of their abilities. Decisions about what goes into the portfolio and which parts of the portfolio to present for assessment should lie with the learner. The assessment of the portfolio will probably be conducted by a teacher although in some circumstances it is possible that a group of peers could conduct or assist in assessment. The portfolios might well contain results of self-assessments and also peer-assessments which could be taken into account during a final assessment. Learners will probably need guidance

---

Making a self-access portfolio

The purpose of a self-access portfolio is for you to demonstrate what you have been doing in self-access learning and the progress you have made. You should collect together things which help you do this. You could include:

- Copies of your study plans.
- Results of tests you have taken (marked by yourself or by a teacher).
- Short paragraphs recording your thoughts about what you learned and how you learned it.
- Your plans for future learning.

In preparing your portfolio think about the following questions. If you do not know the answers find out.

- Why do you need a portfolio?
- How long have you got to produce your portfolio?
- Who will see it?
- What should you put in it?
- What should you leave out of it?
- Do you need to explain what you have put in? How much?
- How will the portfolio be assessed?
- Who will do the assessing?
- What does the assessment count for?

Once you have considered these questions but before you start making your portfolio it would be a good idea to meet with the self-access counsellor to talk about your portfolio.

Figure 11.5.   Worksheet to help students start constructing a portfolio

in constructing a portfolio. They will need to think about the following issues:

- the need for a portfolio
- the time required to produce a portfolio
- their choice of contents
- the criteria for assessment.

It would be useful to provide learners with a worksheet which helps them to begin constructing a portfolio (Figure 11.5).

11.3.6 Advantages and disadvantages

There are advantages and disadvantages to each of the kinds of assessment we have discussed here (see Table 11.3). Whether the former

Table 11.3.   *Characteristics of different kinds of assessment*

	Face validity	Cost effectiveness	Expert authoring	Reliability	Ease of preparation
Teacher-prepared	✓	✗	✓	✓	✓
Generic	✓/✗	✓	✓	✓/✗	✓/✗
Collaborative	✓/✗	✗	✓/✗	✓/✗	✓
Learner-prepared	✗	✓	✗	✗	✗
Portfolio	✓	✓	NA	✓	✗

✓ = possesses this characteristic

✓/✗ = partially possesses this characteristic

✗ = lacks this characteristic

NA = not applicable

outweigh the latter for any particular kind of assessment will depend on the context in which it is being applied. Where possible we recommend that more than one kind of assessment be made available to self-access learners. Where learners are allowed to choose, the pros and cons of the assessment should be explained to them so that learner choice is accompanied by learner responsibility.

Teacher-prepared assessments have a lot of face validity. Many learners expect tests to be prepared by teachers. Providing a marking key will make it easier to score the assessment and can also provide an opportunity to learn from errors. However, preparing a test takes a lot of teacher time and building up a large bank of tests is, therefore, not cost effective. Having used a test once, learners are unlikely to repeat it as they are already familiar with the content. Also, such tests do not encourage learners to think of ways to prepare their own assessments.

The main advantage of generic assessments is that the variety of assessment opportunities is greatly enhanced because learners choose their own topics and questions. In addition, generic assessments are more likely to encourage learners to think of their own ways of self-assessment thus encouraging greater learner independence. Generic assessments require more creative thinking from teachers and this can be more time consuming than constructing a tightly focused test. However, once created, the generic assessment provides a procedure that can be used more than once by the same learners. The disadvantages of generic assessments are that they may be initially less appealing to learners because:

- Self-produced assessments have less face validity than teacher-prepared assessments.
- Learners have to put more effort into generic assessments.
- Scoring in generic assessments can never be so clear cut as when an answer key is available.

Collaborative assessments allow learners to feel involved in the assessment procedure and also allow them greater choice in some or all of the procedure, the content and the marking criteria. However, they can be costly in teacher time as the teachers are slowed down by working with inexperienced collaborators. Also, reliability may be questionable unless the learners have undergone training in assessment techniques.

Learner-prepared assessments are cost effective but may suffer from a lack of expert input, thus making them unreliable and reducing their face validity with users. These problems can be overcome by moving from a totally learner-prepared approach to a collaborative one. While this increases reliability and face validity, it reduces cost effectiveness.

Portfolio assessments allow learners to take responsibility for their own assessment by selecting the content they want to present. At the same time, face validity and reliability remain high because of teacher input into the assessment outcomes. Although portfolios are not particularly easy to produce, their ongoing nature spreads the workload over a period of time and they can be used for a variety of purposes (e.g. reflection on achievement, record keeping).

11.4 The content of assessments

As with other kinds of learning, the breadth of content covered by assessments in self-access learning can vary. Assessments may have a tightly concentrated focus or they may be wider ranging. The former will be small assessments and the latter will be large assessments.

11.4.1 Small assessments

Small assessments take place at the level of a unit of work. When learners come to the end of a worksheet or a videotape they may wish to make a quick assessment of what they have learned. These assessments need to be small so as not to outweigh the time the learners have spent studying. Assessments at unit-of-work level can only be small as they are assessing focused aspects of learning. However, they play an important role as they give the learners an ongoing picture of their progress and encourage frequent reflection; this leads to adjustments of goals and objectives and/or enhanced motivation.

Small assessments will typically be self-assessments or, if working as part of a group, learners may also opt for peer assessments. When assessments are self-administered by learners there are few or no constraints as to when and where they should take place. There is no need to go to an appointed place at an appointed time. Some learners may choose to complete the assessment immediately after finishing a unit of work. Others may choose to take time for reflection on what they have learned and return to the self-assessment on another occasion. In this way learners complete the units of work and take the small assessments at their own pace. There is no need for learners to hurry through work they find difficult in order to be ready for an assessment.

After conducting small assessments learners can choose what they want to do with the results. They may include them in a portfolio of their work, they may choose to discuss their results with a self-access counsellor or their own class teacher or they may choose to keep the results confidential especially if they are discontented with them. One thing they will not be able to do with their results is ignore them. This is what makes small assessments an important part of learners' reflections on their learning.

Some teachers think a disadvantage of self-assessment is that learners can cheat. However, when self-assessment is used within the correct framework of ongoing self-support cheating becomes irrelevant and thus not a disadvantage. If learners record false scores they will be unable to complete subsequent, more difficult, tasks successfully. It seems extremely unlikely that any institution would award a qualification on the basis of self-assessment alone. Therefore, sooner or later cheats will come up against an externally administered assessment at which they fail miserably. In the case of self-access learners who are not aiming at any external assessment – that is those who have chosen self-access study as a method of self-improvement – there is absolutely no advantage to cheating as learners will only be fooling themselves about their abilities. So, it is not true that cheating is a major problem with self-assessments; however, it is important to point out the reasons for this to the learners because for some of them cheating may have become habitual.

11.4.2 Large assessments

At given points in their study, learners may wish to assess their overall learning gain. For example, at the end of an academic year they may wish to assess all they have learned in that period. Alternatively, an institution may impose formal assessment on self-access learners. This kind of assessment will cover a wider range of topics and take considerably more time than a small assessment. If the assessment leads to an award of some kind – for example it might contribute to the assessment of a student's performance in a language course – it is likely that the institution will insist on all or most of the assessment being carried out by teachers. Even where no award is to be made, learners may prefer to be assessed by qualified staff so that they have an expert opinion of their performance. This opinion could become an important document to include in a portfolio when applying for jobs or seeking further education opportunities.

Large assessments need some consideration if they are to be effective measures of self-access learning. If these assessments become standard tests in which all the candidates answer the same questions, the wash-back effect will be that all self-access learners study the same material and attempt to learn the same things regardless of their needs, wants and abilities. If self-access learners are to be encouraged to develop individually and to gradually move towards greater autonomy, then their assessments (both large and small) must not become standardised. To make large assessments fit comfortably into a scheme of self-access learning they need to be much more flexible than language-course examinations.

Large assessments need to be modular so that learners can choose the assessments they wish to undertake. For example, they may choose to be assessed on reading and writing but not speaking and listening. Within modules there would also be choices so that, for example, within a reading module a learner may choose to be assessed on speed reading or reading academic texts (see Figure 11.6). The module would also offer choices of the language level at which the learner wished to be assessed. By recording the choices learners made and the scores they achieved, such an assessment would allow learners a relatively high level of autonomy in their learning while still resulting in a recognised measurement of their achievement.

Of course, such a system still imposes some constraints on how self-access learners can spend their time. In an ideal world, it might be argued, self-access learners should have no assessment constraints

Self-access assessments: reading module

Instructions: In the table below select up to three items on which you want to be assessed and submit the form to your self-access counsellor one week before the test date. Note that some items are not available (N.A.).

NAME:

	Beginners	Elementary	Lower Intermediate	Upper Intermediate	Advanced	Professional English
Skimming						
Scanning						
Speed reading	*N.A.*	*N.A.*				
Newspapers	*N.A.*					*N.A.*
Textbooks	*N.A.*					*N.A.*
Novels	*N.A.*	*N.A.*				*N.A.*
Academic articles	*N.A.*	*N.A.*	*N.A.*			*N.A.*
Manuals	*N.A.*	*N.A.*				
Technical reports	*N.A.*	*N.A.*				
Legal texts	*N.A.*	*N.A.*	*N.A.*			
Scientific reports	*N.A.*	*N.A.*				

Figure 11.6. Example of choices available in one self-access assessment module

placed on them and be allowed to develop their learning interests completely autonomously. However, in the real world students need evidence of academic achievement. This is produced through assessments. Incorporating assessments into self-access learning ensures it is brought into the mainstream of students' academic life. If this does not happen self-access learning will be sidelined and will eventually be eliminated through economic necessity or lack of student interest.

11.4.3 Public examinations

Large assessments could also be public examinations for which learners enrol and use self-access to prepare. Public examinations are not assessments of self-access learning and as such we will not discuss them here. However, it should be noted that, where such examinations are targeted by users of self-access facilities, suitable materials should be made available. The learners should also be made aware that they need to adapt their learning approach to focus more on what they *need to learn* (for the exam) than on what they *want to learn*.

11.5 The administration of assessments

There are four main modes of administration of assessment of self-access learning. Assessments can be administered externally, collaboratively by a learner and teacher, by oneself or by peers. These four modes are summarised in Table 11.4. External assessments have no input from learners. They are administered by teachers or as public examinations. Collaborative assessments involve combined input from a teacher and a learner who negotiate criteria for assessment. Haughton and Dickinson (1989), for example, describe one form of collaborative assessment system in which postgraduate students negotiate with their tutors their final grades for written assignments. In self- and peer-assessments the learner plays a central role in the assessment procedure. An example can be seen in Murphey (1994). He explains a self-assessment procedure in which students are paired randomly and score themselves on how well they are able to explain language items to their partners. There is no teacher intervention. The aim of the procedure is to develop students' awareness that 'the most important evaluation is ultimately what they think of themselves' (Murphey 1994: 14).

Some studies in formal education report that self-assessment is unreliable (e.g. Blue 1988; Janssen-van Dieten 1989; Pierce et al. 1993). Harris (1997) points out that in most studies where self-assessment has been questioned, the learners have received no training. In fact, Janssen-van Dieten (1989) identifies this as a cause of the unreliability of self-assessment. Thomson (1996) also reports that learners engaged in self-assessment wanted more support. Other studies have shown self-assessment to be reliable (e.g. Bachman and Palmer 1989; Blanche 1990). Dickinson (1987) suggests that self-assessment can be used as a complement to teacher assessment rather than an alternative. This is supported by a study (Thomson 1996) in which it was found that results of self-assessments did not correlate well with those of formal

Table 11.4. *Modes of administration of self-access assessments*

Mode of administration	Description
External	• These assessments are most often used as a basis on which to award credit in an institution or public examination. They are conducted in examination conditions which are identical for all candidates. The assessments are prepared by experts in the field (usually teachers) and are marked by the same or similar people. • To make the assessments relevant to self-access learning they must be modularised and sub-modularised to the lowest level. Learners must be allowed to choose in which sub-modules they wish to be assessed. • Because of the modularisation and the high degree of choice offered to learners, these assessments need to have a detailed way of reporting which records achievement at sub-module level.
Collaborative	• May be prepared by teachers or learners but are administered through a process of negotiation.
Self	• May be prepared by teachers, by students or by a combination of both but are administered by the learners themselves. • Self-assessment may not be acceptable to institutions as a basis on which to make awards although it may be considered as part of an assessment system. Self-assessment is most likely to be used for learners' own information and for the construction of portfolios profiling progress and achievement.
Peer	• May be prepared by teachers, by students or by a combination of both but are administered by the learners to each other. • Peer-assessments are most commonly used for small assessments although there is some evidence of their successful use as a credit awarding mechanism (although not in a self-access context).

assessments but that the self-assessments served an important function in involving learners in their learning.

Peer-assessment has long been a part of classroom practice although it may not be recognised specifically as a form of assessment by the teachers who use it. It is common, for example, to ask students to review drafts of each other's written work and much has been said about this as a classroom practice (e.g. Jacobs 1989; Mittan 1989; Lockhart and Ng 1993). This, and similar practices, could be facilitated among self-access learners by providing sets of marking criteria or encouraging learners to develop criteria.

In general, credit-awarding bodies are reluctant to accept self- and peer-assessment as a basis on which to award credit. Haughton and Dickinson (1989: 236) label this phenomenon 'the problem of certification'. The problem arises perhaps because it is difficult to set and maintain standards when self-assessment takes place. It may also be due to traditional attitudes to assessment about both the content of assessments and how assessments should be conducted. Thus, it may be necessary to accept that assessments which earn learners credit of some kind are probably totally, or almost totally, externally administered to ensure their validity.

Assessments conducted mostly for the learner's own information are better administered as self-assessments or peer-assessments. This makes greater logistic sense but also allows the learner a greater degree of privacy concerning assessment outcomes. In this way assessments become a tool to facilitate reflection and ultimately development, rather than a tool to describe and categorise the learner.

As we have shown, the administrators of self-access assessments need not only be teachers (or other external agents). Assessments can also be administered by learners either to themselves or to each other. The mode of administration may change depending on the purpose of the assessment. It is important that teachers and learners are made aware of the differences and select the appropriate mode for what they are trying to achieve.

11.6 Using the results of assessments

11.6.1 Learner reflection

A key to becoming more independent in learning is reflection about learning. Assessments provide an opportunity for reflection. They can help learners to gain a clearer picture of their abilities, encourage reflection on learning and provide evidence of their achievements. In this way assessments also help learners to see the value, or lack of value, of self-access learning activities they have engaged in. Results of assessments should not be the only factor taken into account when learners make decisions about how to improve their approaches to learning but they can make an important contribution. The results of assessments can be a useful starting point for discussions with self-access counsellors.

11.6.2 Administrative uses of the results

The results of self-access assessments could become a useful tool for administrative purposes (e.g. justifications of expenditure). However, teachers and/or self-access centre managers need to make policy decisions about how assessment results are to be used. In this context it is relevant to consider using the results of different kinds of assessments in different ways.

If the main purpose of small assessments is to encourage learner reflection and development then the nature of the assessments should be non-threatening and the results should remain private unless the learners wish to share them. Confidentiality is not an issue when learners undertake self-assessment and is unlikely to be a problem where peer-assessment takes place. However, where assessments are conducted by, marked by or in some way involve teachers then the teachers need to be aware of the importance of confidentiality to the success of the system. If teachers break their learners' trust – by, for example, recording results of small assessments as a performance indicator or using them for streaming – learners will stop using assessments as a tool for reflection and only submit to those assessments where they can score highly.

Large assessments are likely to serve a different function from small assessments and the results may be used in different ways. With all assessments the ways in which the results are used must be made clear to the learners. They should be informed whether the results will:

- become part of an official record
- be made public (e.g. posted on a notice board)
- contribute to statistical analyses
- be used for evaluating self-access learning and facilities
- be made available to learners for their own use (e.g. to include in portfolios).

11.7 Summary

There are various kinds of assessment relevant to a self-access learning context. They may be teacher-prepared, generic, learner-prepared or use a portfolio approach. There are also different modes of administration. Assessments may be administered by external agents, collaboratively, self-administered or peer-administered. In addition, the function of the assessment may vary. Self-access learning assessments may be categorised broadly into 'small assessments' and 'large assessments'. The former are short, focused and usually related to a unit of work. They tend to be private to the individual and serve the purpose of updating the individual's own picture of his or her abilities and needs, and encourage reflection by the learner. The latter are more broadly focused and tend to follow institutional norms. Their function is to measure and record an individual's abilities and performance.

It is important for teachers and learners to understand the uses to which different kinds of self-access assessments can be put and to gain the fullest benefit from them. It is extremely important that confidentiality be maintained where assessments have been undertaken by learners for purposes of reflection and not as a measure of performance which will be entered on their academic record.

11.8 Tasks

1. Design a generic assessment which focuses on a language skill which would be of use to learners you are familiar with (see example in Figure 11.3).
2. Look at the self-assessment worksheet in Figure 11.1 and prepare one which assesses a different grammar point. Also prepare the answer sheet.
3. If you are learning a foreign language write your own learner-prepared assessment for something you are currently learning.

11.9 For discussion

1. What proportion of a learner's self-access time should be taken up with assessment? Why?
2. In a situation with which you are familiar, what kinds of assessment would you introduce and what would be their purposes?
3. How would you encourage self-assessment with learners that you know? Would they accept self-assessment? Why or why not?

12 Evaluation of self-access language learning

12.1 Introduction

In Chapter 11 we looked at ways of measuring what learners' learn through self-access language learning (SALL). In this chapter we look at ways of measuring whether SALL and self-access centres are effective and efficient. This is an important issue because, as with most educational innovations, SALL needs to be shown to be effective in achieving its goals. Institutions, moreover, are also looking for value for money and expect efficiency. In some cases institutions may demand that SALL be shown to be more effective and more efficient than other approaches to learning.

In 1987, Dickinson suggested that there had been very little research into the effectiveness of what he terms self-instruction in language learning. The situation remains largely one of uncertainty about the effectiveness of SALL although there have been some attempts to define more clearly what to evaluate (e.g. Miller and Gardner 1994) and how to evaluate (e.g. Darasawang 1996; Riley 1996). There have also been a small number of evaluations made public (e.g. Star 1994; Dam and Legenhausen 1996; Gardner and Miller 1997; Karlsson et al. 1997).

Star (1994) gives two reasons why the evaluation of SALL systems is a difficult task. She points out that self-access systems are 'highly complex' (Star 1994: 158) and also that each system is unique. In educational terms the purpose of evaluation is to improve learning and teaching and this has been stated, explained and developed by many writers (e.g. Nunan 1988b; Thorpe 1988). In the case of self-access, however, the situation is somewhat different. First, the main focus is on learning rather than teaching. Second, while the enhancement of learning is of paramount importance, issues related to the management of resources and people must also be considered. This distinction in the purposes of evaluation in SALL has been recognised by a number of authors (e.g. Esch 1989; Star 1994). It is reflected in the distinction we draw here between evaluating effectiveness and evaluating efficiency. However, we argue that the two areas are not as clearly defined as may have been suggested in the past. There is an important interaction between them and also some overlap.

In this chapter we look first at the reasons why it is important to conduct evaluations of SALL and self-access facilities. Next we discuss the issues of effectiveness and efficiency, what they mean and how their meanings may vary according to context. Then we look at the decisions which need to be made about what to evaluate and which tools to use. Finally, we provide a step-by-step guide to conducting an evaluation.

12.2 Reasons for evaluating self-access learning

All systems designed to promote learning need to be evaluated periodically but especially when they are new. Although SALL has been in use for quite some time in a small number of institutions it is now being promoted more widely. SALL is quite unlike traditional teaching and, therefore, challenges the status quo. Consequently, teachers and administrators who have no personal experience of SALL may be wary of it and, as explained in Chapter 1, may have reasons why they do not wish to develop or promote SALL.

Controlling resources, time and students' education through a system which may have been tried but rarely tested is a risk. Evaluation can reduce this risk in two ways. First, evaluations conducted by other institutions can be used as evidence for deciding on the suitability of self-access for similar circumstances. This is especially useful when proposing the establishment of SALL within an institution. Second, evaluations conducted within an institution can be used as evidence for deciding whether self-access is a successful use of the institution's resources and contributes meaningfully to students' education. If the evaluations are negative then an institution's use of SALL needs to be re-examined or even abandoned. If they are positive they can be used to support the continued existence of SALL within an institution or even to support its expansion.

Evaluations of self-access learning are also important for learners. They are, after all, the bearers of the greatest risk in being subjected to, or subjecting themselves to, a new approach to their learning. Learners (and in the case of young learners also their families) should be given an opportunity to understand the benefits of SALL and to ask questions about it. Making available the results of evaluations in a format in which they can be understood by a general audience is an important step in helping learners understand the functions and benefits of SALL. Information from evaluations can be presented either as graphical representations of the use of self-access facilities and materials (see, for example, Figure 12.1) or as quotations from learners and teachers (see, for example, Figure 12.2). Ways in which this information can be disseminated are listed in Table 12.1.

Table 12.1. *Ways in which information from evaluations can be disseminated*

- notice boards
- in-house magazines
- information sheets to students and/or parents
- electronic posting of results (Internet sites or e-mail)
- announcements on a school tannoy system
- summary sheets for teachers with suggestions for learner training

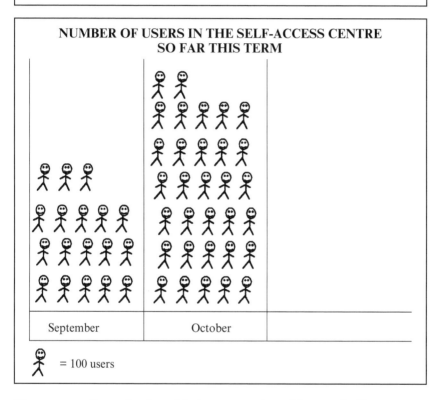

Figure 12.1. *Example of graphical representation of the use of self-access facilities and materials*

In the first chapter of this book we discussed the grounds on which the introduction or continuation of self-access learning may be questioned. These issues (summarised in Table 1.6) should be seen as targets by evaluators. A well-executed evaluation will provide a reliable basis from which the stakeholders can make their own judgements about the value of SALL.

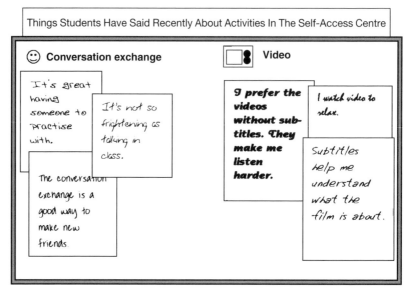

Figure 12.2.   *Example of using evaluative comments from users on a notice board*

12.3 Measuring efficiency and effectiveness

Both efficiency and effectiveness are key elements in measuring the success of self-access facilities. Efficiency is a measure of the relationship between output and cost. Effectiveness is a measure of the meeting of pre-set goals. Some aspects of self-access learning that could be measured to indicate efficiency and effectiveness are listed in Tables 12.2 and 12.3 respectively.

12.3.1 Efficiency

The evaluation of efficiency is important mostly for administrative reasons because it demonstrates that resources are being used optimally, that is, wastage has been eliminated. This is an important point for institutions where budgets need to be stretched to their limits.

Increasing efficiency is important because:

- A larger number of learners can be given access to self-access learning.
- A wider range of materials and activities can be developed.
- Teachers' time is used to the best advantage of learners.
- Unused materials or facilities can be replaced with popular ones.

Table 12.2. *Measures of efficiency of self-access*

Purpose	What to examine
To evaluate the quality of management	<ul><li>how decisions are made</li><li>cost (in staff time) of the decision-making process</li><li>speed at which decisions are implemented</li><li>ways in which funding is secured</li><li>ways in which funding is spent</li></ul>
To evaluate value for money of materials and equipment	<ul><li>frequency of use of different resources compared with their cost</li><li>the relative costs of in-house production versus purchased materials</li></ul>
To evaluate value for money of staffing	<ul><li>number of student-hours facilitated per staff hour</li><li>number of student-hours facilitated without staff presence</li><li>quantity of materials produced by staff</li></ul>
To evaluate the deployment of resources (material and human) throughout the academic year	<ul><li>patterns of usage of facilities on a daily, weekly, monthly and annual basis</li><li>patterns of expenditure on consumables and utilities</li><li>patterns of student requests for help, special materials or workshops</li><li>management/staff responses to recognised patterns</li></ul>
To evaluate return on the overall cost of self-access	<ul><li>number of student-hours facilitated compared with overall cost of self-access facilities</li><li>the cost of self-access learning compared with classroom teaching</li><li>the number of hours a self-access facility is available to students</li></ul>
To evaluate the responsiveness of self-access to student needs	<ul><li>number of different ways in which student feedback is obtained</li><li>the impact of student feedback on the system</li><li>the speed with which staff respond to student feedback</li></ul>

Table 12.3   *Measures of effectiveness*

Purpose	What to examine
To evaluate whether self-access facilitates learning	• learning gain (or loss)
To evaluate whether appropriate learning practices occur in self-access learning	• the learning strategies of self-access learners • learners' behaviour
To evaluate whether self-access encourages learners and teachers to change their approaches to learning/teaching	• changes in learning strategies • changes in teaching strategies • changes in attitudes and behaviour of learners and staff over a period of time
To evaluate whether learners and teachers value self-access	• attitudes of learners to self-access learning • attitudes of teachers (both in and outside the SAC) to self-access learning • learners' motivation • consistency with which students return voluntarily to self-access learning
To evaluate whether self-access learning develops autonomy in learners	• the level of individualisation achieved • the ways in which learners take responsibility for their own learning • the quantity and quality of learner reflection about their learning • the outcomes of learner reflection • the degree of independence learners achieve over a period of self-access learning
To evaluate the role self-access plays in enhancing classroom learning	• links between taught materials/activities and those of self-access learning • the degree to which learners recognise links • the relationship between using self-access learning and performance in classroom activities • the degree to which teachers recognise links

- Streamlining of administrative work releases time for pedagogical activities.
- Funding bodies value operations which use resources economically.

The measurement of efficiency can be achieved using quantitative measures and is relatively easy. Various things are counted and then a formula is applied. Examples of formulas contributing to the measurement of efficiency are shown in Figures 12.3 and 12.4.

If the formula in Figure 12.3 was applied to SALL and also to taught courses, a comparison of the cost of the two approaches could be made. However, while such a comparison would give useful information about the relative cost of SALL it would say nothing about the quantity or quality of learning. Measures of efficiency demonstrate how resources are being spent but not to what effect.

12.3.2 Effectiveness

If evaluations are to examine the part that self-access learning plays in learners' development they need to consider effectiveness as well as efficiency.

Measuring effectiveness is important because:

- Measures of effectiveness indicate good and bad practices as well as areas needing further development. This will lead to development of new learning materials and activities.
- If self-access learning is shown to be effective more teachers are likely to encourage their students to make use of it, thus exposing them to a wider range of learning opportunities.
- If learners see evidence that SALL is effective they are more likely to want to make use of it.

Measuring effectiveness is more difficult than measuring efficiency and it is perhaps for this reason that very little progress has been made in measuring the effectiveness of SALL. Whereas efficiency can be measured entirely using quantitative data, measures of effectiveness need to make use of quantitative and qualitative data. This means that in addition to counting things, the quality of experiences also needs to be considered. Prostano and Prostano (1987) suggest looking at user attitudes, user behaviour and SAC staff attitudes. Similar sources of information were used by Gardner and Miller (1997) in a study in which they developed a multidimensional methodology which integrates quantitative and qualitative data collection techniques. Riley (1996: 264) concludes that research into SALL cannot be 'exclusively "qualitative" or "quantitative"'.

12.3.3 The interaction between efficiency and effectiveness

In evaluating SALL facilities efficiency and effectiveness cannot be considered independently because they interact. Measuring efficiency without relating it to effectiveness will say nothing about pedagogical achievement. Measuring effectiveness without relating it to efficiency

$$\frac{\text{Total hours spent by all students in a SAC over one year}}{\text{Total hours spent by all teachers in a SAC over one year}} = \frac{\text{No. of student-hours}}{\text{facilitated per staff-hour}}$$

Figure 12.3.   A formula for measuring the efficiency of the use of SAC staff hours

$$\frac{\text{Total hours spent by learners using video equipment}}{\text{(Quantity of video equipment)} \times \text{(hours the SAC is open)}} \times 100 = \frac{\text{Percentage capacity to which video equipment is being used}}{}$$

Figure 12.4.   A formula for measuring the efficiency of the use of video equipment in a SAC

tells us nothing about the 'cost' of achieving that effectiveness. Raddon and Dix (1989: 256) remind us of the importance of 'the relationships between the cost of a service and any perceived or measured benefits to its users'.

12.4 The focus and effect of evaluations

Evaluations can be narrowly focused or widely focused. The former concentrate on one specific aspect of self-access (e.g. what learners do with newspapers) or perhaps on a closely related group of aspects (e.g. the different types of text learners use and the reading strategies associated with each type). Widely focused evaluations encompass a range of aspects (e.g. the types of learner using the SALL facilities, the amount of time they spend, and the kinds of activity they engage in). Narrowly focused evaluations can be conducted in greater depth. Widely focused evaluations are usually not in-depth studies unless substantial resources are made available for the evaluation. It should also be remembered that in-depth evaluations tend to disrupt learners' work patterns more than superficial studies. In-depth studies within a narrow focus tend to disrupt a limited number of learners and for a short period. When in-depth studies are extended across a wide range of areas the level of disruption may become unacceptable to learners.

Learners who feel they are 'suffering' at the hands of evaluators may, if their level of autonomy allows, remove themselves from the ranks of unwilling participants. If they do not have the autonomy to make that move they may, at least, be hostile to evaluators. Anecdotally we are aware of more than one situation in which zealous evaluators of self-access facilities have antagonised their sources of information. Where hostility arises among learner or staff informants it may be difficult to conduct an objective in-depth evaluation. It may also lead to the data becoming tainted by negative attitudes which may not have existed before the evaluation began.

Having seen the hostility that over-evaluation can cause we must also point out the effect it can have on study habits. To a certain extent, all learners are looking for confirmation that they are doing the right things. This may be more evident in some cultures than others but will, in any case, be heightened in self-access learning especially when learners are new to it. It is possible that when completing questionnaires or being interviewed for evaluations, learners look for clues to the 'right' self-access behaviour. If they find (or think they find) those clues they may change their study behaviour. In self-access learning where learners are encouraged to be independent, it is desirable that they make changes to their study behaviour. However, this should be as a result of reflection on their learning experiences not as a result of trying to see what is behind evaluative questions. Perhaps a way of preventing this situation is to make learners aware that the purpose of an evaluation is to find out what is happening, not to find out if they are doing the 'right' things.

12.5 Deciding what to evaluate

As has been illustrated above, large-scale evaluations can be disruptive and costly in resources or, alternatively, they may provide limited information. It is important, therefore, to conduct evaluations which minimise disturbance to learners but maximise the gathering of meaningful information. In balancing costs and disruption against usefulness, prospective evaluators need to consider the purpose of their evaluation and design it accordingly. Table 12.4 suggests the purposes for four different types of evaluation defined by their combinations of depth of study and range of focus. The uses to which different types of evaluations are put are varied. Some examples of evaluations which may be conducted under the four types are also shown in Table 12.4.

12.6 Matching evaluations to self-access goals

Teachers and managers involved with self-access learning have, or should have, goals. An evaluation can take one or more of these goals and can attempt to assess whether they are being met fully, partially or not at all. Lai (1994), for example, shows how one goal of her self-access

Table 12.4. *The attributes of four types of evaluation*

Type of evaluation		Purpose	Disruption to learners	Cost	Quantitative data	Qualitative data	Examples of uses
Superficial study	narrow	not clear, perhaps a pilot study	minimal	cheap and cheerful	✓	✗	• A quick survey of one aspect of self-access • To decide where to focus a more detailed evaluation
	wide	to gain an overview of everything	low	medium	✓	✗	• A wide-ranging questionnaire to see how self-access facilities are being used • A head count of users in each section of a SAC each day
In-depth study	narrow	detailed understanding of one area	relatively little	acceptable	✗	✓	• Observations of users to assess the impact of a recent innovation • A case study of a particular group of self-access learners
	wide	detailed understanding of many areas	potentially great	very high	✓	✓	• An ethnographic study of the behaviour and attitudes of self-access learners • A series of focus group discussions about the relationship between self-access learning and classroom teaching

---

Stage 1: Presentation
Staff present their self-access goals.
This includes:
- short- and long-term goals
- an explanation of the goals
- how they see their goals changing over time

↓

Stage 2: Negotiation
The external agent and the staff work together to define manageable
evaluation processes and to establish achievable criteria.

↓

Stage 3: Evaluation
The external agent:
- collects data from a variety of sources
- matches findings to the criteria negotiated in Stage 2 (with the purpose of
  evaluating the level of success in achieving the goals)
- reports on the findings

Figure 12.5.   A three-stage system of evaluation

centre is to meet the needs of students. Evaluations are used to 'confirm
the reliability of needs analysis' (Lai 1994: 151).

There is some similarity between evaluating the achievement of goals
and Woolls' (1994) proposal for evaluating the quality of management.
She suggests comparing 'What is' with 'What should be'. The difference
is the measure of quality. The greater the difference the lower the
quality.

The problem for self-access is in establishing the 'What should be'.
There seems to be considerable disagreement about this in the literature
as we have shown elsewhere in this book. There may also be disagreement between teachers and administrators within an institution.
There may even be disagreement among teachers themselves. The best
equipped people to establish the 'What should be' are the teachers
involved with self-access learning. However, allowing a group of people
to establish their own goals and then conduct their own evaluation to
show they have achieved those goals is likely to provide very positive but
not necessarily useful results. In any event such a system deserves to be
regarded with suspicion as it has no element of monitoring by an external
agent. Perhaps the solution is a three-stage system involving collaboration between an external agent and self-access staff (see Figure 12.5).

Table 12.5.   *Data collection tools*

Data collection tools		Quantitative data	Qualitative data	Examples
Questionnaires	Yes/no, true/false Likert-scale sections	✓	✗	On a scale of 1 (lowest) to 5 (highest) how useful is the work you do in self-access?
	Open-ended sections	✗	✓	What do you like most about self-access and why?
Interviews	Structured	✓	✓	Name the five things you like about self-access
	Open	✗	✓	What do you like about self-access and why?
Observations	Head counts	✓	✗	Note how many students use video per day.
	Record behaviour	✓	✓	Note what students do with video.
Participation		✗	✓	Become a learner and record actions, feelings, etc.
Focus groups (discussions with groups of learners)		✗	✓	Is self-access useful? Why / Why not?
Language tests		✓	✓	As a measure of learning gain.
Documentation		✓	✓	Proposal for setting up a SALL programme.

12.7 Evaluation tools

The choice of tools for collecting evaluative data will depend, at least to some extent, on the purpose of the evaluation and the way in which the evaluators intend to use the data. Table 12.4 indicates the types of evaluation in which quantitative and qualitative data collection are appropriate. Table 12.5 shows the most common types of data collec-

Table 12.6. *Sources of data for an evaluation of self-access learning*

Source	Kind of data
Learners	Attitudes, behaviour, beliefs, abilities, needs, learning goals, study plans, achievements, self-assessments, reflections on own performance
Staff	Attitudes, behaviour, beliefs, standards, assessments, reflections on the performance of self-access facilities, reflections on the performance of self-access learners
Administrators	Attitudes, quantities, finances
Documents	Mission statement of the institution, mission statement of self-access facilities, goals of self-access facilities, future plans, past history, floor plans, descriptions of self-access facilities

tion tools and the kind of data they collect. McCall (1992: 44) points out that 'results are often influenced by the technique chosen'.

12.8 Sources of data

There are a number of different sources of evaluative data as shown in Table 12.6. It is unlikely that an evaluation will achieve its full potential if it makes use of only one source. Dam (1995) discusses an evaluative method which appears initially to rely solely on a single source, that is, students answering questions about SALL. However, most significantly, she sees evaluation as 'a collaborative, ongoing process for the teacher and her learners' (Dam 1995: 58). It is important to see that even if only one set of people answer questions, another set of people (in this case teachers) respond to the data thereby including themselves as a source of data for the evaluation.

Single source evaluations may result in a skewing of the data which gives a false picture. Evaluators should attempt to triangulate their data by seeking alternative viewpoints which can be used to gain a more balanced view of the situation. For example, the following sources might be used to find out which self-access facilities are most popular and why:

- Ask learners which facilities they use most and why.
- Ask staff which facilities seem to be used most and what they think the learners are doing.

- Conduct an observation of the facilities and count usage.
- Conduct random questioning of users of facilities which have been identified as popular, asking users what they are doing and why.

With these sources of data it would be possible to compare learners' perceptions of what they do regularly with those of staff. It would also be possible to compare these perceptions with head counts of usage and observations of behaviour. Such an evaluation will give a clearer picture of what facilities are being used and for what purpose. It will also lead to a clearer understanding of whether learners and staff are fully aware of what is happening. This information will provide a better basis for decision-making than only a head count. As a result of this evaluation self-access managers/staff will be able to decide which facilities need more resources and/or improved materials, and where staff awareness needs to be raised possibly leading to staff training, where students need better information and perhaps training about what they can do with certain facilities. In addition, useful information has been gleaned that could be used in a report to a funding body about what is happening in self-access learning.

12.9 A step-by-step guide to conducting an evaluation of self-access

From the discussion that has taken place in this chapter it is clear that there are a number of decisions and actions which need to be taken to ensure a successful evaluation. They can be summarised as the set of six steps which are shown in Table 12.7. The relationship between these steps and the three-stage system we proposed is also shown in the table.

12.10 Summary

In this chapter we have looked at the evaluation of self-access language learning and have given multiple reasons for conducting such evaluations. We have also shown the differences between effectiveness and efficiency and also that both are important issues for self-access. In the second part of the chapter we looked at the decisions which need to be taken in order to conduct evaluations and the ways in which evaluations can be conducted. We suggested a three-stage system which revolves around interaction between self-access staff and an external agent. Finally, we offered a six-step guide to conducting an evaluation.

Table 12.7.   *A six-step guide to conducting an evaluation of self-access*

Steps to take	Corresponding stages of the three-stage system
Step One: Establish the purpose of the evaluation. It may be one of the following: • to measure efficiency, effectiveness or both • to provide colleagues, administrators, learners or parents with data which supports the use of self-access learning • to investigate in detail one particular area of self-access learning.	Pre-stage 1
Step Two: Identify aspects of self-access which are to be measured. At this stage the evaluator needs to establish the goals which are being pursued in order to measure whether they are being achieved. Examples of aspects of self-access and the purpose of measuring them are in Tables 12.2 and 12.3.	Stage 1
Step Three: Select an appropriate type of evaluation. In making this selection the evaluator must bear in mind the purpose, cost and other factors associated with the evaluation (Table 12.4). **Step Four:** Select appropriate tools. The evaluator should select an appropriate method (or methods) of data collection (Table 12.5) which fits with the purpose of the evaluation and aspects of self-access to be measured. Appropriate sources of information (Table 12.6) should be selected.	Stage 2
Step Five: Conduct the evaluation. This should be done in a way which minimises disruption to learners and staff. **Step Six:** Report the findings. This must be done quickly because as time passes the findings may become less relevant. The report should contain the following: • a statement of what is being evaluated • the purpose of the evaluation • the methods used to conduct the evaluation	Stage 3

Table 12.7. *(contd)*

Steps to take	Corresponding stages of the three-stage system
• a summary of the data collected • interpretations of the data • conclusions and/or recommendations based on the data. Selected findings should also be made available to the learners in a variety of ways (see Table 12.1).	

12.11 Tasks

1. Think of a self-access learning situation with which you are familiar and define at least four of its goals. Say whether they are related to efficiency, effectiveness or both.
2. Write a proposal for an evaluation of a self-access centre which has been open for one year and has never been evaluated. You need to consider:
   • the reason for the evaluation
   • the focus of the evaluation
   • what will be measured
   • how you will conduct the evaluation
   • the data collection tools you will use
   • what you will do with the findings.
3. Write five questions which you would use to evaluate one aspect of self-access language learning. State who the respondents would be.

12.12 For discussion

1. Measuring learning gain is not easy especially when learners are also attending taught courses. How would you deal with this problem?
2. If you were asked to conduct an evaluation of a self-access system, what steps would you take to help you decide the best type of evaluation and the appropriate tools to use?
3. How important is it to conduct evaluations of self-access learning? If there were no evaluations would there be any noticeable effects and what would they be?

Part 3   Case studies

13 Introduction

This part of the book contains four case studies of self-access centres (SACs) from different educational contexts. These case studies illustrate how self-access language learning (SALL) can be implemented in contexts ranging from young learners to adult learners and also how SACs can be established in all kinds of institutions from primary schools to universities and in private language schools. The SACs we look at show how SALL can be established with very different levels of resourcing: some have almost no funding while others have substantial funding; some have full-time staff while others function largely with volunteer efforts.

These case studies have been laid out in a way which illustrates many of the points made in earlier chapters in this book; see Table 13.1.

In the case studies we continue to use the terminology we have developed elsewhere in this book. In the section on 'Type of SAC' we use our typology of self-access systems which is explained in Table 3.1. In the section on 'Staffing and management' we use the typology for models of management explained in Table 4.1.

Each of the case studies is accompanied by a plan and a three dimensional diagram of the SAC. This is intended to make it easier to visualise the way the SAC is laid out and the overall ambience that is created.

Table 13.1.   *Reference guide to case studies and book chapters*

Case study section	Relevant chapter in this book
Reasons for establishing a SAC	1
Type of SAC	3
Staffing and management	4
Learners' beliefs and attitudes	2
Learner profiles	5
Counselling	10
Materials and activities	6, 7 & 9
Assessment and evaluation	11 & 12
Physical settings and resources	8

14 Case study 1: Self-access in a primary school

Name of institution: Sekolah Rendah Kebangsaan (L) Methodist Primary School (SRK)
Location: inner city Kuala Lumpur, Malaysia
Number of staff: 52 teachers, with 14 specialising in English teaching
Number of students: 980
About the students: a multi-racial mix of Malay, Chinese and Indian pupils; aged 7 to 12
Other information: one of the 151 primary schools in Malaysia with a self-access centre
Size of SAC: 56m²

Reasons for establishing a SAC: This centre was established as the result of an initiative of the Ministry of Education in Malaysia. Initially, SALL was established by the setting-up of self-access learning in the specialist teacher-training college in Kuala Lumpur (aided by the British Council). After using self-access in the training of school teachers, it was considered a good idea to establish the facilities in primary and secondary schools.

As stated in the Foreword to the *Teacher's Guide to Self-Access Learning for Malaysian Primary Schools* (1995: iii) 'In the context of the English Language programme for primary schools, SAL refers to the use of self-access learning materials to enable learning to take place independently of teaching. It takes place in conjunction with classroom learning and is complementary to it'. The basic reason for its implementation at SRK is to encourage pupils to enjoy learning English. The SAC was set up in 1993.

Type of SAC: Games arcade and Discount store. This SAC is a Games arcade because it is equipped with games and has lots of pictures on the walls in order to create a 'fun' environment for the pupils. It is also a Discount store as most of the materials have been donated and the budget for buying things for the SAC is very modest.

Staffing and management:
Headmaster (the head of school): makes all decisions related to resources and time-tabling.
Teacher-in-charge: One teacher who has a special interest in SALL has

the tasks of maintaining the centre, decoration, and keeping the other staff and headmaster informed of any changes or requirements.

Fourteen English-subject primary school teachers: All the English teachers are involved in the running, decoration and maintenance of the SAC.

The management of this primary school SAC is of the type identified in Chapter 4 as Democratic. All teachers are involved in the decision-making process which leads to an informed decision being taken by the headmaster.

Use of SAC: The SAC is used by higher form pupils (i.e. 10–12 year olds). It is used every day. Pupils are taken to the SAC by their class teacher for two English class periods (total one hour) each week. The SAC is therefore timetabled for use and is heavily used by the pupils.

Learners' beliefs and attitudes: Teachers have close relationships with their pupils. They know about the pupils' home backgrounds and about their personalities through the day-to-day contact they have with each other. With regard to finding out about pupils' beliefs and attitudes towards SALL, pupils are required to complete a learner's contract once a month. In the contract pupils are asked questions about what they would like to do in the coming month and how they would like to learn English. The teachers (who are also the pupils' SAC counsellors) then look at these contracts with their pupils and try to encourage them to develop their language skills in the areas they show most interest in. By looking at the learners' contracts teachers are also able to identify common areas of language learning which pupils are most interested in. They then try to cater for these areas in the development of SAC materials.

Learner profiles: Pupils develop their learner profiles mainly by collecting their monthly contracts in their folders. Weak pupils are encouraged to have discussions with their teacher about things they might try in order to help them improve their language learning. More able pupils are encouraged to keep a learner's log in which they record what they do in class, in the SAC and elsewhere and how their teacher helps them to learn English.

Counselling: The form of counselling which takes place in this primary-school SAC is mostly teacher initiated. Teachers counsel members of their own classes. This entails motivating pupils to try worksheets, helping them to find appropriate activities, checking that everyone is occupied, keeping noise at an acceptable level (so as not to disturb other nearby classes) and helping to check answers.

Materials and activities: This SAC has no technology. The materials in the centre are all print. Worksheets are prepared by the teachers to accompany the curriculum. There is always a teacher present so help is easily available for pupils having difficulty with the materials. In addition to the worksheets, the centre has a collection of story books and language games. All these are donations from staff, parents and publishers. There is a puppet theatre in one corner and a lot of open space created to allow the pupils to wander around and look at things. The walls are covered with colourful pictures with vocabulary items in Bahasa Malay and their English translations.

Prior to going to the SAC, the pupils are introduced to pair work and group work in class. They are encouraged to help each other learn English. The English teachers introduce the concept of using the SAC to pupils in class first. They ask pupils to guess what a self-access centre might be and talk with them about how they can learn English outside of the classroom. They also ask them to make up a list of advantages of using a SAC. The teachers also tell the pupils about the classification system, and how they can complete worksheets and then check the answers themselves. After the pupils have been introduced to the concepts of self-access in class, they are taken on a tour of the SAC and are shown where everything is located. While in the SAC the teachers talk with their pupils about what kinds of activities they can do, what types of materials are available, how they can get help when in the SAC, and how pupils feel about trying out the activities and materials in the SAC. The pupils are then asked to use the SAC for one class period.

After this first experience of using the SAC, teachers talk with their pupils in class about what they did, what materials they used, what they found interesting, what problems they had and how they feel about using the centre again. This in-class discussion with the pupils is a regular feature of classroom work after the pupils have been in the SAC. Pupils are then shown how to complete simple learner contracts, learner records and activity sheets. They have a notebook and plastic file especially for their SAC work.

Assessment and evaluation: Pupils can check their own answers from the answer keys to exercises, or they can ask their teacher/counsellor to help them. Many of the activities in this centre do not require assessment, e.g. games, the speaking corner and puppet shows. The staff of this centre have stated that they want to allow their pupils freedom to move around and explore things connected with English, to take the focus off English being a classroom subject and to stimulate the pupils' interest in finding out things through English. The focus for most of the materials and activities is therefore very much on a fun type of SAC and using English in a non-classroom setting, which for many of the pupils is novel. Evaluation of SALL occurs by direct observation of pupils in the SAC and by discussions with pupils in class about what they have

Figure 14.1.   Sketch of the SAC at the SRK, Kuala Lumpur

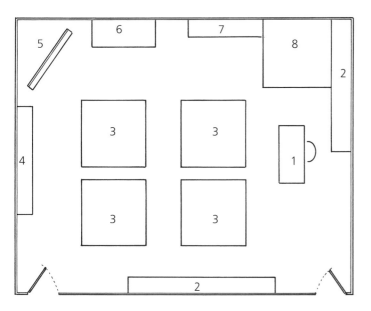

Figure 14.2.   Floor plan of the SAC at the SRK, Kuala Lumpur

done in the SAC. The teachers then report to the headmaster during staff meetings about their pupils' use of the SAC.

Physical settings and resources: The SAC was formally a school classroom and is, therefore, an integral part of the school building. Pupils pass by the SAC on the way to and from other facilities in the school. The SAC has a high profile location: it opens onto the playground and facing opposite is the school canteen. The SAC has an area of approximately 56m². The SAC is open only during school hours, 8am to 2pm.

The environment of this SAC is designed for young learners. In addition to the large pictures on the walls and the puppet theatre there is a table with plastic fruit and vegetables on it; all the SALL materials are in colourful box files. The transformation of a dull classroom into a bright and cheerful SAC was made possible by the volunteer work of the staff. Old school furniture was painted and adapted, bright coloured folders were bought, and local publishers were persuaded to donate posters and pictures. There are low-level desks for the pupils to sit at, and mats on the floor for pupils to lie down on to read books. The SAC looks inviting and comfortable and very different from a standard classroom.

The SAC in this school has the following facilities (see floor plan in Figure 14.2):

1. teacher's desk and chair
2. cupboards and shelving
3. low-level pupil desks
4. box files for storage
5. moveable whiteboard
6. puppet theatre
7. display table
8. speaking/reading corner

15   Case study 2: Self-access in a secondary school

Name of institution: Sekolah Menengah Wangsa Maju 2 Secondary School (SMWM2)
Location: suburb of Kuala Lumpur, Malaysia
Number of staff: 64 teachers, with 11 specialising in English teaching
Number of students: 1,200
About the students: from low socio-economic backgrounds and consisting of all three ethnic groups in Malaysia (Malay, Chinese and Indian)
Other information: This was the first secondary school in Malaysia to set up a dedicated self-access centre (in 1995). Bahasa Malay is the official language used in classes, although with the tri-ethnic mix English is also used between pupils.
Size of SAC: 135m²

Reasons for establishing a SAC: Once SACs were established in primary schools (see Case Study 1), the Department of Education in Malaysia decided to encourage the development of SACs in secondary schools. SMWM2 was chosen as a school in which to begin this. Although the Ministry of Education promoted the establishment of the SAC, no additional funding was given to the school. Instead, the staff and pupils raised funds for the conversion of a classroom into a SAC.

The head of the school, an English teacher herself, was wholeheartedly behind the establishment of a SAC and encouraged her staff, pupils and the Parent Teachers Association to become involved in the project. A great many hours of volunteer work resulted.

The rationale for the establishment of a SAC in SMWM2 as reported in the national press in Malaysia was '[to provide] ... an effective source of motivation for the students to learn the English language ... [to] allow them to learn according to their ability and interest in a tension-free environment' (The Star 1995). Two other reasons for the establishment of the centre, as reported by its coordinator are: to introduce the students to the concept of autonomy and to give them further opportunities to improve their English language proficiency.

Type of SAC: Cash and carry and Supermarket. This SAC is Cash and carry because there is a lot of similar types of material which have been specially prepared to complement the English language syllabus. The students are often directed to this material by their class teachers. It is also a Supermarket type as once students have completed several of the worksheets they are free to browse around and do other activities they are interested in.

Staffing and management:
Head of self-access (an English-language teacher): The head of the SAC is responsible for the overall coordination and running of the centre. She opens the centre each morning and checks the facilities. As her teaching responsibilities do not allow her to spend all her time in the SAC, she shares the general responsibility of the running of the centre with her colleagues and student helpers. The head of the SAC uses the office in the centre for filing and material development.
Six English language teachers: Teachers accompany their classes to the self-access centre. Each teacher contributes to the ongoing materials development of the centre. Two of the teachers have received training in writing SALL materials from the Ministry of Education programmes on self-access. They pass on these skills to their colleagues.
Student self-access prefects: Each class has a self-access prefect. These students help the teachers in monitoring their classmates in the centre and tidying up the SAC after school hours. They also help with the decoration of the SAC and organise SALL activities around the school.

The management of this centre is largely within the Formal model of self-access management (see Chapter 4). It has easily identifiable holders of power. Within the institutional framework of a secondary school this model works well.

Use of SAC: Pupils in the school have access to the SAC. Each class in lower forms is taken there by their class teacher once a fortnight. Students in the higher forms are allowed free access to the centre when it is not being used by a lower-form class. Any student can also use the centre for one hour after school each day.

Learners' beliefs and attitudes: Teachers gauge their students' beliefs and attitudes by the enthusiasm they show when working in the SAC. The teachers also obtain feedback from the SAC prefects who talk with their classmates and then make suggestions to the teachers about what the students would like to do in the SAC. Simple questionnaires are also given to students to find out about their attitudes towards working in the SAC. This information is then shared with members of staff.

Learner profiles: Students are expected to build up a learner profile document while they work in the SAC. In their files, students keep a target sheet (what they hope to achieve while working in the SAC), a contract based on their target sheet, and an exercise book which is used as a learner's log for keeping track of what they have done. This learner profile is constantly referred to by the students when they use the SAC and occasionally looked at by their teachers who may then encourage the students in what they are doing or make suggestions of new targets which may be set.

Counselling: Class teachers, who are present with their students in the SAC, motivate students and encourage them to try out worksheets. They also give help when asked. The teacher also ensures that an acceptable noise level is maintained so as not to disturb other classes. In addition to teacher help, students can get help from the SAC prefects. This may be in the form of asking where something is, or even help with the language as most of the SAC prefects are more able language users. Non-timetabled users of the SAC can get help from any teacher who happens to be in the centre or from their English teacher at other times.

Materials and activities: An English only policy is enforced in the centre. The SAC is well stocked with specially written worksheets covering the four skills. These worksheets complement the work set out in the school curriculum so they have high-face validity for the students. In this way, some of the work students do in the SAC can be seen as complementary to their school studies and so can be justified to anyone (students, parents, other teachers, administrators) who might consider SAC work as 'wasting time'. All students have to attempt one or two worksheets during each visit to the SAC. Then, they are free to do whatever they wish and can make use of the other facilities: TV/video, tape recorders, computers, magazines, language games, etc.

Before their first visit to the SAC, the students receive some basic learner training and orientation in class which consists of talking about their language learning. They do a short quiz when they first visit the SAC. It is a small SAC with clearly labelled sections and materials, and as their class teacher is always on hand to help them, students soon orient themselves to the facility.

Assessment and evaluation: Students can self-assess their work at any time while in the SAC. There are answer keys which accompany each worksheet. The lower form students can also ask their teacher/counsellor and/or the class SAC prefect for help in assessing their work. The higher-form students mostly rely on the answer keys and self- and peer-assessment. In an attempt to evaluate the impact of the SAC on the students' English-language studies, it was found that examination results in the Lower Secondary Certificate increased from a pass rate of 65.5% in 1995 to a pass rate of 77.5% in 1996.

Physical settings and resources: The SAC is situated in the middle of the school premises. Students have to walk past it each day going to and from other classes. The entrance to the SAC is through a short passage

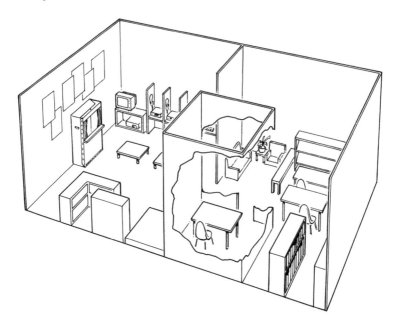

Figure 15.1.   Sketch of the SAC at the SMWM2, Kuala Lumpur

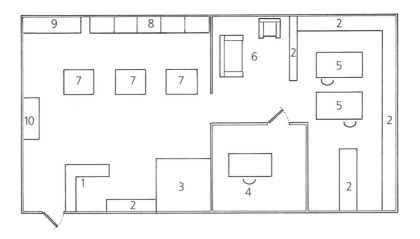

Figure 15.2.   Floor plan of the SAC at the SMWM2, Kuala Lumpur

which has lively notices on the walls advertising the centre. The SAC has been established by merging two classrooms. The total area is around 135m². Most of the area is used as a SAC although there is a small reception area at the entrance and a small office for teachers to use. The office has windows on each side so that even when the teacher is in there they can still observe the students and the students can always see that there is help available. The SAC is open every day during school term from 8am to 1:45pm and for an extra hour after school until 3pm. It is also open on Saturdays.

Pupils were involved in the establishment of the SAC. They helped to clean and prepare the classrooms which were used for the SAC. They painted old school furniture and prepared posters for the walls. The student SAC prefects now help in the daily running of the centre, helping to keep the SAC clean, cataloguing materials and arranging SAC activities for their classmates. This centre was established and continues to operate due to teacher commitment and volunteer student help. In order to raise funds for the SAC, staff and students organise fund raising events. However, the amount of start-up and recurrent funding for this type of centre is small. Most of the technical equipment has been donated.

When in the SAC, students have to take off their shoes and sit on the floor next to low level tables. This creates a less classroom-style environment and allows more students to fit into the space available. Chairs are only available in the computer section and the reading area. The SAC is decorated in a lively manner. Pictures and posters and a lot of colour is used to brighten up the environment and make it welcoming for the students.

The SAC in this school has the following facilities (see floor plan in Figure 15.2):

1. administration counter
2. shelving
3. mini-stage
4. teacher's office
5. tables and chairs
6. soft seating area
7. low-level tables
8. computer section
9. TV/video section
10. puppet theatre

16   Case study 3: Self-access in a university

Name of institution: The Hong Kong University of Science and Technology (UST)
Location: Hong Kong
Number of staff: 3,000, including 53 full- and part-time language instructors
Number of students: 7,000 (full-time and part-time)
About the students: mainly Hong Kong Chinese; some mainland Chinese postgraduates
Other information: The university specialises in science and technical degree programmes. It was purpose built in 1990 and has up-to-date facilities for its staff and students. The Language Centre of the university offers courses in a number of languages, but focuses mainly on English-language courses for first-year undergraduate students. The Self-Access Centre is managed by the Language Centre.
Size of SAC: 300m²

Reasons for establishing a SAC: The impetus for establishing a SAC at UST came directly from the Language Centre of the university. The SAC was established in 1994 to cater for the many and varied language demands of students and staff who work at the university. The students' study for their degree programmes in a second language (English). The SAC aims mostly at individual learners who want flexibility to learn whatever language skills they need at learning paces which suit them. Because of the diverse language-learning requirements of a potentially large group of users, flexibility is a key concept to the rationale of this centre.

Type of SAC: Supermarket, Technology shop and Department store. This SAC is a Supermarket as it holds a wide variety of general language-learning materials that casual users can browse through. It is a Technology shop because it is very well equipped with technological equipment (see Figure 16.2). The centre can also be described as a Department store as it caters to specific groups of learners and holds materials related to their course work.

Staffing and management:
Self-access manager: This post is filled by a senior instructor in the Language Centre. The manager has a reduced teaching timetable in

return for the responsibility of running and managing the SAC. His duties include, planning the use of the centre, making sure everything runs smoothly, coordinating other SAC staff activities, helping in materials writing, budgeting in coordination with the Head of the Language Centre, sorting out problems and trouble shooting, and looking for ways to improve the facility.

Eleven part-time tutors: These tutors are full-time staff members of the Language Centre who opt to work in the SAC as part of their duties. They work in the SAC for six hours per week. Their duties include materials writing, organising special workshops for SAC users, and counselling.

Two administrative staff: The centre has one full-time and one part-time member of administrative staff. These personnel see to the smooth running of the centre, loan out materials, check use of materials, monitor security, and deal with any other administration of the centre.

Technical assistance: A technician and computer officer are based in the SAC. They serve the SAC and the Language Centre.

This SAC operates a combination of the Formal and Democratic models of management (see Chapter 4). It is formal in that positions of authority are established; however, a great deal of democratic power sharing also goes on with the staff and students (via a users' committee) having a say in the direction of the SAC.

Use of SAC: This SAC is open to any student or member of staff of the university. It is also open to the general public, although in practice the university's rural location prevents it from being used by anyone other than those who study or work there. All first-year students are introduced to the SAC as part of their orientation programme and several language courses require the students to make use of the SAC as part of their project work. At any time there is a large number of students in the centre. It is also heavily used at lunchtime and after office hours by staff of the university.

Learners' beliefs and attitudes: The students who use this SAC are mostly Hong Kong Chinese. As a group, they hold certain similar beliefs and attitudes towards language learning and SALL. Teachers ascertain these beliefs and attitudes in three ways. First, a large number of English teachers in the university are Hong Kong Chinese and hold perceptions similar to those of their students. Second, students who attend the SAC are given questionnaires which ask questions like: Do you enjoy learning independently? Do you plan and evaluate your self-access work? Third, in consultation sessions with students counsellors ask them about their beliefs and attitudes and discuss with the students the relevance of working in the SAC.

Learner profiles: Counsellors encourage casual users of the SAC to keep track of their learning. There are learner support documents at the entrance of the SAC which help students to do this. These documents illustrate how to plan, keep track of, assess and evaluate self-access language learning. In a postgraduate language programme the students have to keep a learning portfolio. The students have to spend a minimum of 32 hours in self-access learning. They keep a learner diary, samples of their work and an assessment of this work. Once this is complete the student meets with a counsellor who looks over the portfolio and makes an assessment of the student's progress. This portfolio can then be presented to the student's subject supervisor, or to potential employers, as an indication of the type of language work the student has done.

Counselling: The Language Centre staff who perform part of their duties in the SAC are timetabled for counselling. The SAC has a counsellor's desk (see Figure 16.2) and users of the centre can get practical help or advice on language learning on a drop-in basis. Users can also get help from the administrative and technical staff who work in the reception area.

Materials and activities: Although the primary target language in this SAC is English, there are also a lot of materials to support Mandarin and Cantonese. In addition, there are self-study materials for the following languages: Arabic, Bahasa Indonesia, Bahasa Malaysia, Cambodian, Dutch, French, German, Greek, Hebrew, Hindi, Italian, Japanese, Korean, Nepali, Portuguese, Russian, Spanish, Swahili, Tagalog, Tamil, Thai and Vietnamese.

Most of the English language materials held in the centre are commercially produced. Some of these have been adapted for self-access use. The materials consist of books, worksheets, audiotapes, videotapes, CD-ROMs, Laser Disks, computer programs, magazines and CDs. Students also have access to Satellite TV and the Internet. There are a number of ways in which users can find out about the centre or get help: an orientation video which guides the user through the centre, a user's guide booklet; a set of learner advice sheets which offer practical suggestions of how to structure self-access learning and how to carry out and evaluate learning in various language skills areas, learner training workshops run by the teaching staff, and a consultation service where users can talk to language instructors about their language learning.

One course requires students to carry out a project in which they have to make extensive use of the SAC materials and facilities. In other courses, students are asked to use audio and video materials held in the SAC. In these ways students find out more about the SAC by having to use it.

Assessment and evaluation: Users mostly assess themselves in this SAC. They can also obtain feedback on their work from the counsellor.

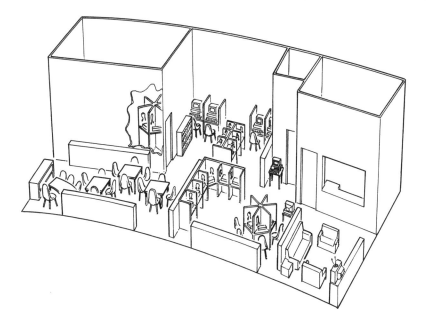

Figure 16.1.   Sketch of the SAC at the UST, Hong Kong

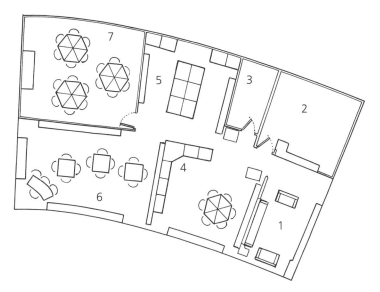

Figure 16.2.   Floor plan of the SAC at the UST, Hong Kong

Students who use the SAC as part of their course-work can also receive comments from their class teachers. From time to time, the users of the SAC are asked to complete questionnaires about it. The management team analyse the responses to these questionnaires and try to accommodate users' requests. Users can also make comments to the counsellors about the facilities and these comments are relayed to the SAC manager at the regular SAC staff meetings.

Physical settings and resources: The SAC covers an area of 300m² in a purpose-built section of the university academic buildings. It is located on the third floor and is accessible by stairs and lifts. It is easy to find and is well signposted. The SAC is open at the following times: Monday to Friday, 9am to 8pm (term time), and 9am to 6pm (vacations); Saturday, 9am to 12pm. During term time a consultation service is available from 1–5pm. The extended opening hours ensure that the SAC is open when users are free to go there.

The SAC is divided into seven sections: The lobby where users can wait or relax by reading magazines, watch satellite TV or listen to CDs via a wireless headset; an audio area designed for listening and speaking activities; a reading/writing area with a CD-ROM computer station (for listening to the pronunciation of words, etc.); a video/multimedia area with VCRs, TVs and caption decoders and computers; a seminar room for small group meetings; an audio-visual/computer laboratory with computers and VCRs; an office for the general support staff.

This SAC is at the high-tech end of self-access facilities. A large start-up budget was allocated along with generous sponsorship so that the latest in computer technology could be bought. The university gave a substantial amount of space for the creation of a specially designed SAC, and staff have reduced workloads to commit their time to the development of the centre.

The SAC in this university has the following facilities (see floor plan in Figure 16.2):

1. lobby
2. office
3. seminar room
4. audio area
5. video/multimedia area
6. reading/writing area
7. AV/computer lab.

17 Case study 4: Self-access in a private language school

Name of institution: Eurocentres Cambridge
Location: Cambridge, UK
Number of staff: approximately 22 full- and part-time teachers but the number varies depending on the time of year and the demand for courses
Number of students: varies
About the students: Multinational. Young adult and adult learners. Students who attend this school are usually 16 years old and above although courses for juniors occasionally take place.
Other information: This is an educational trust school. Classes are mostly mixed nationalities. The policy of the school is that students must not use their native language in the school. All students live with English-speaking host families.
Size of SAC: 300m²

Reasons for establishing a SAC: One of the main reasons for establishing this SAC was that it was company policy. The goals of this policy were to use self-access as an extension to the approach to learning and to allow teachers to use their class time for more enjoyable and less repetitive activities. The specific aims for introducing learners to self-access are (1) to try to unfocus exam-oriented students and encourage them to do things with the language they are learning other than prepare for exams; (2) to increase the variety of learning that is available to learners; (3) to use self-access as a bridge to the environment; and (4) to train students in language-learning skills so that they can continue using these skills once they leave the school and return to their home countries.

Type of SAC: Technology shop, Supermarket. This SAC fits into the Technology shop category because it has a lot of technology (see Figure 17.1). In addition, it is like a Supermarket because it holds a lot of general language-learning materials, games, magazines and newspapers which students can browse through.

Staffing and management:
Director of Studies: Ultimate managerial and financial responsibility rests with this person but it is just one of the many responsibilities generated by a busy school.

Teachers: All teachers who work in the school can take their classes to the SAC and they can also help develop materials for use in the SAC. Some teachers do not use the SAC with their students. They prefer to spend all their time in the classroom. However, as the school has a teacher-pairing scheme, all students will have one teacher who will take them during their timetabled class hours to the SAC for three 50-minute lessons a week.

One full-time administrator: Although this person is not a teacher she has an RSA certificate in TEFL and sees to the day-to-day management of the SAC.

Pedagogical manager: This is a part-time position. The Director of Studies, the Pedagogical manager and the administrator decide together on policy issues. In consultation with teachers the pedagogical manager decides on materials. These decisions are then passed to the administrative manager who arranges purchase of the materials. The pedagogical manager, along with other teachers, also develops special materials for the centre.

Technician: Technical assistance is available but sometimes there is a delay while the computer expert is sent from the central school which is not in the same town. Other technical problems are dealt with by local experts on an ad-hoc basis, with the exception of the language laboratory, which is regularly serviced.

This SAC mainly follows the Formal model of self-access management (see Chapter 4). However, it also contains elements of the Democratic model in that any of the teaching staff in the school can contribute to materials or ideas for activities in the SAC.

Use of SAC: All students who enrol in language courses in the school have timetabled hours in the SAC. It is also available for them to use during lunch breaks, when they have free periods and after school every day from 4pm to 6pm. Students have 25 hours of classes per week of which 3 hours are timetabled in the SAC. When the students attend the SAC as a timetabled part of their studies, the class teacher also attends and the whole class has the SAC to itself. This happens only in the mornings; the SAC is free for anyone to use in the afternoon. The school also runs an autonomous learning scheme. Learners pay a small amount, get one hour of a teacher's time per week and then they can use the SAC whenever they wish for a certain period.

Learners' beliefs and attitudes: Because Eurocentres Cambridge has multinational students, class teachers have to cater to all types of students' beliefs and attitudes. Teachers usually gain an insight into their students' beliefs and attitudes by encouraging class discussions in which students talk about their previous learning and how they feel about learning English. In this way, not only is the teacher sensitised to the students' beliefs and attitudes but so are the other students. All students have a tour of the SAC in their first week of classes. During this tour the teacher will try to find out about the students' attitudes to using such facilities through general chats with them. This informal approach helps the teacher gain an insight into how certain students, or groups of students, may react to working in self-access.

Learner profiles: Students do not keep any written record of their language learning in self-access. Instead, teachers have discussions with the students in class about what they are doing and how successfully they are using the facility. In addition to this, students are asked about opportunities they are taking outside of the school to use their language skills. These discussions help to build up some kind of informal learner profile for the students.

Counselling: As the students' work in the SAC is closely connected with their classroom language learning, the class teacher also acts as their counsellor. Students can also obtain help from the administrator or other teaching staff who are in the SAC at specific times.

Materials and activities: The print materials held in the SAC are flexible and can be added to quickly. Every six months new materials are added to the SAC. The SAC does not cater for many specific courses; it caters mostly for general English and English for Business. The SAC lends out materials to students. Each learner is given two tickets when they begin their course with which they can borrow materials. Not all the materials can be borrowed, but many items can, e.g. books, audiotapes and videotapes. Students can borrow at lunch-time, after school or during the timetabled class time.

Teachers can use the SAC as a teaching centre. For example, they can begin some activity in class, like asking students to prepare interview questions. The activity can then be continued when the class goes to the SAC; for example, the students could record and listen to each other's interviews using facilities in the SAC. The SAC also has a lot of games that can be used for language learning.

Activities for orientation to the SAC include: promotion by the principal during the school's induction programme for new students; class tours of the SAC accompanied by the class teachers; and ad-hoc help from the administration manager for learners who appear to be floundering.

Learner training sheets are provided for the students to take away. There is also a bank of lessons for teachers to use in the classroom or give their students to do in the SAC. These activities have been developed over several years as the centre has developed.

General in-house teacher training takes place every Friday afternoon.

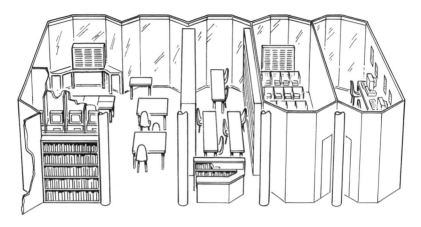

Figure 17.1.   Sketch of the SAC at Eurocentres, Cambridge

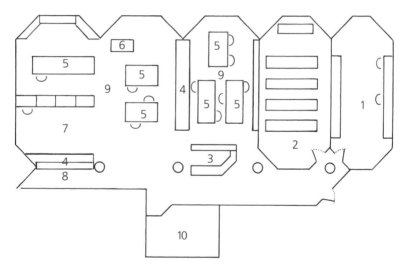

Figure 17.2.   Floor plan of the SAC at Eurocentres, Cambridge

At some of these meetings teachers discuss problems and issues related to their learners' work in the SAC.

Assessment and evaluation: The work undertaken in the SAC is often closely related to classroom language learning so assessment is frequently done by the class teachers. Sometimes students also engage in peer assessment when completing group work with students from other nationalities. Most of the print materials in the SAC have answer keys so students can also undertake self-assessment.

At the end of each course, students are asked to complete an evaluative questionnaire about the course and their experiences in the school. The questionnaire contains a section about self-access language learning and whether the SAC actually helps students. The feedback is usually very positive. The school has identified some groups of learners who enjoy self-access work more than others. For example, Japanese and Taiwanese learners specifically enjoy working in the language laboratory on their own. Latin-American students and Thai secondary-school teachers take to self-access work very easily. Non-academic Swiss learners need a lot of training in order to make use of the facilities. Kuwaiti learners do not like working in the SAC; they tend to prefer classroom-based learning.

Physical settings and resources: The SAC occupies an area of around 300m². It has been purpose built and is an integral part of the language school. It is located on the second floor of the school and is easy to find. The SAC is only open during working hours (8:30am to 6pm weekdays); it is not open during evenings or weekends. The philosophy behind not opening the SAC outside office hours is that the students are in an English-speaking country and so they should exploit the uncontrolled environment, i.e. the native-speaking community, in which they live.

1. computer room
2. language laboratory
3. reception desk
4. shelving
5. desks and chairs
6. counsellor's desk
7. video laboratory
8. easy-reader section
9. language-work areas
10. office

References

Adult Migrant Education Program (AMEP). 1990. National Centre for English Language Teaching and Research (NCELTR): Macquarie University, New South Wales.

Anderson, P. H. 1990. *Planning School Library Media Facilities*. Hamden, CT: Library Professional Publications.

Armanet, C. M. and K. Obese-jecty, 1981. Towards student autonomy in the learning of English as a second language at university level. *ELT Journal* 36(1) 24–8.

Armitage, S. 1992. Using a videotape-based system for management learning. *Interactive Learning Journal* 8 37–44.

Bachman, L. and A. S. Palmer. 1989. The construct validation of self-ratings of communicative language ability. *Language Testing* 6(1)14–29.

Bailly, S. 1995. La formation de conseiller. *Mélanges Pédagogiques* 22 63–83.

Baker, A. 1981. *Ship or Sheep*. Cambridge: Cambridge University Press.

Barnett, A. 1995. Linking SAC tasks to classroom activities. Paper presented at the South-East Asian Seminar on Self-Access Learning, King Mongkut's Institute of Technology, Bangkok, Thailand.

Bateman, G. R. and H. V. Roberts. 1995. Total quality for professors and students. In H. V. Roberts (Ed.) *Academic Initiatives in Total Quality for Higher Education*. Milwaukee, WI: ASQC Quality Press.

BBC / British Council. 1985–6. *Television English*. Videorecording. London: BBC / British Council.

Benson, P. 1997. The philosophy and politics of learner autonomy. In P. Benson and P. Voller (Eds.). *Autonomy and Independence in Language Learning*. London: Longman.

Benson, P. and P. Voller. (Eds.) 1997. *Autonomy and Independence in Language Learning*. London: Longman.

Blanche, P. 1990. Using standardised achievement and oral proficiency tests for self-assessment purposes: the DLIFC study. *Language Testing* 7(2) 202–29.

Block, D. 1991. Some thoughts on DIY materials design. *ELT Journal* 45(3) 211–17.

Blue, G. M. 1988. Self-assessment: the limit of learner independence. In A. Brookes and P. Grundy (Eds.) *Individualisation and Autonomy in Language Learning*. *ELT Documents 131*. London: Modern English Publications in association with the British Council (Macmillan).

Booton, P. and P. Benson. 1996. *Self-access: Classification and Retrieval*. Manchester: British Council.

Boud, D. (Ed.) 1988. *Developing Student Autonomy in Learning*. London: Kogan Page.

Broady, E. and M-M. Kenning. (Eds.) 1996. *Promoting Learner Autonomy in University Language Teaching*. London: Association of French Language Teachers / Centre for Information on Language Teaching and Research.

Brookes, A. and P. Grundy. (Eds.) 1988. *Individualisation and Autonomy in Language Learning*. *ELT Documents 131*. London: Modern English Publications in association with the British Council (Macmillan).

Burton, K. 1989. Bringing about gender equality of opportunity in a special school. In P. Lomax. (Ed.) *The Management of Change*. Clevedon: Multilingual Matters.

Cambridge Key English Test 1. 1997. Cambridge: Cambridge University Press.

Carroll, M. 1994. Journal writing as a learning and research tool in the adult classroom. *TESOL Journal* 4(1) 19–22.

Carvalho, D. 1993. *Self-access: Appropriate Materials*. Manchester: British Council.

Chin, T. M. 1991. Designing and managing a self-access learning system for adult learners. *Guidelines* 13(1) 74–81.

Cotterall, S. and D. Crabbe (Eds.) 1998. *Learner Autonomy in Language Learning: Defining the Field and Effecting Change*. Bochum: Brockineyer.

Crabbe, D. 1993. Fostering autonomy from within the classroom: The teacher's responsibility. *System* 21(4) 443–52.

Dam, L. 1994. How do we recognize an autonomous classroom?. *Die Neuere Sprache* 93(5) 503–27.

Dam, L. 1995. *Learner Autonomy 3: From Theory to Classroom Practice*. Dublin: Authentik.

Dam, L., R. Eriksson, D. Little, J. Miliander and T. Trebbi. 1990. Towards a definition of autonomy. In Proceedings of Developing Autonomous Learning in the F. L. Classroom, 11–14 August 1989, Institutt for praktisk pedagogikk, Universitetet i Bergen, Bergen.

Dam, L. and L. Legenhausen, 1996. The acquisition of vocabulary in an autonomous learning environment – the first months of beginning English. In R. Pemberton, E. S. L. Li, W. W. F. Or and H. D. Pierson (Eds.) *Taking Control: Autonomy in Language Learning*. Hong Kong: Hong Kong University Press.

Darasawang, P. 1996 A proposal to evaluate a learner training programme. In Proceedings of Autonomy 2000: The Development of Learning Independence in Language Learning. King Mongkut's Institute of Technology Thonburi, Bangkok.

de Garcia, R., S. Reynolds, and S. J. Savignon. 1976. Foreign-language attitude survey. *The Canadian Modern Language Review* 32 302–4.

Dennison, W. F. and M. Kelly. 1989. The educational coordinator – Perceptions of an emergent role. *Educational Management and Administration* 17: 151–7.

Dickinson, L. 1987. *Self-instruction in Language Learning*. Cambridge: Cambridge University Press.

Dickinson, L. 1992. *Learner Autonomy 2: Learner Training for Language Learning*. Dublin: Authentik.

References

Dickinson, L. and D. Carver. 1980. Learning how to learn: steps towards self-direction in foreign language learning. *ELT Journal* 35 1–7.

Dickinson, L. and A. Wenden. (Eds.) 1995. Special issue on autonomy. *System* 23(2).

Dwyer, R. 1996. Building thoughts. In D. Gardner and L. Miller (Eds.) *Tasks for Independent Language Learning*. Alexandria, VA: TESOL.

Earley, P. 1993. Developing competence in schools: a critique of standards-based approaches to management development. *Educational Management and Administration* 21(4) 233–44.

Elliot, G. and M. Crossley. 1994. Qualitative research, educational management and the incorporation of the further education sector. *Educational Management and Administration* 22(3) 188–97.

Ellis, G. and B. Sinclair. 1987. Helping learners discover their learning styles. In R. Duda, and P. Riley. (Eds.). *Learning Styles*. Nancy: Presses Universitaires de Nancy.

Ellis, G. and B. Sinclair. 1989. *Learning to Learn English: A Course in Learner Training*. Cambridge: Cambridge University Press.

Esch, E. 1989. Keeping things going: evaluation and development. In D. Little (Ed.) *Self-access Systems for Language Learning*. Dublin: Authentik.

Esch, E. (Ed.) 1994. *Self-access and the Adult Language Learner*. London: CILT.

Esch, E. 1996. Promoting learner autonomy: criteria for the selection of appropriate methods. In R. Pemberton, E. S. L. Li, W. W. F. Or and H. D. Pierson (Eds.) *Taking Control: Autonomy in Language Learning*. Hong Kong: Hong Kong University Press.

Esp, D. 1993. *Competences for School Managers*. London: Kogan Page.

Farmer, R. 1994. The limits of learner independence in Hong Kong. In D. Gardner and L. Miller. (Eds.) *Directions in Self-Access Language Learning*. Hong Kong: Hong Kong University Press.

Flavell, J. H. 1979. Metacognitive and cognitive monitoring: a new area of cognitive-developmental inquiry. *American Psychologist* 34(10) 906–11.

Forrester, J. 1994. Self-access language learning for secondary school students. In D. Gardner and L. Miller (Eds.) *Directions in Self-Access Language Learning*. Hong Kong: Hong Kong University Press.

Gardner, D. 1992. Electronic mail as a tool to enable purposeful communication. *Hong Kong Papers in Linguistics and Language Teaching* 15 73–4.

Gardner, D. 1993a. Copyright, publishers and self-access centres. *Hong Kong Papers in Linguistics and Language Teaching* 16 111–15.

Gardner, D. 1993b. Interactive video in self-access language learning: development issues. In Interactive Multimedia '93, Proceedings of the Fifteenth Annual Conference, Washington, Society for Applied Learning Technology, pp. 150–2.

Gardner, D. 1994. Creating simple interactive video for self-access. In D. Gardner and L. Miller (Eds.) *Directions in Self-Access Language Learning*. Hong Kong: Hong Kong University Press.

Gardner, D. 1995. A methodology for converting teaching materials to self-access learning materials. *Modern English Teacher* 4(3) 53–7.

Gardner, D. 1996. Self-assessment for self-access learning. *TESOL Journal* 5(3) 18–23.

Gardner, D. and R. Blasco García. 1996. Interactive video as self-access support for language learning beginners. In R. Pemberton, E. S. L. Li, W. W. F. Or and H. D. Pierson (Eds.) *Taking Control: Autonomy in Language Learning*. Hong Kong: Hong Kong University Press.

Gardner, D. and L. Miller. (Eds.) 1994. *Directions in Self-Access Language Learning*. Hong Kong: Hong Kong University Press.

Gardner, D. and L. Miller. (Eds.) 1996. *Tasks for Independent Language Learning*. Alexandria, VA: TESOL.

Gardner, D. and L. Miller. 1997. *A Study of Tertiary Level Self-Access Facilities in Hong Kong*. Hong Kong: ESEP, City University of Hong Kong.

Gierse, C. 1993. Idea on how to motivate learner independence. *Modern English Teacher* 2(4) 57–60.

Gremmo, M-J. 1995. Conseiller n'est pas enseigner: Le role du conseiller dans l'entretien de conseil. *Mélanges Pédagogiques* 22 33–61.

Gremmo, M-J. and P. Riley. 1995. Autonomy, self-direction and self access in language teaching and learning: the history of an idea. *System* 23(2) 151–64.

Grenfell, M. 1994. Flexible learning: the teacher's friend?. *Modern English Teacher* 3(4) 7–13.

Harding, E. and A. Tealby. 1981. Counselling for language learning at the University of Cambridge: progress report on an experiment. *Mélanges Pédagogiques* 95–120.

Harris, M. 1997. Self-assessment of language learning in formal settings. *ELT Journal* 51(1) 12–20.

Haughton, G. and L. Dickinson. 1989. Collaborative assessment by masters candidates in a tutor based system. *Language Testing* 5(2) 233–46.

Hitt, P. 1990. Teacher perceptions of management in schools. *Educational Management and Administration* 18(2) 27–9.

Ho, J. and D. Crookall. 1995. Breaking with Chinese cultural traditions: Learner autonomy in English language teaching. *System* 23(2) 235–43.

Hoffman, R. 1993. The distance brings us closer: Electronic mail, ESL learner writers, and teacher. In G. Davis and B. Samways. (Eds.) *Teleteaching*. Amsterdam: North-Holland.

Holec, H. 1980. *Autonomy and Foreign Language Learning*. Strasbourg: Council of Europe.

Holec, H. 1981. *Autonomy and Foreign Language Learning*. Oxford: Pergamon Press.

Holec, H. 1985. Self-Assessment. In Proceedings of Self-Directed Learning and Self Access in Australia: From Practice to Theory, Conference held in 1984 by Council of Adult Education, Melbourne, Australia.

Holec, H. (Ed.) 1988. *Autonomy and Self-directed Learning: Present Fields of Application*. Strasbourg: Council of Europe.

Holmes, G. and A. Neilson. 1989. Training for school management: reflections and suggestions. *Educational Management and Administration* 17 67–70.

Horwitz, E. K. 1985. Using student beliefs about language learning and teaching in the foreign language methods course. *Foreign Language Annals* 18(4) 333–40.

Jacobs, G. 1989. Miscorrection in peer feedback in writing class. *RELC Journal* 20 68–76.

Janssen-van Dieten, A. 1989. The development of a test of Dutch as a foreign language: the validity of self-assessment by inexperienced subjects. *Language Testing* 6(1) 30–46.

Johnson, K. E. 1995. *Understanding Communication in Second Language Classrooms*. Cambridge: Cambridge University Press.

Karlsson, L., F. Kjisik and J. Nordlund. 1997. *From Here to Autonomy*. Yliopistopanino: Helsinki University Press.

Kelly, R. Undated. Interaction for autonomy. Mimeo.

Kelly, R. 1996. Language counselling for learner autonomy: The skilled helper in self-access language learning. In R. Pemberton, E. S. L. Li, W. W. F. Or and H. D. Pierson (Eds.) *Taking Control: Autonomy in Language Learning*. Hong Kong: Hong Kong University Press.

Kennedy, C. 1987. Innovating for a change: teacher development and innovation. *ELT Journal* 44(3) 163–70.

Kennedy, C. 1988. Evaluation of the management of change in ELT projects. *Applied Linguistics* 9(4) 329–42.

Kenny, B. 1993. For more autonomy. *System* 21(4) 431–42.

Kinsella, K. 1996. Designing group work that supports and enhances diverse classroom work styles. *TESOL Journal* 6(10) 24–30.

Kroonenberg, N. 1994. Developing communicative and thinking skills via electronic mail. *TESOL Journal* 4(2) 24–7.

Lai, E. F. K., 1994. Keeping contact with learners. In E. Esch (Ed.) *Self-Access and the Adult Language Learner*. London: Centre for Information on Language Teaching and Research.

Lamb, T. 1996. Self-management in the secondary school language classroom. In Proceedings of Autonomy 2000: The Development of Learning Independence in Language Learning, King Mongkut's Institute of Technology Thonburi, Bangkok.

Lewis, T., J. Woodin and E. St John. 1996. Tandem learning: independence through partnership. In E. Broady and M-M. Kenning (Eds.) *Promoting Learner Autonomy in University Language Teaching*. London: AFLS and CILT.

Little, D. 1986. Interactive video for language learning: the autotutor project. *System* 14(1) 29–34.

Little, D. (Ed.) 1989. *Self-Access Systems for Language Learning: A Practical Guide*. Dublin: Authentik.

Little, D. 1990. Autonomy in language learning: some theoretical and practical considerations. In I. Gathercole (Ed.) *Autonomy In Language Learning*. London: CILT.

Little, D. 1991. *Learner Autonomy 1: Definitions, Issues and Problems*. Dublin: Authentik.

Little, D. 1996. Freedom to learn and compulsion to interact: promoting learner autonomy through the use of information systems and information technologies. In R. Pemberton, E. S. L. Li, W. W. F. Or and H. D. Pierson

(Eds.) *Taking Control: Autonomy in Language Learning*. Hong Kong: Hong Kong University Press.

Little, D., S. Devitt and D. Singleton. 1989. *Learning Foreign Languages From Authentic Texts: Theory and Practice*. Dublin: Authentik.

Littlejohn, A. P. 1983. Increasing learner involvement in course management. *TESOL Quarterly* 17(4) 595–608.

Littlewood, W. 1996. Autonomy in communication and learning in the Asian context. In Proceedings of Autonomy 2000: the Development of Learner Independence in Language Learning, King Mongkut's Institute of Technology Thonburi, Bangkok, pp. 124–40.

Lockhart, C. and Ng, P. 1993. How useful is peer response? *Perspectives: Working papers of the Department of English, City University of Hong Kong* 5 17–29.

McCall, J. 1992. *Self-Access: Setting Up a Centre*. Manchester: British Council.

McDevitt, B. 1996. The Self-Access Language Learning Centre, University of Abertay Dundee: history of a project. *Language Learning Journal* 13 67–9.

McGowan, C. 1989. Setting up a project within a general English programme. *Modern English Teacher* 17(1) 57–63.

Martyn, E. 1994. Self-access logs: promoting self-directed learning. In D. Gardner, and L. Miller (Eds.). *Directions in Self-Access Language Learning*. Hong Kong: Hong Kong University Press.

Middlehurst, R. 1995. Top training: Development for institutional managers. In A. Brew (Ed.) *Directions in Staff Development*. Buckingham: The Society for Research into Higher Education and Open University Press.

Miller, L. 1992. *Self-Access Centres in South East Asia*. Research Report No. 11. Hong Kong: Department of English, City University of Hong Kong.

Miller, L. 1995. Materials production in EFL: a team process. *English Teaching Forum* 33(4) 31–2.

Miller, L. and D. Gardner. 1994. Directions for research into self-access language learning. In D. Gardner and L. Miller (Eds.) *Directions in Self-Access Language Learning*. Hong Kong: Hong Kong University Press.

Miller, L. and R. Ng. 1996. Autonomy in the classroom: peer assessment In R. Pemberton, E. S. L. Li, W. W. F. Or and H. D. Pierson (Eds.) *Taking Control: Autonomy in Language Learning*. Hong Kong: Hong Kong University Press.

Miller, L. and P. Rogerson-Revell. 1993. Self-access systems. *ELT Journal* 47(3) 228–33.

Mittan, R. 1989. The peer review process: harnessing students' communicative power. In D. Johnson and D. Roen (Eds.) *Richness in Writing: Empowering ESL Students*. New York: Longman.

Moore, C. 1992. *Self-Access: Appropriate Technology*. Manchester: British Council.

Munby, J. 1978. *Communicative Syllabus Design: A Sociolinguistic Model for Defining the Content of Purpose-Specific Language Programmes*. Cambridge: Cambridge University Press.

Murphey, T. 1994. Tests: learning through negotiated interaction. *TESOL Journal* 4 2–16.

References

Murphy, R. 1985. *English Grammar in Use*. Cambridge: Cambridge University Press.

Myers, C. 1990. Facilitating learner independence in the adult ESL classroom. *TESL Canada Journal* 8(1) 77–86.

North, S. 1990. Resource materials for library project work. *ELT journal* 44(3) 222– 9.

Nunan, D. 1987. Communicative language teaching: making it work. *ELT Journal* 41(2) 136–45.

Nunan, D. 1988a. *The Learner-Centred Curriculum*. Cambridge: Cambridge University Press.

Nunan, D. 1988b. *Syllabus Design*. Oxford: Oxford University Press.

Nunan, D. 1996. What's my style? In D. Gardner and L. Miller (Eds.) *Tasks for Independent Language Learning*. Alexandria, VA: TESOL.

Nunan, D. 1997. Designing and adapting materials to encourage learner autonomy. In P. Benson and P. Voller (Eds.) *Autonomy and Independence in Language Learning*. London: Longman.

O'Dell, F. 1992. Helping teachers to use a self-access centre to its full potential. *ELT Journal* 46(2) 153–9.

Or, W. W. F. 1994. Helping learners plan and prepare for self-access learning. In D. Gardner and L. Miller (Eds.) *Directions in Self-Access Language Learning*. Hong Kong: Hong Kong University Press.

Oxford, R. L. 1990. *Language Learning Strategies: What every teacher should know*. Boston, MA: Heinle & Heinle.

Oxford, R. L. 1992. Language learning strategies in a nutshell: update and ESL suggestions. *TESOL Journal* 2(2) 18–22.

Pang, T. T. T. 1994. A self-directed project: A critical humanistic approach to self-access In D. Gardner and L. Miller. (Eds.). *Directions in Self-Access Language Learning*. Hong Kong: Hong Kong University Press.

Parker, D. F., S. Hart Kimball, D. J. Brown and D. O. Kaldenberg. 1995. Incorporating total quality into a college of business. In H. V. Roberts (Ed.) *Academic Initiatives in Total Quality for Higher Education*. Milwaukee, WJ: ASQC Quality Press.

Pemberton, R. 1992. *A self-access centre for Hong Kong University of Science and Technology: a preliminary proposal*, Report prepared for The Language Centre Advisory Committee, The Hong Kong University of Science and Technology.

Pemberton, R., E. S. L. Li, W. W. F. Or and H. D. Pierson (Eds.). 1996. *Taking Control: Autonomy in Language Learning*. Hong Kong: Hong Kong University Press.

Pierce, B. N., M. Swain and D. Hart. 1993. Self-assessment, French immersion and locus of control. *Applied Linguistics* 14(1) 25–42.

Prostano, E. T. and J. S. Prostano. 1987. *The School Media Center*. Littleton, CO: Libraries Unlimited.

Pugsley, J. 1991. The rise and call of academic management. *ELT Journal* 45(4) 313–19.

Raddon, R. and P. Dix. 1989. *Planning Learning Resource Centres in Schools and Colleges*. Aldershot: Gower.

Rendon, M. 1995. Learner autonomy and co-operative learning. *English Teaching Forum* 33(4) 41–3.

Richards, J. C. and C. Lockhart. 1994. *Reflective Teaching in Second Language Classrooms*. Cambridge: Cambridge University Press.

Riley, P. 1981. Pedagogical implications of the use of authentic documents. CRAPEL (mimeo).

Riley, P. 1988. The ethnography of autonomy. In A. Brookes and P. Grundy (Eds.) *Individualisation and Autonomy in Language Learning. ELT Documents 131*. London: Modern English Publications in association with the British Council (Macmillan).

Riley, P. 1993. Notes on the design of self-access systems. *Mélanges Pédagogiques* 22 105–21.

Riley, P. 1996. The blind man and the bubble: researching self-access. In R. Pemberton, E. S. L. Li, W. W. F. Or and H. D. Pierson (Eds.) *Taking Control: Autonomy in Language Learning*. Hong Kong: Hong Kong University Press.

Riley, P. 1997. The guru and the conjurer: aspects of counselling for self-access. In P. Benson and P. Voller (Eds.). *Autonomy and Independence in Language Learning*. London: Addison Wesley Longman.

Rogerson-Revell, P. and L. Miller. 1994. Developing pronunciation skills through self-access learning. In D. Gardner and L. Miller. (Eds.) *Directions in Self-Access Language Learning*. Hong Kong: Hong Kong University Press.

Ruechakul, P. 1996. Moving towards independent learning at Chaiwanwithaya Secondary School by establishing a self-access centre. In Proceedings of Autonomy 2000: The Development of Learning Independence in Language Learning, King Mongkut's Institute of Technology Thonburi, Bangkok.

Sallis, E. 1993. *Total Quality Management in Education*. London: Kogan Page.

Scott, P. 1989. Accountability, responsiveness and responsibility. In R. Glatter (Ed.) *Educational Institutions and Their Environments: Managing the Boundaries*. Milton Keynes: Open University Press.

Self-Access Learning: For English Language in Malaysian Primary Schools (Teacher's Guide). 1995. Cetakan Pertama: PPK.

Sharkey, J. 1995. Helping students become better learners. *TESOL Journal* 4(2) 18–22.

Sheerin, S. 1989. *Self-Access*. Oxford: Oxford University Press.

Sheerin, S. 1991. Self-access: State-of-the-art-article. *Language Teaching* 24(3) 143–57.

Sheerin, S. 1997. An exploration of the relationship between self-access and independent learning. In P. Benson and P. Voller (Eds.) *Autonomy and Independence in Language Learning*. London: Longman.

Simmons, D. 1996. A study of strategy use in independent learners. In R. Pemberton, E. S. L. Li, W. W. F. Or and H. D. Pierson (Eds.) *Taking Control: Autonomy in Language Learning*. Hong Kong: Hong Kong University Press.

Sinclair, B. and G. Ellis. 1984. Autonomy begins in the classroom. *Modern English Teacher* 11(4) 45–7 and p. 36.

Star, M. 1994. Learning to improve: evaluating self-access centres. In

D. Gardner and L. Miller (Eds.) *Directions in Self-Access Language Learning*. Hong Kong: Hong Kong University Press.

The Star, Malaysia. 1995. First SAC centre at secondary school. 9 September 1995.

Stein, B. L. and R. W. Brown. 1992. *Running a School Library Media Center*. New York: Neal-Schuman.

Stern, H. H. 1975. What can we learn from the good language learner? *The Canadian Modern Language Review* 31 304–18.

Sturtridge, G. 1992. *Self-access: Preparation and Training*. Manchester: British Council.

Thom, D. J. 1993. *Educational Management and Leadership*. Calgary: Detselig.

Thomson, C. K. 1992. Learner-centred tasks in the foreign language classroom. *Foreign Language Annals*. 25(6) 523–31.

Thomson, C. K. 1996. Self-assessment in self-directed learning: issues of learner diversity. in R. Pemberton, E. S. L. Li, W. W. F. Or and H. D. Pierson (Eds.) *Taking Control: Autonomy in Language Learning*. Hong Kong: Hong Kong University Press.

Thorpe, M. 1988. *Evaluating Open and Distance Learning*. London: Longman.

Tibbetts, J. 1994. Materials production for self-access centres is secondary schools. In D. Gardner and L. Miller (Eds.) *Directions in Self-Access Language Learning*. Hong Kong: Hong Kong University Press.

Tudor, I. 1996. *Learner-Centredness as Language Education*. Cambridge: Cambridge University Press.

Veado, M., V. Siqueira and G. Jones. 1993. No turning back: the experience of running a self-access centre for young learners. *Modern English Teacher* 2(1) 59–64.

Victori Blaya, M. 1996. Fostering awareness of person, task and strategy knowledge in autonomous learning. In Proceedings of Autonomy 2000: the Development of Learning Independence in Language Learning, King Mongkut's Institute of Technology Thonburi, Bangkok.

Victori, M. 1992. *Investigating the metacognitive knowledge of students of English as a second language*. Unpublished Masters thesis, University of California, Los Angeles, CA.

Victori, M. and W. Lockhart. 1995. Enhancing metacognition in self-directed language learning. *System* 23(2) 223–34.

Voller, P. and V. Pickard. 1996. Conversational exchange: a way towards autonomous language learning. In R. Pemberton, E. S. L. Li, W. W. F. Or and H. D. Pierson (Eds.) *Taking Control: Autonomy in Language Learning*. Hong Kong: Hong Kong University Press.

Wenden, A. 1986. Helping language learners think about learning. *ELT Journal* 40(1) 3–12.

West-Burnham, J. 1992. *Managing Quality in Schools: A TQM Approach*. London: Longman.

White, R. V. 1988. *The ELT Curriculum: Design, Innovation and Management*. Oxford: Basil Blackwell.

White, R., M. Martin, M. Stimson and R. Hodge. 1991. *Management in English Language Teaching*. Cambridge: Cambridge University Press.

Willing, K. 1988. *Learning Styles in Adult Migrant Education*. Adelaide: National Curriculum Resource Centre for the Adult Migrant Education Program.

Willing, K. 1989. *Teaching How to Learn*. Sydney: NCELT, Macquarie University.

Wolverton, M. 1995. The business college at Arizona State University: Taking the quality to heart. In H. V. Roberts (Ed.) *Academic Initiatives in Total Quality for Higher Education*. Milwaukee, WI: ASQC Quality Press.

Woolls, B. 1994. *The School Library Media Manager*. Englewood, CO: Libraries Unlimited.

Wynn, R. and C. W. Guditus. 1984. *Team Management: Leadership by Consensus*. Columbus, OH: Charles E. Merrill Publishing.

Index

activities for: advance learners, 136; diverse groups of learners, 136; groups, 133–5, 136; individuals, 130–1; intermediate learners, 135; pairs, 132–3; young learners, 135

activities: learner support, 123–9

activities: level, 157

activities: project work, 165–72

adapting materials, 100

Adult Migrant Education Programme, 2, 52

advanced learners: activities, 136

alternative methods of counselling, 196–201

American learners, 11

Anderson, P.H., 66, 80

answer keys, 97, 99

Armanet, C.M., 147, 170–2

Armitage, S., 100

Asia, 31

Asian learners, 42

assessment methods: the pros and cons, 214–16

assessment portfolio starter sheet, 214

assessment: self-, 206–17; administration, 220–2; as feedback to learners, 206; characteristics, 206–16; cheating, 217; choices, 205–6; content, 216–20; face validity, 215, 216; formal, 218; modes, 221; peer, 217; privacy, 223; purposes, 205–6, 207; SALL in isolation, 206

assessment: size: large, 218–19; small, 217

assessment: types : collaborative, 208, 211–13, 215–16; generic assessments, 208–11, 214–16; learner-generated, 208, 213, 214–16; portfolio, 208, 213–14; teacher-generated, 208, 214–16

assessment: use of results, 222–3

attitudes to self-access: institutional, 11; learners and teachers, 12, 479

Australia, 2, 39, 40, 43, 52

Australian Adult Migrant Education Program (AMEP), 2, 52, 54, 57, 58, 64

authentic materials: definition, 101; sources, 102–4; supporting, 104–5

autonomous learners, 67

autonomy, 67, 47; developing, 8

avoiding chaos, 141

awareness raising, 34, 124–5

Bachman, L., 220

Bailly, S., 184

Baker, A., 208

BALLI, 457, 50

Barnett, A., 185

Bateman, G.R., 71

BBC, 100

Benson, P., 1, 6

Blanche, P., 220

Blasco García, R., 100

Block, D., 105

Blue, G.M., 220

Booton, P., 1

Boud, D., 6

Brazil, 56, 172

British Council, 2, 55, 100, 146

Broady, E., 1

Brookes, A., 1

Brown, R.W., 66

Burton, K., 67

Cambridge Key English Test 1., 208

Carroll, M., 176–7, 177

Carvalho, D., 1

Carver, D., 43, 44

case studies of self-access centres, 241–61

categorising self-access, 51

Centre de Researches et d'Applications Pédagogiques en Langues (CRAPEL), 2, 54

characteristics of self-access, 811

cheating, 217–18

checklist for materials development, 120

Chin, T.M., 147

classroom self-access, 139–43

clubs, 137

Index

Index